Miss Fr

Syracuse

Poim cann

420, 216

When distant hills she
And you I cannot see
Remember it is Betsy
That always thinks of

Think of me

A

PRACTICAL GRAMMAR

OF THE

ENGLISH LANGUAGE,

FOR THE

USE OF SCHOOLS OF EVERY GRADE.

BY

THOS. W. HARVEY, A. M.

WILSON, HINKLE & CO.,

CINCINNATI: NEW YORK:

137 WALNUT ST.   28 BOND ST.

PREFACE.

In the preparation of this treatise, the ever-recurring wants and requirements of the class-room have been kept constantly in view. The aim of the author has been to make a *practical text-book*—a useful manual for the learner, not a reference book for the learned.

The whole plan of the work is in accordance with the educational doctrine that accuracy and facility in the use of language, both spoken and written, are the ends to be secured by the study of grammar: that to secure these ends, a thorough acquaintance with the elements, forms, structure, and laws of our mother tongue, is indispensable; and that a practical knowledge of these can be acquired only by patient, persistent exercise in the analysis and synthesis of syllables, words, and sentences.

The author has endeavored to present the subject in a simple, concise, and perspicuous manner. He has purposely avoided the discussion of mere theories; preferring, rather, a plain didactic statement of his own views. Experience has taught him that such discussions serve only to confuse and discourage the beginner, and are of questionable utility to the advanced student. Neither the erudition of the teacher, nor the exhaustive completeness of the text-book used, can compensate for the lack of *drill* in the class-room.

The distinguishing features of this treatise, to which special attention is invited, are the following:

1. The methodical arrangement and logical development of the subjects discussed.

2. The brevity, clearness, and uniformity of the rules and definitions.

3. The simple yet complete system of Analysis.

4. The great variety of carefully prepared MODELS FOR PARSING AND ANALYSIS. By these models, the pupil is taught how to parse every kind of word, and how to analyze every kind of sentence.

5. The abundance of appropriate exercises and illustrations, systematically arranged, and numbered for convenient reference.

6. The definite statement or clear indication of opinion upon those points which annoy and perplex both pupil and teacher.

7. The practical character and systematic classification of the instruction and exercises in False Syntax.

8. The lucid and comprehensive treatment of Punctuation and Prosody—both important subjects, too much neglected in most schools.

9. The superior mechanical execution of the work.

Actuated by a desire to render the labor of the class-room more pleasant and effective, by furnishing an attractive means for instruction in a useful branch of study, the author ventures the hope that this treatise will commend itself to the favorable notice and consideration of his fellow-teachers.

CONTENTS.

PROSODY.

ENGLISH GRAMMAR.

1. Definitions.

1. **A Word** is the sign of an idea.

2. **Language** is the expression of thought by means of words. It may be either *spoken* or *written.*

3. **Spoken Language** is the expression of ideas by the voice.

4. **Written Language** is the expression of ideas by the use of written or printed characters representing sounds.

5. **Grammar** treats of the principles and usages of language.

6. **English Grammar** teaches how to speak and write the English language correctly.

7. English Grammar is divided into four parts: *Orthography, Etymology, Syntax,* and *Prosody.*

8. **Orthography** treats of elementary sounds, letters, syllables, and spelling.

9. **Etymology** treats of the classification, derivation, and properties of words.

10. **Syntax** treats of the construction of sentences.

11. **Prosody** treats of the quantity of syllables, of accent, and of the laws of versification.

(7)

PART I.

ORTHOGRAPHY.

2. Definitions.

1. **Orthography** treats of elementary sounds, letters, syllables, and spelling.

2. An **Elementary Sound** is one which can not be separated into two or more distinct sounds.

3. A **Letter** is a character used to represent either an elementary sound, or a combination of elementary sounds; as, *a, x.*

4. A **Syllable** is a sound or a combination of sounds uttered with one impulse of the voice; as, *man, man-ner.*

5. A **Word** is either a syllable, or a combination of syllables; as, *hat, men-tion, phi-los-o-phy.*

3. Elementary Sounds.

1. There are forty elementary sounds in the English language.

2. They are divided into *Vowels* and *Consonants.* Consonants are subdivided into *Subvocals* and *Aspirates.*

3. **Vowels,** or **Vocals,** are those sounds which are made with the vocal organs open, and consist of pure tone only. They are also called *Tonics.*

4. **Subvocals** are those sounds which are obstructed by the vocal organs, in the process of articulation. They are sometimes called *Subtonics.*

5. **Aspirates** are mere emissions of breath, articulated by the lips, tongue, teeth, and palate. They are sometimes called *Atonics*.

TABLE OF ELEMENTARY SOUNDS.

4. Vowels.

a	long,	as in	late.	i	long, as in	time.
a	short,	"	hat.	i	short, "	tin.
a	middle,	"	ask.	o	long, "	cold.
a	Italian,	"	arm.	o	short, "	hot.
a	broad,	"	all.	oo	long, "	ooze.
e	long,	"	eve.	oo	short, "	book.
e	short,	"	ell.	u	long, "	lute.
				u	short, "	cup.

5. Consonants.

1. **Consonants** may be divided into six classes, viz.:

Labials, or *lip-sounds*, which are made by the lips;

Linguals, or *tongue-sounds*, made by the tongue;

Linguo-dentals, or *tongue-teeth-sounds*, made by the tongue and teeth;

Linguo-nasals, or *tongue-nose-sounds*, articulated by the tongue, the sound passing through the nose;

Palato-nasals, or *palate-nose-sounds*, made by the palate, the sound passing through the nose;

Palatals, or *palate-sounds*, made by the palate.

2. The *Subvocals* are arranged on the left of the page, and the corresponding *Aspirates* on the right.

Labials.

b,	as in	bib,	p,	as in	lip,
v,	"	save,	f,	"	life,
w,	"	way,	wh,	"	when.
m,	"	am,			

Linguo-Dentals.

d, as in lid,	**t,** as in tat,
th, " with,	**th,** " myth,
j, " jar,	**ch,** " rich,
z, " size,	**s,** " hiss,
zh, " azure,	**sh,** " hush.

Linguals.

l, as in lull,	
r, " roar.	(Have no corresponding aspirates.)

Linguo-Nasal.

n, as in man.	(Has no corresponding aspirate.)

Palato-Nasal.

ng, as in song.	(Has no corresponding aspirate.)

Palatals.

g, as in nag,	**k,** as in kick,
y, " yes,	**h,** " how.

Rem.—The sounds represented by *l, m, n,* and *r,* are sometimes called *liquids,* because they easily unite with other consonant sounds.

6. Letters.

1. There are twenty-six letters in the English alphabet. As there are more elementary sounds than letters, it becomes necessary that some letters represent more than one sound. Letters also combine to represent sounds for which there are no single representatives. Letters and combinations of letters are often used as substitutes for other letters.

7. Diphthongs, Digraphs, and Trigraphs.

1. A **Diphthong** consists of two vowels sounded together in the same syllable.

Rem.—There are two diphthongal sounds, represented by four diphthongs, viz.: *ou, ow, oi, oy,* as in *foul, now, boil, cloy.*

2. A **Digraph** consists of two vowel letters written together in the same syllable, one only being pronounced, or both representing a single elementary sound.

Rem.—There are twenty-four digraphs, viz.: *aa,* Canaan; *ai,* gain; *ao,* gaol; *au,* maul; *aw,* maw; *ay,* may; *ea,* meat; *ee,* need; *ei,* ceiling; *eo,* people; *eu,* feud; *ew,* new; *ey,* they; *ie,* lief; *oa,* coat; *oe,* foe; *oi,* avoirdupois; *oo,* moon; *ou,* tour; *ow,* flow; *ua,* guard; *ue,* sue; *ui,* guise; *uy,* buy.

3. A **Trigraph** consists of three vowel letters written together in the same syllable, one only being pronounced, or the three together representing a single vowel sound, or diphthong.

Rem. 1.—There are seven trigraphs, viz.: *aye,* aye; *awe,* awe; *eau,* beau, beauty; *eou,* gorgeous; *eye,* eye; *ieu,* lieu; *iew,* view.

Rem. 2.—In such words as *Christian, alien, union, i* does not form a digraph with the following vowel, but is a substitute for *y.* In the unaccented terminations *cean, cial, sion, tion,* the combinations *ce, ci, si, ti,* are substitutes for *sh.*

Rem. 3.—In such words as *herbaceous, gracious, precious, e* and *i* do not form trigraphs with the following vowels, but the combinations *ce, ci* are substitutes for *sh.*

8. Double Consonants.

Double Consonants consist of two consonant letters written together in the same syllable, representing a single elementary sound.

Rem.—They are *ch,* chord; *gh,* laugh; *ph,* physic; *sh,* hush; *th,* thin, this; *wh,* when; *ng,* sing.

9. Substitutes.

A **Substitute** represents a sound usually represented by another letter or combination of letters.

A *long* has four substitutes: *ê*, tête; *ei*, feint; *ey*, they; *ao*, gaol.

A *middle* has two substitutes: *e*, there; *ei*, heir.

A *broad* has two substitutes: *o*, cord; *ou*, sought.

E *long* has three substitutes: *i*, marine; *ie*, fiend; *ay*, quay.

E *short* has four substitutes: *ay*, says; *u*, bury; *i*, irksome; *ie*, friend.

I *long* has three substitutes: *y*, thyme; *ei*, Steinway; *oi*, choir.

I *short* has six substitutes: *y*, hymn; *e*, England; *u*, busy; *o*, women; *ee*, been; *ai*, captain.

O *long* has three substitutes: *eau*, beau; *ew*, sew; *oa*, goal.

O *short* has two substitutes: *a*, what; *ow*, knowledge.

U *long* has five substitutes: *eau*, beauty; *ieu*, lieu; *iew*, view; *ew*, new; *ui*, suit.

U *short* has three substitutes: *e*, her; *i*, sir; *o*, son.

F has two substitutes: *gh*, laugh; *ph*, philosophy.

J has two substitutes: *g*, rage; *di*, soldier.

S has two substitutes: *c* before *e*, *i*, and *y*; *z*, quartz.

T has one substitute: *ed* final, after any aspirate except *t*.

V has two substitutes: *f*, of; *ph*, Stephen.

W has one substitute: *u*, quick. It is understood before *o* in *one*, *once*.

X is used as a substitute for *ks*, as in *wax;* *gz*, as in *exact;* *ksh*, as in *noxious*.

Y has one substitute: *i*, alien. It is frequently understood before *u*, as in *verdure*.

Z has three substitutes: *c*, sacrifice; *s*, his; *x*, Xenia.

CH has one substitute: *ti*, question.

SH has six substitutes: *ce*, ocean; *ci*, facial; *si*, losion; *ti*, motion; *ch*, chaise; *s*, sugar.

ZH has four substitutes: *si*, fusion; *zi*, brazier; *z*, azure; *s*, rasure.

NG has one substitute: *n*, generally before palatal sounds; as in *ink*, *uncle*, *conquer*.

10. Forms of the Letters.

1. Letters are of different styles; as, Roman, *Italic*, *Script*, 𝕺𝖑𝖉 𝕰𝖓𝖌𝖑𝖎𝖘𝖍.

2. Types for printing are of various sizes:

Great Primer,
English,
Pica,

Small Pica,
Long Primer,
Bourgeois,
Brevier,

Minion,
Nonpareil,
Agate,
Pearl,
Diamond.

3. Letters are used either as capital letters or as lower-case, or small letters.

11. Capital Letters.

I. The first word of every sentence, or the first word after a full pause, should begin with a capital letter.

Ex.—Winds blow. Snow falls. The heavens are aflame.

II. The first word after an introductory word or clause may begin with a capital letter.

Ex.—"*Resolved*, That the sum of $3000 be appropriated," &c.

"*Be it enacted by the General Assembly of the State of Ohio*, That section fourteen," &c.

III. Each new line or paragraph of an enumeration of particulars, arranged in lines or paragraphs, should begin with a capital letter.

Ex.—"These expenditures are in proportion to the whole expenditures of government,

In Austria, as thirty-three per cent.:
In France, as thirty-eight per cent.:
In Great Britain, as seventy-four per cent."

IV. The first word of a direct quotation, or of an important statement, a distinct speech, &c., should begin with a capital letter.

Ex.—"When thou saidst, Seek ye my face, my heart said unto thee, Thy face, Lord, will I seek." "Dora said, 'My uncle took the boy.'" "One truth is clear: Whatever is, is right."

V. The first word in every line of poetry should begin with a capital letter.

Ex.—"Put your best foot foremost, or I fear
That we shall miss the mail: and here it comes
With five at top; as quaint a four in hand
As you shall see—three piebalds and a roan."

"Faith, he's got the Knicker-
Bocker Magazine."

VI. Proper names of persons, places, months, days, &c., should begin with capital letters.

Ex.—James, Emma, Boston, July, Wednesday, James Monroe, O. W. Holmes.

VII. Titles of honor or distinction, used alone or accompanied by nouns, should begin with capital letters.

Ex.—*Earl* Russell; the *Duke* of York; *Mr.* Wilson, *Mrs.* Smith; *Dr.* Johnson; *Gen.* Harrison; *Sir* Robert Peel; George the *Third;* Charles the *Bold;* "O had I a thousand a year, *Gaffer* Green;" "The *Elder* spake as follows."

VIII. Names of things personified become proper nouns in sense, and should begin with capital letters.

Ex.—"Come, gentle *Spring!* ethereal *Mildness!* come."

"In *Misery's* darkest cavern known,
His useful care was nigh,
When hopeless *Anguish* poured his groan,
And lonely *Want* retired to die."

IX. Words or phrases used as names for particular objects should begin with capital letters.

Ex.—The Falls; Yellow Creek; the Havana; the City of Brotherly Love; the Cape of Good Hope; John o' Groat's House; the

Round Tower; the Sailor's Home; "I have read 'The Tent on the Beach.'"

X. All appellations of the Deity should begin with capital letters.

Ex.—God; the Most High; the Supreme; the Infinite One; Divine Providence; the Father, the Son, and the Holy Ghost; our Lord Jesus Christ.

XI. A common word must sometimes begin with a capital letter, to show its reference to the Deity.

Ex.—"The *Hand* that made us is divine."

"The spangled heavens, a shining frame,
Their great *Original* proclaim."

Rem.—A word that describes rather than denotes a name of the Deity, and a pronoun whose expressed antecedent is the name of the Deity, usually require no capitals; as, "O *thou merciful* God!" "The *all-powerful* Lord of *lords;*" "God provides for all *his* creatures."

XII. Nouns denoting the race or nation of individuals should begin with capital letters.

Ex.—The French; the Spaniards; the English; the Anglo-Saxons.

XIII. Words derived from proper names should begin with capital letters.

Ex.—American, Mainote, Danish, Johnsonian, Icelandic.

Rem.—When such words become common nouns by losing their reference to their original proper nouns, they should not begin with capital letters; as, a louis d' or; a guinea; china-ware.

XIV. Words of special importance may begin with capital letters.

Ex.—The Tariff; the Sub-Treasury Bill; the Commissioner of Common Schools; "Be prepared for the Great Day;" "Angler's Companion: a Complete and Superior Treatise on the Art of Angling."

XV. In natural history, *generic* names, or names of genera, should commence with capital letters. *Specific* names, or names of species, if derived from proper nouns, should also commence with capitals: otherwise with small letters. Scientific terms are usually printed in italics.

Ex.—*Rosa Gallica, Rosa alba; Anomma Burmeisteri, Anomma rubella; Spongites Townsendi, Spongites flexuosus.*

XVI. The pronoun *I* and interjection *O* should be capitals.

Ex.—   "Sleep, O gentle Sleep,
    Nature's soft nurse, how have I frighted thee."

GENERAL REMARKS.

1. Indirect quotations, or words quoted as the peculiar language of authors, should not begin with capital letters; as, "A man is an 'individual,' or a 'person,' or a 'party.'" "A fine house is always a 'palatial residence.'"

2. The pronouns *he, his, him, thy,* and *thee,* referring to names of the Deity, in sentences where their antecedents are understood, or when they are used for emphasis, may sometimes begin with capital letters; as, "The hope of my spirit turns trembling to *Thee;*" "Trust in *Him,* for *He* will sustain thee."

3. In writing many compound names of places, usage is not uniform. When the parts remain separate, or are connected by a hyphen, each should begin with a capital letter: when the parts are consolidated, but one capital letter should be used; as, New Castle, New-Castle, Newcastle.

4. In phrases or sentences used as headings or titles, nouns, adjectives, participles, or other important words, only, should begin with capital letters: unimportant words and connectives should begin with small letters.

5. In advertisements, show-bills, &c., different styles and sizes of type are frequently used, and the liberty of capitalizing is carried to an indefinite extent.

6. Names, signs, titles, and mottoes, designed to attract attention, are printed in various styles; most frequently in capitals.

12. Exercises to be Corrected.

1.—it is a pleasant thing to see the sun. man is mortal. flowers bloom in summer.

2.—*Resolved*, that the framers of the constitution, &c.

3.—The town has expended, the past year,
  for grading streets, $15,000 :
  for public buildings,   15,000.

4.—He said "you are too impulsive;" Remember the maxim, "a penny saved is a penny earned."

5.—"The day is past and gone;
  the evening shades appear;
 O may we all remember well
  the night of death draws near."

6.—James and samuel went to baltimore last august; The general assembly meets on the first monday in february.

7.—The bill was vetoed by the president; John Jones, esq.; Richard the third; "The opposition was led by lord Brougham."

8.—"When music, heavenly maid, was young,
  While yet, in early Greece, she sung,
  The passions, oft, to hear her shell,
  Throng'd around her magic cell."

9.—The central park; the Ohio river; I have read "great expectations;" the mountains of the moon are in Africa.

10.—The lord shall endure forever; Remember thy creator; divine love and wisdom; "The ways of providence."

11.—"I know that my redeemer liveth; " "I am the way, the truth, the life;" "The word was made flesh."

12.—Those are chinamen; the turcomans are a wandering race; the gypsies of Spain; the indians are fast disappearing.

13.—The swiss family Robinson; a russian serf; "The rank is but the Guinea's stamp;" a Cashmere shawl; a Damask rose.

14.—The emancipation proclamation; the art of cookery, (a title); the Missouri compromise; the whisky insurrection; "A treatise on the science of education and the art of teaching."

16.—i don't like to study grammar. i write correct enough, now. o, how i wish school was out!
   H. G. 2.

13. Italics, Small Capitals, etc.

I. Emphatic words, phrases, and clauses are frequently printed in italics.

Ex.—"Do not you *grieve* at this?" "The truth is, his lordship *weeps for the press, and wipes his eyes with the public.*"—*Curran.*

II. Words borrowed from foreign languages should be printed in italics.

Ex.—"Each word stood quite *per se.*"—*Lamb.* "This odd *quid pro quo* surprised me into vehement laughter."—*Walpole.*

III. The names of authors, annexed to selections from their writings, are usually printed in italics.

Ex.—"His coward lips did from their color fly."—*Shakspeare.*

IV. Parenthetical words and phrases are frequently printed in italics.

Ex.—Old gentleman (*looking quite unconcerned*), "Run away, has she?"

V. Names of ships, books, newspapers, and periodicals are frequently printed in italics or small capitals.

Ex.—"The *Quaker City* has arrived." "The JOURNAL is committed to no such policy as that."

VI. Names of important personages are frequently printed in small capitals.

VII. Words requiring special emphasis are frequently printed in small capitals or capitals.

Ex.—"I brand him as a *rogue*, a THIEF, a COWARD."—*Placard.*

Rem. 1.—Italicized words in the Bible are those supplied by translators to explain the original.

Rem. 2.—In manuscripts, one line drawn under a word indicates *italics;* two lines, SMALL CAPITALS; three lines, CAPITALS.

Rem. 3.—In this work, **full-faced types** are also used for distinction.

14. Syllables.

1. A Syllable may be composed,

1. Of a vowel, digraph, or trigraph; as, *o*-men, *ou*-ranography, *eau*-de-cologne.

2. Of a vowel or diphthong, with one or more consonants prefixed or affixed; as, l-*o*, b-*oy*, *a*-m, *a*-nd.

3. Of a vowel or diphthong, with one or more consonants prefixed and affixed; as, *b*-a-*d*, *fr*-a-*nk*.

2. A vowel sound is an essential part of a syllable.

3. Synthesis is the process of combining elementary sounds.

4. Analysis is the process of separating a syllable or word into its elementary sounds.

15. Models for Analyzing Syllables.

Model I.

Lo.—Give both sounds in quick succession, **L-o,** and pronounce the word.

Model II.

Lo . . . is a syllable, containing two elementary sounds.
L . . . . is a consonant-subvocal-lingual. (*Give its sound.*)
o . . . . is a vowel, long sound. (*Give its sound.*)

Model III.

Clank.—Give the five sounds in quick succession, **c-l-a-n-k,** and pronounce the word.

Model IV.

Clank is a syllable, containing five elementary sounds.
c . . . . is a consonant-aspirate-palatal, substitute for *k*. (*Give its sound.*)
l . . . . is a consonant-subvocal-lingual. (*Give its sound.*)
a . . . . is a vowel, short sound. (*Give its sound.*)
n . . . . is a consonant-subvocal-palatal-nasal, substitute for *ng*. (*Give its sound.*)
k . . . . is a consonant-aspirate-palatal. (*Give its sound.*)

Model V.

Boy.—Give the three sounds in quick succession, **b-a-i,** and pronounce the word.

Model VI.

Boy. . is a syllable, containing three elementary sounds.
B . . . . is a consonant-subvocal-labial. (*Give its sound.*)
oy . . . is a diphthong, representing *a* broad, and *i* short. (*Give the sound of each in quick succession.*)

Model VII.

View.—Give the two sounds in quick succession, **v-u,** and pronounce the word.

Model VIII.

View . is a syllable, containing two elementary sounds.
V . . . . is a consonant-subvocal-labial. (*Give its sound.*)
iew . . is a trigraph, equivalent to *u* long. (*Give its sound.*)

Note.—Either set of models may be used in analyzing syllables. The models for complete analysis need not be used after the classification of elementary sounds shall have been thoroughly learned.

Analyze the following words, omitting all silent letters:

And, fly, warm, elm, fin, sing, wax, when, sue, light, pot, home, zinc, valve, kid, ask, sun, goat, jolt.

Form syllables by prefixing a consonant to **a, ay, eau, oy ;**

By prefixing two or more consonants to **e, oo, aw, i ;**

By affixing one, two, or more consonants to any of the vowels or diphthongs.

16. Words.

1. A **Word** may consist of one, two, or more syllables.

A word of *one* syllable is called a **monosyllable**; as, *care, man.*

A word of *two* syllables is called a **dissyllable**; as, *care-ful, man-ly.*

A word of *three* syllables is called a **trisyllable**; as, *care-ful-ness, man-li-ness.*

A word of *four or more* syllables is called a **polysyllable**; as, *com-mu-ni-ty, ec-cen-tric-i-ty.*

2. **Accent** is a stress of voice placed upon a particular syllable. It may be either **primary** or **secondary,** the *primary* being the more forcible.

3. Every word of more than one syllable has one of its syllables accented.

4. In words having both a *primary* and a *secondary* accent, the secondary occurs nearest the beginning; as, *in''-compatibil' ity, in''comprehen'sible.*

17. Models for Analyzing Words.

Tree . . . . is a word of one syllable: therefore a *monosyllable.*

Nature . . . . . is a word of two syllables: therefore a *dissyllable.* It is accented on the first syllable.

Commotion . . is a word of three syllables: therefore a *trisyllable.* It is accented on the second syllable.

Indefatigable is a word of six syllables: therefore a *polysyllable.* Its secondary accent is on the first syllable, and its primary accent on the third.

Note.—A word having been analyzed according to one of these models, analyze each syllable according to the preceding models. In separating a word into syllables, divide it as it is pronounced. In writing, never divide a syllable at the end of a line. Each line should end with a word or an entire syllable.

Analyze the following words:

Sand, lead, sack; unction, famous, greatly; endeavor, infamous, candidly; unpopular, information, gratuitous; domestication, interrogation, incredulity; incomprehensible, indefensibleness; incompatibility, incompassionately.

Write each of these words on your slates, and divide them into syllables, marking the accented syllables.

Correct the accent in the following words:

Advertise′ment, prima′ry, contra′ry, legis′lature, lamen′table, seconda′ry, infa′mous, armis′tice, admi′rable, interest′ing.

Change the accent of the following words to the second syllable, and give the meaning of each word before and after the change:

In′sult, fer′ment, reb′el, rec′ord, pre′lude, con′jure, en′trance, es′cort, in′crease, in′valid, ob′ject, in′cense, es′say.

18. Classes.

1. **Words** are either *Primitive* or *Derivative*.

2. A **Primitive** or **Radical** word is one in no way derived from another in the same language; as, *mind, faith.*

3. A **Derivative** word is one formed by joining to a primitive some letter or syllable to modify its meaning; as, *re*-mind, faith-*ful.*

4. A **Compound** word is one formed by uniting two or more primitive or derivative words; as, *man-worship, Anglo-Saxon.*

5. A **Prefix** is that part of a derivative word which is placed before the radical; as, *re*-call, *sub*-join.

6. A **Suffix** is that part of a derivative word which is placed after the radical; as, faith-*ful*, change-*able.*

7. Prefixes and suffixes are called **Affixes.**

Note.—The meaning and use of affixes should be learned from some work prepared for that purpose.—*See De Wolf's Instructive Speller and Hand-Book of Derivative Words.*

PART II.

ETYMOLOGY.

19. Definitions.

1. **Etymology** treats of the classification, derivation, and properties of words.

2. With reference to meaning and use, words are divided into nine classes, called **Parts of Speech**; viz., *Noun, Adjective, Pronoun, Verb, Participle, Adverb, Preposition, Conjunction, Interjection.*

3. A **Noun** is a name; as, *house, Charlotte, magnetism.*

4. An **Adjective** is a word used to describe or define the meaning of a noun; as, *fine* houses; *studious* pupils; *animal* magnetism.

5. A **Pronoun** is a word used instead of a noun; as, *his* house; *my* book; *your* children; "*Whom* did *you* see?"

6. A **Verb** is a word which expresses being, action, or state; as, I *am;* George *writes;* the house *stands.*

7. A **Participle** is a word derived from a verb, partaking of the properties of a verb and of an adjective or a noun; as, "A light, *shining* from afar;" "A letter, *written* in haste."

8. An **Adverb** is a word used to modify the meaning of a verb, adjective, participle, or an adverb; as, "He runs *swiftly;*" "You are *very* kind;" "The letter was written *hastily.*"

9. A **Preposition** is a word used to show the relation between its object and some other word; as, "The house stands *on* the hill."

10. A **Conjunction** is a word used to connect words, sentences, or parts of sentences; as, "John *and* Elisha are brothers." "Winds blow *and* rains descend."

11. An **Interjection** is a word used to denote some sudden or strong emotion; as, *O, ah, alas, pshaw.*

THE NOUN.

20. Oral Lesson.

Write on your slates the names of five objects in the school-room. These words, as you perceive, are not the objects themselves, but their *names.* They are called *Nouns,* which means *names.* Now write the names of five objects not in the school-room. What are these words called? *Ans.*—Nouns. Why? *Ans.*—Because they are names. Write the names of five of your school-mates. What are these words called? *Ans.*—Nouns. Why? *Ans.*—Because they are names.

Are there not other names by which your school-mates are called? *Ans.*—Yes; they may be called *girls* and *boys.* Can the name "girl" be applied to all the girls in the room? *Ans.*—Yes. Can the name "Sarah" be applied to all the girls in the room? *Ans.*—It can not. Why? *Ans.*—All the girls are not named "Sarah." There are Mary, and Charlotte, and Jane, and Susan, and many other names for girls.

We have, then, two kinds of Nouns, or names. One kind can be applied to each one of a class, and the other kind can be applied to a particular one only. The first kind are called *Common Nouns,* and the second *Proper Nouns.* What kind are the names *horse, book, boy, girl, map, blackboard? Ans.*—Common Nouns. Why? *Ans.*—Because they can be applied to each one of a class. What kind are the names *John, Charles, Washington, Boston, Europe? Ans.*—Proper Nouns. Why? *Ans.*—Because they can be applied to particular persons, or particular places, only.

21. Definition.

A **Noun** is a name; as, *desk, Richard, goodness, army.*

22. Classes.

1. There are two classes of Nouns : *Common* and *Proper.*

2. A **Common Noun** is a name which may be applied to any one of a kind or class of objects; as, *boy, child, book, radiation.*

3. A **Proper Noun** is the name of some particular person, place, people, or thing; as, *Charles, Cincinnati, The French, The Sun.*

Rem. 1.—*Common nouns* have meaning, and admit of definition. Most *proper nouns* originally had meaning, but it is not taken into consideration in applying them; and, therefore, they do not admit of definition. There are about 30,000 common nouns, and 70,000 proper nouns, in the English language.

Rem. 2.—Whenever a *proper noun* assumes a meaning, so that it can be applied to each individual of a class, it becomes a *common noun;* as, "He is the *Cicero* of our age;" "Bolivar was the *Washington* of South America;" "He piled *Ossa* upon *Pelion* to accomplish his purpose."

Rem. 3.—Whenever a *common noun* is used to distinguish one individual from another of the same class, it becomes a *proper noun;* as, *The Havana; The Falls; The Laurel Ridge.*

Rem. 4.—When two or more words form but one name, they are taken together as one noun; as *New York; Niagara Falls; John Milton; Lord Bacon; Chief Justice Chase.*

4. **Common Nouns** may be divided into four classes: *Class Nouns, Abstract Nouns, Collective Nouns,* and *Verbal Nouns.*

5. **Class Nouns** are names which can be applied to each individual of a class or group of objects; as, *horse, apple, man.*

H. G. 3.

6. An **Abstract Noun** is the name of a quality considered apart from the object in which it is found; as, *brightness, brittleness, cohesion.*

7. A **Collective Noun** is a name singular in form, though denoting more than one; as, *herd, jury, swarm, school, assembly.*

8. A **Verbal Noun** is the name of an action, or a state of being; as, *singing, standing, seeming.*

Rem. 1.—Words, phrases, and clauses, used as nouns, or in the relations in which nouns occur, are called **substantives,** and when thus used have all the properties of nouns.

Rem. 2.—Such words as *mass, heap, furniture,* names of collections of objects without life, are *class* nouns, not *collective* nouns. They are sometimes called **mass nouns.**

23. Properties.

The **Properties** of the Noun are *Gender, Person, Number,* and *Case.*

24. Gender.

1. **Gender** is a distinction of nouns and pronouns with regard to sex.

2. There are four genders: *Masculine, Feminine, Common,* and *Neuter.*

3. The **Masculine Gender** denotes males; as, *father, uncle, king, governor.*

4. The **Feminine Gender** denotes females; as, *mother, aunt, queen, governess.*

5. The **Common Gender** denotes either males or females, or both; as, *parent, children, bird, cattle.*

6. The **Neuter Gender** denotes neither males nor females; as, *stove, city, pen, ink, tree, house.*

Rem. 1.—By a figure of speech called *Personification*, gender is sometimes ascribed to inanimate objects. They should then be regarded as either masculine or feminine.

Ex.—"The *ship* has lost *her* rudder." "The meek-eyed morn appears, *mother* of dews." "The *sun* in *his* glory; the *moon* in *her* wane."

Rem. 2.—When masculine or feminine qualities are ascribed to animals, they are regarded as either masculine or feminine.

Ex.—"The *nightingale* sings *her* song." "The *lion* meets *his* foe boldly." "The *fox* made *his* escape."

Rem. 3.—Nouns used to denote both genders, though strictly applicable to males only, or females only, are usually regarded as masculine.

Ex.—"*Heirs* are often disappointed." "The *English* are a proud people." "The *poets* of America."

Rem. 4.—The distinction of gender is not observed in speaking of inferior animals, and sometimes even of children.

Ex.—"The *bee* on *its* wing." "The *child* in *its* cradle."

7. There are three ways of distinguishing the masculine and feminine genders:

1. By using different words:

Ex.—Bachelor, maid, spinster; bridegroom, bride; brother, sister; boy, girl; cock, hen; drake, duck; earl, countess; father, mother; gentleman, lady; hart, roe; male, female; man, woman; Mr., Mrs.; Sir, Madam; nephew, niece; son, daughter; uncle, aunt; Charles, Caroline; Augustus, Augusta.

2. By different terminations:

Ex.—Abbot, abbess; baron, baroness; host, hostess; actor, actress; prior, prioress; benefactor, benefactress; executor, executrix; murderer, murderess; sorcerer, sorceress.

3. By prefixes and suffixes:

Ex.—Man-servant, maid-servant; he-bear, she-bear; male-descendant, female-descendant; cock-sparrow, hen-sparrow; Mr. Smith, Mrs. Smith, Miss Smith; pea-cock, pea-hen.

25. Person.

1. **Person** is that property of a noun or pronoun which distinguishes the speaker, the person spoken to, and the person or object spoken of.

2. There are three persons: *First, Second,* and *Third.*

3. The **First Person** denotes the speaker; as, "*I, Abraham Lincoln,* President of the United States." "Many evils beset *us* mortals."

4. The **Second Person** denotes the person addressed; as, "*James,* be more careful." "*Fellow Citizens,* the crisis demands the utmost vigilance."

5. The **Third Person** denotes the person or object spoken of; as, "*Milton* was a poet;" "*Rome* was a *city* of *flame.*" "I am reading *Tennyson's Poems.*"

Rem. 1.—The writer or speaker often speaks of himself, or the person he addresses, in the third person; as, "*Mr. Johnson* has the pleasure of informing *Mr. Mason* that he has been elected Honorary Member of the Oriental Society."

Rem. 2.—A noun in the predicate is of the third person, though the subject may be of the first or second.

Ex.—"*You* are the *man* wanted." "*We* are *strangers.*" "*I* am *he* whom you saw."

26. Number.

1. **Number** is that property of a noun which distinguishes one from more than one.

2. There are two numbers: *Singular* and *Plural.*

3. The **Singular Number** denotes but one; as, *apple, flower, boy, girl.*

4. The **Plural Number** denotes more than one; as, *apples, flowers, boys, girls.*

27. Formation of the Plural.

1. Nouns whose last sound will unite with *s*, form their plurals by adding *s* only to the singular; as, book, *books;* boy, *boys;* desk, *desks.*

2. Nouns whose last sound will not unite with *s*, form their plurals by adding *es* to the singular; as, church, *churches;* box, *boxes;* witness, *witnesses.*

3. Nouns ending in *y* preceded by a consonant, change *y* into *ies;* as, glory, *glories;* mercy, *mercies.*

4. Most nouns ending in *f* or *fe*, change these endings into *ves;* as, beef, *beeves;* wife, *wives.*

5. Most nouns ending in *o* preceded by a consonant, add *es;* as, cargo, *cargoes.* Nouns ending in *o* preceded by a vowel, add *s;* as, folio, *folios.*

6. Some nouns form their plurals irregularly; as, man, *men;* ox, *oxen;* tooth, *teeth;* mouse, *mice.*

7. Letters, figures, marks and signs add *'s;* as, "Mind your *p's* and *q's;*" the 9's and 11's; the *'s; the +'s; "Those ƺ's and ϑ's."

8. In compound words, the part which is described by the rest is generally pluralized; as, *brothers*-in-law, *courts*-martial, *wagon-loads*, ox-*carts.*

9. Compound words from foreign languages form their plurals according to (1) and (2); as, *tête-à-têtes, piano-fortes, ipse-dixits, scire-faciases.*

10. Some compound words have both parts made plural; as, man-servant, *men-servants;* knight-templar, *knights-templars;* ignis-fatuus, *ignes-fatui.*

11. Compound terms composed of a proper noun and a title, may be pluralized by adding a plural termination to either the name or the title, but not to both; as, the Miss *Browns*, the *Misses* Brown; the *Messrs.* Thompson: "May there be *Sir Isaac Newtons* in every science."

12. When the title is preceded by a numeral, the name is always pluralized; as, the three Miss *Johnsons;* the two Dr. *Bensons;* the two Mrs. *Kendricks.*

13. Some nouns have two plurals, but with a difference in meaning; as, brother, *brothers* (of the same family), *brethren* (of the same society); die, *dies* (stamps for coining), *dice* (for gaming); fish, *fishes* (individuals), *fish* (quantity, or the species); genius, *geniuses* (men of genius), *genii* (spirits); index, *indexes* (tables of contents), *indices* (algebraic signs); penny, *pennies* (pieces of money), *pence* (how much in value); pea, *peas* (individuals), *pease* (in distinction from other vegetables).

14. Proper nouns, and words generally used as other parts of speech, are changed as little as possible, and usually add *s* only in forming their plurals; as, Mary, *Marys;* Sarah, *Sarahs;* Nero, *Neros;* "The novel is full of *ohs, bys, whys, alsos,* and *nos.*" There is good authority, however, for using *Maries, Neroes, whies, noes.*

15. Many nouns from foreign languages retain their original plurals, changing *us* to *i; um* and *on* to *a; is* to *es* or *ides; a* to *œ* or *ata;* and *x* to *ces* or *ices;* as, calculus, *calculi;* arcanum, *arcana;* criterion, *criteria;* thesis, *theses;* ephemeris, *ephemerides;* nebula, *nebulæ;* calix, *calices;* index, *indices.*

28. General Remarks on Number.

1. Abstract nouns, and names of material substances, have no plural forms, as, *silver, vinegar, hemp, tar, frankness, darkness.* When different kinds of the same substance are referred to, a plural form may be used; as, *sugars, vinegars, wines, oils.*

2. Some nouns have no singular forms; as, *ashes, assets, bellows, billiards, compasses, clothes, drawers, lees, scissors, shears, tongs. News* and *molasses* have the plural form, but are regarded as singular. *Lungs, bowels,* and a few others, have a singular form denoting a part of the whole; as, "The left *lung.*"

3. Some nouns have no singular forms, but are singular or plural in meaning; as, *alms, amends, corps, mumps, measles, nuptials, odds, riches, series, suds, tidings, wages,* and some others.

4. The names of some of the sciences are either singular or plural in meaning, according as they denote the science, or the objects of which the science treats; as, *ethics, mechanics, mathematics, optics, pedagogics, physics,* &c.

5. Some nouns are alike in both numbers; as, *sheep, deer, vermin, couple, salmon, trout, dozen, gross, hose, yoke.*

29. Case.

Case is the relation of a noun or pronoun to other words. Nouns have four cases: *Nominative*, *Possessive*, *Objective*, and *Absolute*.

30. Nominative Case.

The **Nominative Case** is the use of a noun or pronoun as the subject or the predicate of a proposition.

Ex.—"The *sun* is shining." "That man is a *sailor*." In the first sentence, "sun" is in the nominative case, because it is used as the *subject* of the proposition; in the second, "sailor" is in the nominative case, because it is used as the *predicate* of the proposition.

31. Possessive Case.

1. The **Possessive Case** is the use of a noun or pronoun to denote ownership, authorship, origin, or kind.

Ex.—*Susan's* book; *Gray's* Botany; the *sun's* rays; *boys'* hats; *men's* clothing.

2. The Possessive Case *Singular* is formed by annexing *'s* to the nominative; as, *John's*, *Clarence's*.

3. The Possessive Case *Plural* is formed by annexing the apostrophe only, when the nominative plural ends with *s*; as, boys'; "The Ohio State *Teachers'* Association."

Rem. 1.—Plural nouns not ending with *s*, form their possessive case by annexing *'s*; as, *men's* hats; *children's* shoes.

Rem. 2.—In *compound names*, the possessive sign is annexed to the last word; as, "*Daniel Webster's* speeches:" in *complex names* it is annexed to the last word; as, "The *Bishop of Dublin's* palace:" in a *series of terms*, and common possession, it is annexed to the last term; as, "*Day & Martin's* Blacking," in a *series of terms*, and separate possession, it is annexed to each term; as, "*Webster's* and *Worcester's* Dictionaries."

Rem. 3.—When a noun in the possessive case is limited by a noun in apposition with it, or by a descriptive phrase, the possessive sign is annexed to the noun immediately preceding the object possessed, though not always to the name of the possessor; as, "Her Majesty, *Queen Victoria's* government;" "The captain of the *Fulton's* wife died yesterday." Here "captain" is in the possessive case, and "Fulton" in the objective, governed by the preposition "of."

Rem. 4.—In compound words, the sign of possession is placed at the end; as, "The *knight-templar's* costume;" "My *brother-in-law's* residence."

Rem. 5.—"For *conscience'* sake," "For goodness' sake," &c., are idiomatic exceptions to the general rule for forming the possessive case singular.

Rem. 6.—The sign ('s), is a contraction of *is* or *es;* as, *John's, King's;* anciently written *Johnis, Kingis,* or *Johnes, Kinges.*

32. Objective Case.

The **Objective Case** is the use of a noun or pronoun as the object of a transitive verb in the active voice, or of a preposition.

Ex.—"John studies *grammar.*" "The book is on the *table.*" In the first sentence, "grammar" is the object of the transitive verb "studies;" in the second, "table" is the object of the preposition "on."

Rem. 1.—Nouns of *measure, quantity, time, distance, value,* or *direction,* are in the objective case without a governing word; as, "The lake is ten *miles* long;" "The child is six *months* old;" "He is worth a hundred thousand *dollars;*" "That is a ten *horse-power* engine;" "The men traveled *north.*"

Rem. 2.—A noun or pronoun used to complete the meaning of a transitive verb is called a **direct object:** when added to a verb to denote that *to* or *for* which any thing is or is done, or that *from* which any thing proceeds, it is called an **indirect object.** When an indirect object precedes the direct, the preposition should be omitted; when it follows, it should be expressed; as, "I gave *him* an apple;" "I gave an apple *to him.*"

33. Absolute Case.

The **Absolute Case** is the use of a noun independent of any governing word.

Ex.—*"John,* bring me a book;" "Your *fathers,* where are they?" *"Honor* being lost, all is lost."

Rem.—A noun may be in the **absolute case,**

1. *By direct address;* as, *"Charles,* come to me." This use is sometimes called the **Vocative Case.**

2. *By mere exclamation;* as, "Oh, Popular *Applause!"*

3. *By pleonasm,* or by placing the noun before the sentence in which an affirmation is made concerning it; as, *"Gad,* a troop shall overcome him."

4. *With a participle;* as, "The *sun* being risen, we pursued our journey."

34. Nouns in Apposition.

A noun limiting the meaning of another noun, denoting the same person, place, or thing, is, by apposition, in the same case.

Ex.—"Washington the *general* became Washington the *states-man."* "We visited New York, the *metropolis* of the United States." "In her brother *Abraham's* house."

35. Declension.

The **Declension** of a noun is its variation to denote *number* and *case.*

Examples.

	Singular.	*Plural.*		*Singular.*	*Plural.*
Nom.	Boy,	Boys,	*Nom.*	Fly,	Flies,
Poss.	Boy's,	Boys',	*Poss.*	Fly's,	Flies',
Obj.	Boy.	Boys.	*Obj.*	Fly.	Flies.
Nom.	Charles,	——	*Nom.*	Goodness,	——
Poss.	Charles's,	——	*Poss.*	Goodness',	——
Obj.	Charles.	——	*Obj.*	Goodness.	——

36. Parsing.

Parsing consists (1) in naming the part of speech; (2) In telling its properties; (3) In pointing out its relation to other words; (4) In giving the rule for its construction.

37. Order of Parsing.

1. A Noun, and why?
2. Common or Proper, and why?
3. If Common, whether a Class Noun, &c., and why?
4. Gender, and why?
5. Person, and why?
6. Number, and why?
7. Case, and why?
8. Rule for construction.

38. Models for Parsing.

I. "*Mary* sings."

Mary ... is a *noun;* it is a name: *proper;* it is the name of a particular person: *feminine gender;* it denotes a female: *third person;* it denotes the person spoken of: *singular number;* it denotes but one: *nominative case;* it is used as the *subject* of the proposition "Mary sings." Rule I. "The subject of a proposition is in the nominative case."

II. "Horses are *animals.*"

Animals . is a *noun;* (why?): *common;* it can be applied to any one of a class or kind: *common gender;* it denotes either males or females: *third person;* (why?): *plural number;* it denotes more than one: *nominative case;* it is used as the *predicate* of the proposition "Horses are animals." Rule II. "A noun or pronoun, used as the predicate of a proposition, is in the nominative case."

III. "The poet *Milton* was blind."

Milton .. is a *noun;* (why): *proper;* (why?): *masculine gender;* it denotes a male: *third person;* (why?): *singular number;*

(why?): *nominative case*, in apposition with "poet." Rule IV. "A noun or pronoun, used to limit the meaning of a noun or pronoun, by denoting the same person, place, or thing, is in the same case."

IV. "*Henry's* lesson is learned."

Henry's . is a *noun;* (why?): *proper;* (why?): *masculine gender,* (why?): *third person;* (why?): *singular number;* (why?): *possessive case;* it denotes possession, and modifies "lesson." Rule III. "A noun or pronoun, used to limit the meaning of a noun denoting a different thing, is in the possessive case."

V. "John studies *grammar*."

Grammar is a *noun;* (why?): *common;* (why?): *neuter gender;* (why?): *third person;* (why?): *singular number;* (why?): *objective case;* it is used as the object of the transitive verb "studies." Rule VI. "The object of a transitive verb in the active voice, or its participles, is in the objective case."

VI. "The book lies on the *table*."

Table . . . is a *noun;* (why?): *common;* (why?): *neuter gender;* (why?): *third person;* (why?): *singular number;* (why?): *objective case;* it is used as the object of the preposition "on." Rule VII. "The object of a preposition is in the objective case."

VII. "*William*, open the door."

William . is a *noun;* (why?): *proper;* (why?): *masculine gender;* (why?): *second person;* (why?): *singular number;* (why?): *absolute case;* it is the name of a person addressed. Rule V. "A noun or pronoun used independently, is in the absolute case."

39. Exercises.

1. Nominative Case. 1. The wind blows. 2. The sun shines. 3. Horses run. 4. Rain descends. 5. The vessel sails. 6. Scholars study. 7. Grass grows. 8. Fire burns. 9. Liberty is sweet. 10. St. Helena is an island. 11. Lead is a metal. 12. Water is a liquid. 13. Cicero was an orator. 14. Webster was a statesman. 15. Grammar is a science. 16. Birds are animals.

2. Possessive Case. 1. The storm's fury is past. 2. Henry's health is good. 3. The king's palace is on fire. 4. Mary's task is done. 5. Byron's poems are published. 6. Jane borrowed Sarah's book. 7. Mr. Johnson sells boys' hats. 8. The defeat of Xerxes' army was the downfall of Persia.

3. Objective Case. 1. John struck James. 2. Joseph bought the book. 3. The widow lost her son. 4. Peter studies algebra. 5. The horse kicked the boy. 6. The man wrote a letter. 7. A dog bit a man. 8. Samuel lives over the river. 9. Martha went with Susan. 10. The house stands on the hill. 11. James is going to Cincinnati. 12. The boy ran by the mill.

4. Absolute Case. 1. The rebellion being ended, the army disbanded. 2. Henry being away, the work was not done. 3. "Friends, Romans, Countrymen! lend me your ears!" 4. "To arms! they come! the Greek! the Greek!" 5. "My daughter! oh, my daughter!" 6. "Your fathers, where are they?" 7. "My son, have you seen him?"

Parse all the nouns in the following sentences:

1. Boys like to play. 2. The Atlantic Ocean is three thousand miles wide. 3. Johnson the doctor is a brother of Johnson the lawyer. 4. Shakspeare lived in Queen Elizabeth's reign. 5. "Ah, Warwick! Warwick! wert thou as we are!"

6. Temperance is a virtue. 7. King Agrippa, believest thou the prophets? 8. The inferior animals are divided into five classes: quadrupeds, fowls, fishes, reptiles, and insects. 9. The little army fought bravely on that day. 10. Where are the Platos and Aristotles of modern times? 11. I have seen Mr. Squires, the bookseller and stationer.

Correct all errors in the following sentences:

1. I have two brother-in-laws. 2. There were three knight-templars in the procession. 3. Nebulas are sometimes called stardust. 4. I saw the two Mrs. Jackson. 5. The Friends' are holding a meeting: some people call them Quaker's. 6. He called at Steele's the banker's. 7. The Jones' were all there.

8. The boys slate was broken. 9. The mens' wages should be paid promptly. 10. The colonel's of the 7th regiment's horse ran away. 11. She is reading in her sister's Susan's book. 12. He studied O. B. Pierce' Grammar. 13. The fellows impudence was intolerable. 14. He has octavoes, quartoes, and folioes, among his books.

THE ADJECTIVE.
40. Oral Lesson.

Here are some apples, nice for eating: what shall we call them? *Ans.—Ripe* apples. I have just eaten one, and it tasted sweet: what else can we call them? *Ans.—Sweet* apples. They are quite soft: what else can we call them? *Ans.—Mellow* apples. Write on your slates, "*Ripe, sweet, mellow* apples." All these words denote some quality of the apples: what shall we call them? *Ans.— Quality-words.* A very good name.

Let us count the apples: *one* apple, *two* apples, *three* apples, *four* apples. Let us also number them: the *first* apple, the *second* apple, the *third* apple, the *fourth* apple. Write these numbers on your slates, as I write them on the blackboard—*one, two, three, four: first, second, third, fourth.* What shall we call these words? *Ans.— Number-words.*

When I speak of the apple nearest me, I say, "*This* apple;" when of one farther from me, "*That* apple." Do the words *this* and *that* denote any *quality* of the apples? *Ans.—*They do not. What do they do, then? *Ans.—*They point them out. Very well: what shall we call them? *Ans.—Pointing-out-words.*

You see that all the words we have used, in some manner describe "apples." Some denote quality: some, number: some merely point out. What is the word "apple?" *Ans.—*A noun. Then they all describe a noun. We will call those words which describe or limit the meaning of nouns, *Adjectives.* What are all of these words? *Ans.—*Adjectives.

The "quality-words" we will call *Descriptive Adjectives,* because they describe by denoting some quality. The "number-words" and "pointing-out-words" do not denote quality. We will call them *Definitive Adjectives.*

Write "This is a good book." What is "good?" *Ans.—*An adjective. Why? *Ans.—*It describes the word "book." What kind? *Ans.—*Descriptive. Why? *Ans.—*It denotes a quality belonging to the book. Write "These two books are mine." What are "these" and "two?" *Ans.—*Adjectives. Why? *Ans.—*They describe "books." What kind? *Ans.—*Definitive. Why? *Ans.—* They define without denoting any quality.

Write "Every man can do some good." What are "every" and "some?" *Ans.—*Adjectives. Why? *Ans.—*They limit nouns. What kind? *Ans.—*Definitive. Why? *Ans.—*They define without denoting any quality.

41. Definition.

An **Adjective** is a word used to describe or define the meaning of a noun; as, *wise* men, *that* book, *three* steamships, the *fourth* stanza.

Rem.—The English language has about 7,000 adjectives.

42. Classes.

Adjectives may be divided into two general classes: *Descriptive* and *Definitive.*

43. Descriptive Adjectives.

1. A **Descriptive Adjective** describes the meaning of a noun by denoting some quality belonging to it.

Ex.—A *round* table, a *square* table, a *sour* apple, a *sweet* apple, a *good* boy, a *bad* boy, an *Italian* sunset, *twinkling* stars, *thick-warbled* songs.

2. There are three kinds of Descriptive Adjectives: *Common, Proper,* and *Participial.*

3. A **Common Adjective** is any ordinary epithet; as, *good, hard, broad, flexible.*

4. A **Proper Adjective** is an adjective derived from a proper noun; as, *French, American, Websterian.*

5. A **Participial Adjective** is a participle placed before the noun which it describes; as, a *shining* light, *echoing* shouts, a *written* agreement.

Rem. 1.—Words commonly used as other parts of speech, sometimes perform the office of descriptive adjectives, and should be parsed as such.

Ex.—A *gold* ring, a *silver* cord, the *California* pine, a *make-believe* patriot, *double-distilled* nonsense. "The West is as truly *American,* as genuinely *Jonathan,* as any other part of our country."

Rem. 2.—An adjective is frequently limited by a word joined to it by a hyphen. The compound term thus formed is called a compound adjective, and should be parsed as a single word.

Ex.—A *high-sounding* title, an *ill-matched* pair.

Rem. 3.—Participial adjectives are derived directly from verbs. Participles usually follow the nouns they describe.

Rem. 4.—When a descriptive adjective represents a noun understood, or not expressed, the article must be prefixed; as, "*The wise* are provident;" "*The good* are happy." Adjectives thus used should be parsed as "*adjectives used as nouns.*"

Tell which of the adjectives in the following sentences are Common, Proper, and Participial:

1. The unfortunate man was a hard-working mechanic. 2. The fields looked beautiful. 3. English books are costly. 4. The howling storm is passed. 5. The soil is very productive. 6. The water falls into a marble basin. 7. I prefer a New England winter to an Australian summer.

44. Definitive Adjectives.

1. A **Definitive Adjective** limits or defines the meaning or application of a noun without expressing any of its qualities.

Ex.—*The* Ohio, *that* man, *three* dollars, the *third* seal, a *two-fold* reference. "*All* men are mortal." "*Each* soldier received his pay."

2. Definitive Adjectives are divided into three classes: *Articles, Pronominal Adjectives,* and *Numeral Adjectives.*

45. Articles.

1. **The** is called the *Definite Article,* because it definitely points out the object which it defines or restricts; as, "*The* book is on *the* table;" "*The* horse ran over *the* bridge."

2. **A** or **An** is called the *Indefinite Article,* because it defines or restricts in an indefinite or general manner; as, "*A* book is on *a* table;" "*A* horse ran over *a* bridge."

3. **An** should be used before words beginning with a vowel sound; **A** before words beginning with a consonant sound. They are spoken of as *one* article, because they are merely a later and an earlier form of the same word.

Rem. 1.—The *definite* article is used,

1. To point out a particular object or class of objects, or a particular individual or portion of a class; as, "*The* sun and *the* moon;" "*The* Turks and *the* Greeks are at war;" "*The* rich and *the* poor here meet together."

2. To distinguish an object from another having the same name; as, *Mississippi*, the name of a State; *the Mississippi*, the name of a river: *Robert Fulton*, the name of a person; *the Robert Fulton*, the name of a steam-boat.

3. To point out an object as familiarly known or spoken of, or as preëminently distinguished; as, "*The Hibernia* sailed yesterday;" "*The Capitol* is a noble building;" "*The* immortal *Washington*."

Rem. 2.—The *indefinite* article is used to show that no particular one of a class is meant—the leading idea being *any* or *one;* as, *a* man, *i. e.*, *any* man, or *one* man; "*A* picture hangs on the wall," *i. e.*, *one* picture. "Bring me *a* book," *i. e.*, *any* book.

Rem. 3.—The *indefinite* article may be used,

1. To point out a single individual; as, *a* plum, *i. e.*, *one* plum; *a* horse, *i. e.*, *one* horse; *an* ox, *i. e.*, *one* ox.

2. To point out a single sum or aggregate; as, *a* dozen apples, *a* few dimes, *a* hundred dollars, *a* wealthy people.

Rem. 4.—An article sometimes limits, not a noun alone, but a noun as limited by other words; as, "*The old men* retired early; *the young men* remained until midnight." The article here limits the complex ideas "old men" and "young men." "*An early spring* is no sign of *a fruitful season*." The article here limits the complex ideas "early spring" and "fruitful season."

46. Pronominal Adjectives.

1. **Pronominal Adjectives** are definitives, most of which may, without an article prefixed, represent a noun understood; as, *all* men, *each* soldier, *yonder* mountain.

2. They may be divided into three classes: *Demonstratives, Distributives*, and *Indefinites*.

47. Demonstratives.

1. **Demonstratives** point out objects definitely. They are *this, that, these, those, former, latter, both, same, yon, yonder*.

2. **This,** (plural **these,**) distinctly points out an object as near in place or time; as, "*This* desk and *these* books."

3. **That,** (plural **those,**) distinctly points out an object as not near, or not so near as some other object; as, "*That* desk and *those* books."

4. In speaking of two objects, *that* should refer to the former, and *this* to the latter; as, "*These* horses are larger than *those*."

5. **Former** and **latter** are used to designate which of two objects previously mentioned is referred to; as, "The cry of danger to the *Union* was raised to divert their assaults upon the *Constitution*. It was the *latter*, and not the *former*, which was in danger."

6. **Both** implies *not only the one but the other also ;* as, "*Both* forts were taken;" "James and Silas were *both* tardy."

7. **Same** denotes an identical or similar object; as, "That is the *same* man we saw yesterday;" "Both tables are made of the *same* wood."

8. **Yon** and **yonder** point out some object in sight; as, "*Yon* house on the hill;" "*Yonder* mountain is a volcano."

48. Distributives.

1. **Distributives** represent objects as taken separately. There are four distributives: *each, every, either, neither.*

2. **Each** can be applied to one of two or any greater number; as, "*Each* warrior drew his battle blade;" "Useless *each* without the other."

3. **Every** can be applied to one of more than two individuals only; as, "They received *every* man a penny;" "*Every* person in the room was astonished."

4. **Either** can be applied to one of two objects only; as, "*Either* of the two roads leads to town;" "You may have *either* house."

5. **Neither** means *not either ;* as, "Which of the two shall I take? both? one? or *neither ?*"

49. Indefinites.

1. **Indefinites** refer to objects in a general way, without pointing out any one in particular. The principal indefinites are *all, any, another, certain, divers, enough, few, little, many, much, no, none, one, own, other, several, some, sundry, which, whichever, whichsoever, what, whatever, whatsoever.*

2. **All** describes objects taken together; as, "*All* the years of man's life;" "*All* men are mortal."

3. **Any** denotes a single one of many; as, "Have you *any* wheat to sell?" "Neither go into the town, nor tell it to *any* in the town."

4. **Another, or other,** denotes something distinct from something else of the same kind; as, "He took *another* road;" "He will let out his vineyard to *other* husbandmen."

5. **Certain** denotes *one* or *some* in an indefinite sense; as, "And I, Daniel, was sick *certain* days;" "I shall not vote for a *certain* individual."

6. **Divers** means *unlike, various, numerous;* as, "A prey of *divers* colors of needle-work;" "*Divers* miracles."

7. **Enough** denotes a *sufficiency;* as, "I have *enough* for my brother;" "*Enough* has been said already."

8. **Few** denotes *not many, a small number;* as, "Many shall be called, but *few* chosen;" "I have a *few* old books."

9. **Little** means small in quantity, amount, or duration; as, "A *little* learning is a dangerous thing;" "A *little* sleep, a *little* slumber, a *little* folding of the hands to sleep."

10. **Many** denotes a large number; as, "*Many* men of *many* minds;" "The mutable, rank-scented *many*."—*Shakspeare.*

11. **Much** denotes a large quantity; as, "There is *much* wealth in this town;" "Thou shalt carry *much* seed out into the field, and shalt gather but little in."

12. **No** means *not any, none.* As a noun it means one who votes in the negative; as, "The *noes* have it."

13. **None** means *not one,* or *not any;* as, "Ye shall flee when *none* pursueth you;" "Thou shalt have *none* assurance of thy life."

14. **One** corresponds to *another;* as, "They love *one another*," *i e.*, each person loves the other.

15. **Own** implies possession with emphasis or distinction; as, "My *own* home;" "Our *own* dear mother."

16. **Several** denotes any small number more than two; as, "*Several* victories." Also, *single, individual;* as, "I'll kiss each *several* paper for amends."

17. **Some** denotes a certain but indeterminate number or quantity; as, "*Some* money;" "I have brought *some* books."

18. **Sundry** means *various, divers;* as, "So teach *sundry* grammarians."

19. **What** and **which,** and their compounds, point out objects *definitely* or *indefinitely;* as, "*What* lesson shall we learn tomorrow?" "He told me *which* of the two did it."

50. Numeral Adjectives.

1. **Numeral Adjectives** are those which express number and order definitely; as, *four, fourth, fourfold.*

2. They are divided into three classes: *Cardinal, Ordinal,* and *Multiplicative.*

3. **Cardinal Numerals** denote simply the number of objects; as, *two, thirteen, fifty, a thousand.*

4. **Ordinal Numerals** mark the position of an object in a series; as, *second, thirteenth, fiftieth, the thousandth.*

5. **Multiplicative Numerals** denote how many fold; as, *twofold, fourfold.*

GENERAL REMARKS.

1. When a noun, limited by either a descriptive or a definitive adjective, is some indefinite word, or has been previously used in the same sentence, it may be omitted; as, "The cedars highest on the mountain are the *smallest;*" "The *foremost* horse is a better animal than the *hindmost.*" "Give me *this* book, and you may have *that.*"

2. *Such, many, only, but, much,* and *not,* when used alone limit plural nouns only. When followed by the indefinite article *a* or *an,* the phrases *such a, many a,* &c., limit singular nouns; as, "If you repay me not on *such a* day;" "*Many a* time;" "He is *but a* man;" "*Not a* drum was heard." These phrases should be parsed as single words.

3. When. definitive adjectives are used in connection with descriptive, the former should be placed first; as, "*That* valuable property;" "*Ten* small houses."

4. When cardinal and ordinal numerals are used together, the latter should be placed first; as, "The *last* two days;" "The *first* three chapters."

5. A *cardinal* numeral used as a noun, requires no article: an *ordinal* should have the article prefixed; as, "Were not *ten* cleansed?" "The *tenth* was rescued."

6. *Each other* and *one another* are sometimes called **reciprocals,** because they are reciprocally related; as, "They mutually assist *each other;*" "They help *one another.*"

7. Adjectives which vary in form to denote number, should agree in that property with the nouns they limit. Say, "*this* sort," not "*these* sort."

8. Other parts of speech should not be improperly used as adjectives. Say "*these* books," not "*them* books;" "His voice sounds *harsh,*" not "*harshly.*"

51. Comparison.

1. **Comparison** is a variation of the adjective to express different degrees of quality; as, *wise, wiser, wisest; good, better, best.*

2. There are three **Degrees of Comparison**: the *Positive,* the *Comparative,* and the *Superlative.*

3. The **Positive** degree ascribes to an object the simple quality, or an equal degree of the quality; as, "A *mild* winter;" "She is as *good* as she is *beautiful.*"

4. The **Comparative** degree ascribes to one of two objects a higher or lower degree of the quality than that

expressed by the positive; as, "A *milder* winter than usual;" "Mary is *less studious* than Emma."

5. The **Superlative** degree ascribes the highest or lowest degree of the quality to one of more than two objects; as, "The *mildest* winter ever known;" "The *least skillful* rider could do no worse."

Rem. 1.—The suffix *ish,* and the words *rather, somewhat,* &c., denote the possession of a little of the quality; as, *bluish, rather* young, *somewhat* uncomfortable.

Rem. 2.—The words *altogether, far, by far, vastly, much, very, exceedingly, a most, a little, too, very, slightly, greatly,* &c., denote a high degree of the quality without implying comparison; as, *very* useful, *exceedingly* welcome, *a most* valuable invention.

Rem. 3.—Adjectives denoting qualities which can not exist in different degrees, can not, with propriety, be compared—though some writers, not taking them in their full sense, often use them in the comparative and superlative degrees.

Ex.—Blind, deaf, perfect, right, level, square, straight, perpendicular, equal, naked, honest, sincere, hollow, empty, dead. "My *sincerest* regards." "Our sight is the *most perfect* of our senses."

52. Of Comparatives and Superlatives.

1. In **Ascending** comparison, the comparative and superlative degrees are regularly formed,

1st. By adding to the positive of monosyllables, *r* or *er* for the comparative, and *st* or *est* for the superlative; as, *wise, wiser, wisest; hard, harder, hardest.*

2d. By prefixing to the positive of adjectives of more than one syllable, *more* for the comparative, and *most* for the superlative; as, *honorable, more honorable, most honorable.*

Rem. 1.—Most adjectives of two syllables ending in *y* or *le,* after a consonant, or accented on the second syllable, form their comparative and superlative degrees like monosyllables; as, *holy, holier, holiest; gentle, gentler, gentlest.*

Rem. 2.—Some adjectives of two syllables, ending in a vowel or liquid sound, form their comparative and superlative degrees like monosyllables; as, *handsome, handsomer, handsomest; narrow, narrower, narrowest.*

Rem. 3.—Some words are expressed in the superlative degree by adding the suffix *most;* as, *hindmost, innermost.*

2. In **Descending** comparison, the comparative is formed by prefixing *less,* and the superlative by prefixing *least,* to the positive; as, *wise, less wise, least wise.*

3. Some adjectives are compared *irregularly;* as, *good, better, best; bad, worse, worst.*

Rem. 1.—Poets sometimes compare monosyllables by prefixing *more* and *most;* as, "A foot *more light,* a step *more true.*"

Rem. 2.—When monosyllabic and polysyllabic adjectives come together, the monosyllables are placed first, and all are compared by prefixing *more* and *most;* as, "The *more nice* and *elegant* parts;" "The *most rude* and *barbarous* people."

Rem. 3.—Adjectives should not be doubly compared; as, "A *more healthier* climate;" "After the *most strictest* sect of our religion, I lived a Pharisee."

53. Order of Parsing.

1. An Adjective, and why?
2. Descriptive or Definitive, and why?
3. Compare it, if it admits of comparison.
4. Degree of comparison, and why?
5. What does it describe or define?
6. Rule.

54. Models for Parsing.

I. "*Every diligent* boy received *merited* praise."

Every . . . is an *adjective;* it is a word used to describe or define the meaning of a noun: *definitive;* it defines without expressing any quality: *distributive pronominal;* it represents objects taken separately: it can not be compared, and belongs to "boy." Rule XII. "An adjective or participle belongs to some noun or pronoun."

Diligent . is an *adjective;* (why?): *descriptive;* it describes a noun by denoting some quality: *common;* it is an ordinary epithet: *compared, pos.* diligent, *comp.* more diligent, *sup.* most diligent: *positive degree,* and belongs to "boy." Rule XII.

Merited . is an *adjective;* (why?): *descriptive;* (why?): *participial;* it is a participle placed before the noun it limits: *compared, pos.* merited, *comp.* more merited, *sup.* most merited: *positive degree,* and belongs to "praise." Rule XII.

II. *"Many a fine* intellect is buried in poverty."

Many a . . is an *adjective;* (why?): *definitive;* (why?): *indefinite pronominal;* it refers to objects in a general way: it can not be compared, and belongs to "intellect." Rule XII.

Fine . . . . is an *adjective;* (why?): *descriptive;* (why?): *common;* (why?): *compared, pos.* fine, *comp.* finer, *sup.* finest: *positive degree,* and belongs to "intellect." Rule XII.

III. *"The first two* engravings are *American harvest* scenes."

The . . . . is an *adjective;* (why?): *definitive;* (why?): *definite article;* (why?): it can not be compared, and belongs to "engravings." Rule XII.

First . . . . is an *adjective;* (why?): *definitive;* (why?): *numeral;* it denotes number: *ordinal;* it marks the position of an object in a series: it can not be compared, and belongs to "engravings." Rule XII.

Two . . . . is an *adjective;* (why?): *definitive;* (why?): *numeral;* (why?): *cardinal;* it denotes the number of objects: it can not be compared, and belongs to "engravings." Rule XII.

American is an *adjective;* (why?): *descriptive;* (why?): *proper;* it is derived from a proper noun: it can not be compared, and belongs to "scenes." Rule XII.

Harvest . is an *adjective;* (why?): *descriptive;* (why?) *common;* (why?): it can not be compared, and belongs to "scenes." Rule XII.

IV. "The weather is *pleasant.*"

Pleasant . is an *adjective;* (why?): *descriptive;* (why?): *common;* (why?): *compared, pos.* pleasant, *comp.* more pleasant; *sup.* most pleasant: *positive degree,* and belongs to "weather." Rule XII.

55. Exercises.

Parse the nouns and adjectives in the following sentences:

1. A loud report was heard. 2. Fearful storms sweep over these beautiful islands. 3. Life is but a vapor. 4. These walks are quiet and secluded. 5. I feel sad and lonely. 6. The fields look green. 7. He took a twofold view of the subject. 8. Bright and joyful is the morn. 9. The steak was cooked rare.

10. Either road leads to town. 11. Each soldier was a host in himself. 12. Both horses are lame. 13. Such a law is a disgrace to any state. 14. Repeat the first four lines in concert. 15. My drowsy powers, why sleep ye so? 16. Homer was a greater poet than Virgil. 17. One story is good until another is told. 18. Silver and gold have I none. 19. The Australian gold fields are very extensive. 20. The floor was formed of six-inch boards.

> 21. My opening eyes with rapture see
> The dawn of this returning day.

> 22. With many a weary step, and many a groan,
> Up the high hill he heaves a huge round stone.

> 23. Strong Creator, Savior mild,
> Humbled to a little child,
> Captive, beaten, bound, reviled—
> Jesus! hear and save.

Exercises to be corrected:

1. Put them books on the table. 2. You may have either of them six apples. 3. Neither of my three hats is large enough. 4. That book you are now reading was printed in 1578. 5. These men we saw yesterday were Italians. 6. He gave a reward to all of the four men. 7. None of the two young ladies is very beautiful.

8. There are less boys in school now than formerly.—(*Less* suggests *quantity—fewer* suggests *number.*) 9. I have caught less fish than you. 10. They worship both the sun, moon, and stars. 11. There is no glory in doing what every body can do. 12. Such persons as desire may remain.—(Do not use *such* instead of *all.*) 13. The gravel walk was rolled smoothly. 14. I like our now minister very much. 15. The eggs were boiled hardly. 16. John reads too loudly.

17. The relative should be placed as nearly as possible to its antecedent. 18. Often touching will soil silver. 19. There are not fewer than ten tons of iron in that bridge. 20. Every member are expected to contribute something. 21. Sing the two first and the two last verses.

22. You may have the peaches on the three first trees in them two rows. 23. The former of them five sentences is incorrect. 24. I never saw a more happier man. 25. Worser evils than poverty can be imagined. 26. That was the most unkindest cut of all. 27. He is the awkwardest, backwardest boy in school.

28. I do not like these kind of apples. 29. I would rather have a squarer box. 30. Which is meanest, a miser or a thief? 31. Jacob loved Joseph more than all his children. 32. None of our family was at the party last evening. 33. That man occupies the largest storeroom of any in the town.

THE PRONOUN.

56. Oral Lesson.

Notice what I write: "John took John's hat, and put John's hat on John's desk." Do you think this is a correct sentence? *Ans.*—No, sir, we do not. What words are unnecessarily repeated? *Ans.*—"John" and "hat." Write the sentence on your slates as you think it should be written. Sarah, you may read what you have written. (Sarah reads "John took his hat, and put it on his desk." The teacher writes it on the blackboard.) Now, the words used in the place of "John" and "hat," are called *Pronouns*, which means "instead of nouns." What shall we call all words used instead of nouns? *Ans.*—Pronouns.

I will write again: "*I* write, *you* read, but *he* whispers." What are the words "I," "you," and "he"? *Ans.*—Pronouns. Why? *Ans.*—Because they are used instead of nouns. What *person* is "I"? *Ans.*—*First person*, because it stands for the person speaking. What *person* is "you"? *Ans.*—*Second person*, because it stands for the person spoken to. What *person* is "he"? *Ans.*—*Third person*, because it stands for the person spoken of. Those words which show by their form the *person* of the nouns they represent are called *Personal Pronouns*. What kind of pronouns are these words? *Ans.*—Personal Pronouns.

Write this sentence: "The man who was with me is a lawyer." What is "me"? *Ans.*—A pronoun. What other pronoun is there in the sentence? *Ans.*—"Who." That is right—and what word does "who" stand for? *Ans.*—Man. But "who" can be used to represent the *first, second,* or *third* person; as, "I *who* speak to you;" "You *who* listen;" "He *who* whispers." It does not change its

H. G. 5.

form to denote person, but *relates* to some noun, and must be of the same person and number as the noun to which it relates. It is therefore called a *Relative Pronoun*. What shall we call all similar words? *Ans.*—Relative Pronouns.

Write this sentence: "Who has lost a pencil?" The word "who" is here used in asking a question. We will call it an *Interrogative Pronoun*. What shall we call those pronouns which are used in a similar manner? *Ans.*—Interrogative Pronouns.

Write this sentence: "That book is mine." What two words can I use instead of "mine?" *Ans.*—"My book." "Mine," then, stands for both the possessor and the thing possessed. We will call it a *Possessive Pronoun*. What shall we call all words used in a similar manner? *Ans.*—Possessive Pronouns.

57. Definition.

1. A **Pronoun** is a word used instead of a noun; as, *his* book, *my* house; "*Whom* did *you* see?"

2. The **Antecedent** of a pronoun is the noun, or equivalent expression, instead of which the pronoun is used. It usually precedes, but sometimes follows the pronoun.

Ex.—"The poor *widow* lost *her* only son." Here "widow" is the antecedent of "her." "True to *his* flag, the *soldier* braved even death." "Soldier" is the antecedent of "his."

3. The Antecedent may be a noun, a different pronoun, a phrase, or a clause.

Ex.—"A *pupil that* is studious will learn." "Pupil" is the antecedent of "that." "*He who* runs may read." "He" is the antecedent of "who." "He desired *to pray*, but *it* was denied him." "To pray" is the antecedent of "it." "*He has squandered his money*, and he now regrets *it*." "He has squandered his money" is the antecedent of "it."

4. The Antecedent may be omitted; in which case it is said to be understood.

Ex.—"*Who* steals my purse steals trash." "The person," or "he," understood, is the antecedent of "who."

58. Properties.

1. The **Properties** of a Pronoun are *Gender, Person, Number,* and *Case.*

2. The *gender, person,* and *number* of a pronoun are always the same as those of its antecedent, but its *case* depends upon the construction of the clause in which it is found.

59. Classes.

Pronouns are divided into four classes: *Personal, Possessive, Relative,* and *Interrogative.*

60. Personal Pronouns.

1. **Personal Pronouns** both represent nouns, and show by their form whether they are of the first, second, or third person. They are either *Simple* or *Compound.*

2. The **Simple Personal Pronouns** are *I, thou, he, she,* and *it,* with their declined forms, *we, our, us, my, mine, ye, you, your, thy, thine, thee, his, him, her, its, they, their, them.*

3. The **Compound Personal Pronouns** are formed by adding *self* or *selves* to some form of the Simple Personals; as, *myself, yourselves, himself, themselves.*

61. Declension.

1. The Simple Personal Pronouns are declined as fol lows:

First Person.

	Singular.		Plural.
Nom.	I,	*Nom.*	We,
Poss.	My or mine,	*Poss.*	Our,
Obj.	Me.	*Obj.*	Us.

Second Person.

	Singular.	*Plural.*		*Singular.*	*Plural.*
Nom.	Thou,	Ye,	*Nom.*	You,	You,
Poss.	Thy or thine,	Your,	*Poss.*	Your,	Your,
Obj.	Thee,	You.	*Obj.*	You,	You.

Third Person.

	Singular.				*Plural.*
	Mas.	*Fem.*	*Neut.*		*Neut. or Com.*
Nom.	He,	She,	It,	*Nom.*	They,
Poss.	His,	Her,	Its,	*Poss.*	Their,
Obj.	Him,	Her,	It.	*Obj.*	Them.

2. The Compound Personal Pronouns are declined as follows:

First Person.

	Singular.		*Plural.*
Nom. & Obj.	Myself.	*Nom. & Obj.*	Ourselves.

Second Person.

	Singular.		*Plural.*
Nom. & Obj.	Thyself or Yourself.	*Nom. & Obj.*	Yourselves.

Third Person.

	Singular.		*Plural.*
	Mas., Fem. & Neut.		
Nom. & Obj.	{ Himself, Herself, Itself.	*Nom. & Obj.*	Themselves.

GENERAL REMARKS.

1. *Mine* and *thine* were formerly used before words commencing with a vowel sound, in preference to *my* and *thy*. They are still used thus in poetry; as, "*Thine* eyes I see thee raise."

2. *Thou, thy, thine, thee, thyself,* and *ye,* though habitually used by the Friends, and frequently in poetry, in the Bible, and other sacred writings, are now seldom used except in solemn style

They may be regarded as antiquated forms. *You, your, yours,* and *yourself,* are now preferred.

3. *You,* originally plural, and still plural in its grammatical relations, is used to represent singular as well as plural nouns.

4. *We* is often used in place of *I,* in royal proclamations, editorials, and when the speaker or writer wishes to avoid the appearance of egotism; as, "*We,* George III, King of Great Britain and Ireland, do proclaim," &c. "*We* formerly thought differently, but have changed *our* mind."

5. *It* is sometimes used in the nominative without referring to any particular antecedent; and in the objective for euphony alone; as, "*It* thunders;" "*It* seems to me;" "*It* is a true saying;" "Come and trip *it* on the green."

6. The compound personal pronouns are used in the nominative and objective cases only. To express emphatic distinction in the possessive case, the word *own* is used instead of *self* or *selves;* as, "Let every pupil use his *own* book;" "Successful merchants mind their *own* business, not that of their neighbors."

7. The English language being destitute of a pronoun of the third person singular and common gender, usage has sanctioned the employment of the masculine forms *he, his, him,* for that purpose; as, in speaking of scholars generally, we say, "A thorough scholar studies *his* lesson carefully."

8. When reference is made to an assemblage containing males only, or females only, the masculine or feminine forms should be used, as the case may require.

9. When pronouns of different *persons* are used, the *second* should precede the *third,* and the *third* the *first;* as, "*You,* and *he,* and *I* were boys together."

62. Order of Parsing.

1. A Pronoun, and why?
2. Personal, and why?
3. Simple or Compound.
4. What its antecedent?
5. Gender, person, and number? Rule.
6. Decline it.
7. Case, and why?
8. Rule.

63. Models for Parsing.

I. "*I* have seen *him*."

I . . . . is a *pronoun;* (why?): *personal;* it shows by its form whether it is of the first, second, or third person: *simple;* its antecedent is the name, understood, of the person speaking: —— *gender, first person, singular number*, to agree with its antecedent: Rule IX. "Pronouns must agree with their antecedents in gender, person, and number:" declined, *singular, nom.* I, *poss.* my, *obj.* me; *plural, nom.* we, *poss.* our, *obj.* us: *nominative case;* (why?): Rule I.

Him . . . . . is a *pronoun;* (why?): *personal;* (why?): *simple;* its antecedent is the name, understood, of the person spoken of: *masculine gender, third person, singular number*, to agree with its antecedent: Rule IX: declined, *sing., nom.* he, *poss.* his, *obj.* him; *plural, nom.* they, *poss.* their, *obj.* them: *objective case;* (why?): Rule VI.

II. "James, lend *me your* book."

Me . . . . is a *pronoun;* (why?): *personal;* (why?): *simple;* its antecedent is the name, understood, of the speaker: —— *gender, first person, singular number*, to agree with its antecedent: Rule IX: *decline it: objective case*, it is the *indirect object* of transitive verb "lend." Rule VI.

III. "The soldiers helped *themselves*."

Themselves is a *pronoun;* (why?): *compound personal;* it is formed by adding *selves* to one of the declined forms of a simple personal: its antecedent is "soldiers:" *masculine gender, third person, plural number*, to agree with its antecedent: Rule IX: *decline it: objective case*, it is the object of the transitive verb "helped." Rule XI.

IV. "I, *myself*, heard him say so."

Myself . . . . is a *pronoun;* (why?): *compound personal;* (why?): its antecedent is the name, understood, of the speaker: —— *gender, first person, singular number*, to agree with its antecedent: Rule IX: *decline it: nominative case*, in apposition with "I:" Rule IV.

64. Exercises.

Parse the nouns, personal pronouns, and adjectives in the following sentences:

1. He and I attend the same school.   2. She gave her sister a new book.   3. Have you seen him to-day?   4. I saw it with my own eyes.   5. You, yourself, told me so.   6. The wicked is snared in the work of his own hands.   7. I bought the book, and read it. 8. They live in our house.

9. I see them on their winding way.   10. For we dare not make ourselves of the number, or compare ourselves with some that commend themselves: but they, measuring themselves by themselves, and comparing themselves among themselves, are not wise.

> 11. My country, 't is of thee,
>   Sweet land of liberty,
>   Of thee, I sing.

> 12. Thou great Instructor, lest I stray,
>   Teach thou my erring feet thy way.

Correct the following sentences:

1. Him and me both study grammar.   2. I and he were playmates.   3. Her and my aunt are great friends.   4. Every person should try to improve their mind and heart.   5. Each scholar should try to learn their lessons.   6. Those molasses, they cost one dollar a gallon.   7. Many a thoughtless youth make good business men—but it is after they have reformed.

8. Both John and Samuel got his lesson.   9. If a fish is caught foul, they are more difficult to land.   10. People should be kind to each other.   11. Did you see which of the scholars finished their examples first?   12. Every boy and girl shall have their reward. 13. Let the President and the Senate make such appointments as it pleases.   14. If any member of the congregation wishes to connect themselves with this church, they will please come forward while the choir sings.

15. They had some victuals left, and we ate it.   16. Every person and every thing was in its proper place.   17. The hen-hawk caught a hen, and killed her on her own nest.   18. The earth is my mother, and I will repose on its bosom.   19. It is me, and not her, who you wish to see.   20. If any passenger has not paid his fare, they will come up to the captain's office and pay it.

65. Possessive Pronouns.

1. **Possessive Pronouns** are words used to represent both the possessor and the thing possessed. They are *mine, thine, his, hers, ours, yours, theirs.*

2. To denote emphatic distinction, *my own* is used for *mine, his own* for *his, thy own* for *thine, our own* for *ours, your own* for *yours, their own* for *theirs.*

Ex.—"This book is *my own;*" "Stand, the ground's *your own.* my braves!" "Do not borrow or lend pencils: each scholar should have one of *his own.*"

Rem.—Two sets of models are given for parsing Possessive Pronouns. Both methods are sanctioned by good authorities.

66. Order of Parsing.

1. A Pronoun, and why?
2. Possessive, and why?
3. What is its antecedent?
4. Gender, person, and number, and why? Rule.
5. Case, and why? Rule.

67. Models for Parsing.

I. "That book is *hers,* not *yours.*"

FIRST METHOD.

Hers . . . . is a *pronoun;* (why?): *possessive;* it represents both the possessor and the thing possessed; its antecedent is "book;" *neuter gender, third person, singular number,* to agree with its antecedent: Rule IX: *nominative case,* it is used as the predicate of the proposition "That book is hers:" Rule II.

Yours . . . is parsed in a similar manner; equivalent to "your book."

SECOND METHOD.

Hers . . . is a *pronoun;* (why?): *possessive;* (why?): it is equivalent to "her book." Parse "her" as a personal pronoun in the possessive case, according to Rule III, and "book" as predicate-nominative, according to Rule II.

II. "The ground's *your own*."

Your own is a *pronoun;* (why?): *possessive;* (why?): its antecedent is "ground:" *neuter gender, third person, singular number;* (why?): *nominative case;* it is used as the predicate of the proposition "The ground's your own." Rule II.

Your own is a *pronoun;* (why?): *possessive;* (why?): it is equivalent to "your ground." Parse "your" as a personal pronoun in the possessive case, according to Rule III, and "ground" as the predicate-nominative, according to Rule II.

68. Exercises.

Parse the possessive pronouns in the following sentences:

1. The farm is neither his nor theirs. 2. Is that horse of yours lame yet? 3. I did not hear that lecture of yours last evening. 4. He is an old friend of ours. 5. This book is not mine; it must be his or hers. 6. That carriage of theirs is a very fine one. 7. Friend of mine, why so sad?

Exercises to be corrected:

1. That horse is his'n. 2. Is that book your'n or her'n? 3. I think it is her'n. 4. He had no team; so he borrowed our'n. 5. Your hat is not so pretty as her'n. 6. We'uns are better off than you'uns. 7. You'uns are a low set.

69. Relative Pronouns.

1. A **Relative Pronoun** is used to represent a preceding word or phrase, called its antecedent, to which it joins a limiting clause; as, "The man *whom* you saw is my father."

Rem. 1.—The **antecedent** is a word or phrase on which the relative clause depends. It may be either a *definite* or an *indefinite* object. When the object is indefinite, the relative clause stands alone; as, "*Who* steals my purse steals trash."

Rem. 2.—The difference between personal and relative pronouns is shown by the following distinctions: 1. Personal pronouns have a distinct form for each grammatical person; as, first person, *I;*

second person, *thou*, or *you;* third person, *he*, *she*, or *it:* the relatives do not change their form for person. 2. A personal pronoun may be the subject of an independent sentence; as, "*He* is well:" a relative can never be thus used; it is always found in a dependent clause; as, "Laws *which* are unjust should be repealed."

Rem. 3.—Relatives serve two purposes in a sentence: one, to represent nouns in any relation; the other, to join a limiting clause to the antecedent. The first is a *pronominal*, the second, a *conjunctive* use.

2. Relative Pronouns are either *Simple* or *Compound*.

3. The **Simple Relatives** are *who*, used to represent persons; *which* and *what*, to represent things; *that*, to represent both persons and things; and *as*, to take the place of *who*, *which*, or *that*, after *such*, *many*, and *same*.

Rem. 1.—*What* is sometimes used as a definitive adjective, as well as a relative, in the same sentence: in which case it is placed before the noun it limits; as, "I send you *what* money I have," *i. e.*, "I send you *the* money *which* I have." When the noun it limits is understood, *what* takes its place, and should be parsed, first as a pronominal adjective, and secondly as a relative.

Rem. 2.—*That* is a *relative* when *who*, *whom*, or *which* can be substituted for it; as, "He *that* [*who*] is slow to wrath, is of great understanding." It is a *pronominal adjective* when it immediately precedes a noun, expressed or understood; as, "*That* book is yours;" "I did not say *that*." It is a *conjunction* when it joins a dependent clause to its principal; as, "I know *that* my Redeemer liveth."

Rem. 3.—*What*, when a relative, can be changed into *that which*, or *the thing which;* as, "Tell me *what* [*that which*] you know;" "I got *what* [*the thing which*] I desired." *That*, or *the thing*, should be parsed as the antecedent part of *what*, and *which* as the relative. The antecedent part, *that*, is usually a pronominal adjective, either limiting a noun expressed, or representing it understood.

Rem. 4.—Besides being a *relative*, *what* may be an *interrogative pronoun;* as "*What* did you say?"—a *pronominal adjective;* as, "*What* book have you?"—an *interjection;* as, "*What!* is thy servant a dog, that he should do this?"—an *adverb;* as, "*What* [*partly*] by force, and *what* by fraud, he secures his ends."

70. Declension.

Singular and Plural.			*Singular and Plural.*
Nom.	Who,	*Nom.*	Which,
Poss.	Whose,	*Poss.*	Whose,
Obj.	Whom.	*Obj.*	Which.

The **Compound Relatives** are formed by adding *ever*, *so*, and *soever* to the simple relatives. They are *whoever*, *whoso*, *whosoever*, *whichever*, *whichsoever*, *whatever*, and *whatsoever*.

Rem.— *Whoever*, *whoso*, and *whosoever*, are equivalent to *he who*, or *any one who;* as, "*Whoever* studies will learn," *i. e.*, "*Any one who* studies will learn." *Whichever* and *whichsoever* are equivalent to *any which;* as, "*Whichever* way you may take will lead to the city," *i. e.*, "*Any* way *which* you may take," &c. *Whatever* and *whatsoever* are equivalent to *any thing which;* as, "I am pleased with *whatever* you may do," *i. e.*, "I am pleased with *any thing which* you may do." Compound relatives are indeclinable, and should be parsed like the simple relative *what*.

71. Order of Parsing.

1. A Pronoun, and why?
2. Relative, and why?
3. Name its antecedent.
4. Simple or Compound?
5. Gender, person, and number, and why? Rule.
6. Decline it.
7. Case, and Rule.

72. Models for Parsing.

I. "A man *who* is industrious, will prosper."

Who .... is a *pronoun;* (why?): *relative;* it represents a preceding word or phrase, to which it joins a limiting clause: its antecedent is "man:" *simple: masculine gender, third person, singular number*, to agree with its antecedent: Rule IX: *nominative case;* it is used as the subject of the subordinate proposition "who is industrious:" Rule I.

II. "I am he *whom* ye seek."

Whom ... is a *pronoun;* (why?): *relative;* (why?): its antecedent is "he:" *simple: masculine gender, third person, singular number;* (why?): Rule IX: *objective case;* it is the object of the transitive verb "seek:" Rule VI.

III. "Happy is the man *that* findeth wisdom."

That .... is a *pronoun;* (why?): *relative;* (why?): its antecedent is "man:" *simple: masculine gender, third person, singular number;* (why?): Rule IX: *nominative case;* it is the subject of the subordinate proposition "That findeth wisdom:" Rule I.

IV. "The horse *which* you sold me is lame."

Which ... is a *pronoun;* (why?): *relative;* (why?): its antecedent is "horse:" *simple: masculine gender, third person, singular number;* (why?): Rule IX: *objective case;* it is the object of the transitive verb "sold:" Rule VI.

V. "I remember *what* you said."

What .... is a *pronoun;* (why?): *relative;* (why?): it is equivalent to *that which*—"*that*" being the *antecedent* part, and "*which*" the *relative.* Parse "*that*" as a "pronominal adjective used as a noun," in the objective case after "remember."

Which ... is a *pronoun* (why?): *relative;* (why?): its antecedent is "that:" *neuter gender, third person, singular number;* (why?): *objective case;* object of the transitive verb "said:" Rule VI.

VI. "That is the man *whose* house we occupy."

Whose ... is a *pronoun;* (why?): *relative;* (why?): its antecedent is "man:" *masculine gender, third person, singular number;* (why?): Rule IX: *possessive case;* modifies "house:" Rule III.

VII. "*Whoever* studies will learn."

Whoever. is a *pronoun;* (why?): *relative;* (why?): *compound;* it is equivalent to *he who,* or *any one who*—"*he*" being the *antecedent* part, and "*who*" the *relative.* Parse "*he*" as a personal pronoun, subject of "will learn," or "*one*" as a "pronominal adjective used as a noun," subject of "will learn," and "*who*" as a relative, by preceding models.

VIII. "*Whatever* purifies sanctifies."

Whatever is a *pronoun;* (why?): *relative;* (why?): *compound;* it is equivalent to *that which.* Parse "*that*" and "*which*" according to Model V—"*that*" being the subject of "sanctifies," "*which*" of "purifies."

IX. "*Whoso* keepeth the law is a wise son."

Whoso... is a *pronoun;* (why?): *relative;* (why?): *compound;* it is equivalent to *he who,* or *any one who.* Parse according to Model VII.

X. "As many *as* came were baptized."

As ...... is a *pronoun;* (why?): *relative;* (why?): its antecedent is "many:" *simple: common gender, third person, plural number;* (why?): Rule IX: *nominative case;* it is used as the subject of the subordinate proposition "as came," *i. e.,* who came: Rule I.

73. Exercises.

Parse the relative pronouns in the following sentences:

1. Those who sow will reap. 2. He that hateth, dissembleth with his lips. 3. They that forsake the law, praise the wicked; but such as keep the law, contend with them. 4. There is no class of persons that I dislike so much as those who slander their neighbors. 5. The house which you admire so much, belongs to the man whom we see yonder.

6. Whatever is, is right. 7. Whatsoever ye shall ask in my name, that will I do. 8. He will do what is right. 9. This is the dog that worried the cat that killed the rat that ate the malt that lay in the house that Jack built. 10. A kind boy avoids doing whatever injures others.

Correct the following sentences:

1. Tell me who you saw. 2. Those which are rich should assist the poor. 3. I am the chap what is not afraid of ghosts. 4. I gave all what I had. 5. This is the man who we sent for. 6. The dog whom you bought, was stolen.

7. Who went with me, I shall not tell. 8. I am happy in the

friend which I have long proved. 9. Whom, when they had scourged him, they let him go. 10. They compose the easiest that have learned to compose. 11. Do you know who you are talking to? 12. They are the sort of people who I do not like. 13. This is the child who was lost.

74. Interrogative Pronouns.

1. The **Interrogative Pronouns** are *who, which,* and *what,* when used in asking questions; as, "*Who* goes there?" "*Which* is yours?" "*What* did you say?"

2. The **Subsequent** of an Interrogative Pronoun is that part of the answer which is represented by it. An Interrogative must agree with its subsequent in gender, person, and number.

Rem. 1.—*Who* seeks to designate some person: *which,* to distinguish a certain individual from others: *what,* to describe the character or occupation of the person inquired for; as, "*Who* is that gentleman?"—Mr. Webster.—"*Which* one?"—Daniel Webster.—"*What* is he?"—An eminent lawyer and statesman.

Rem. 2.—When a definite object is referred to, *which* and *what* are pronominal adjectives, limiting the name of the object inquired for; as, "*Which* lesson shall we learn?" "*What* book shall we study?" When an indefinite object is referred to, the interrogative takes its place; as, "*Which* is mine?" "*What* say you?"

Rem. 3.—The interrogatives *who* and *which* are declined like relative pronouns.

Rem. 4.—Apply Rule IX in parsing interrogatives, changing "antecedents" to "subsequents."

75. Order of Parsing.

1. A Pronoun, and why?
2. Interrogative, and why?
3. Name its subsequent, if expressed.
4. Gender, person, and number. Rule.
5. Decline it.
6. Case, and why? Rule.

76. Models for Parsing.

I. "*Who* goes there?"

Who .. is a *pronoun;* (why?): *interrogative;* it is used in asking a question: its subsequent is indefinite: *gender* and *person* indeterminate: *singular number*, to agree with its subsequent: Rule IX: *nominative case;* it is used as the subject of the sentence "Who goes there?" Rule I.

II. "*Which* is yours?"—The large one.

Which is a *pronoun* (why?): *interrogative;* (why?): its subsequent is "one:" *neuter gender, third person, singular number;* (why?): Rule IX: *nominative case;* it is used as the subject of the sentence "Which is yours?" Rule I.

III. "*What* is that man?"—A blacksmith.

What . is a *pronoun;* (why?): *interrogative;* (why?): its subsequent is "blacksmith:" *masculine gender, third person, singular number;* (why?): Rule IX: *nominative case;* it is used as the predicate of the sentence "What is that man?" Rule II.

77. Exercises.

Parse the interrogative pronouns in the following sentences:

1. Who saw the horse run? 2. Whose house is that on the hill yonder? 3. Whom did he call?—James. 4. For whom did he inquire? 5. Which will you have, the large or the small book?

6. Whom did you take me to be? 7. What shall I do?—Wait. 8. What can be more beautiful than that landscape? 9. Which is the lesson? 10. Who told you how to parse "what"?

Parse the relative and interrogative pronouns in the following sentences:

1. Who is in the garden?—My father. 2. I do not know who is in the garden. 3. Tell me what I should do. 4. What vessel is that? 5. Always seek for what you need the most.

6. Whose house was burned last night?—Mr. Hubbard's. 7. The boy closed the shutters, which darkened the room. 8. What is his name? 9. Whoever enters here should have a pure heart. 10. I gave all that I had.

Correct the following sentences:

1. Whom do you suppose it was?   2. Who do you suppose it to be?   3. Those who consider themselves a good critic are not so considered always by others.   4. One should not think too favorably of themselves.   5. Do you know who you are talking to?

6. The army was cut up, or at least they suffered much.   7. Be sure to tell nobody whom you are.   8. Each of the sexes should be kept within their proper bounds.   9. The council were divided in its estimates.   10. No one could have acted more gallantly than him who bore the standard of the legion.

11. I wish I was her.   12. Many a youth have injured their prospects for life by one imprudent step.   13. The moon appears, but the light is not his own.   14. Between he and I there is some disparity of years, but none between he and she.

15. Whom say the people that I am?   16. Every one of those pleasures that are pursued to excess, convert themselves into poison.   17. They that honor me, I will honor.   18. The very men that had fought in the Peninsular war, and who had received the plaudits of all Europe, were defeated at New Orleans.

19. She was a conspicuous flower, which he had sensibility to love, ambition to attempt, and skill to win.   20. Those lots, if they had been sold sooner, they would have brought more money. ˙

Parse the nouns, pronouns, and adjectives in the following sentences:

1. Virtue is the condition of happiness.   2. Ye are the light of the world.   3. That garment is not well made.   4. One ounce of gold is worth sixteen ounces of silver.   5. The prayers of David, the son of Jesse, are ended.   6. Every man went to his own house. 7. The army is loaded with the spoils of many nations.   8. Be of the same mind one toward another.

9. He sacrificed every thing he had in the world: what could we ask more?   10. Who's here so base that would be a bondman? 11. I speak as to wise men: judge ye what I say.   12. Liberty was theirs as men: without it they did not esteem themselves men. 13. The death of Socrates, peacefully philosophizing with his friends, is the most pleasant that could be desired.   14. I was a stricken deer, that left the herd long since.

15. O Popular Applause! what heart of man
     Is proof against thy sweet, seducing charms?

16. Beauty is but a vain, a fleeting good:
     A shining gloss, that fadeth suddenly.

17. What black, what ceaseless cares besiege our state:
    What strokes we feel from fancy and from fate.

18. Unveil thy bosom, faithful tomb;
    Take this new treasure to thy trust;
    And give these sacred relics room
    To slumber in the silent dust.

19. Thy spirit, Independence, let me share,
    Lord of the lion-heart and eagle-eye:
    Thy steps I'll follow with my bosom bare;
    Nor heed the storm that howls along the sky.

20.   The gay will laugh
    When thou art gone; the solemn brood of care
    Plod on, and each one as before will chase
    His favorite phantom: yet all these shall leave
    Their mirth and their employment, and shall come
    And make their bed with thee.—*Bryant.*

THE VERB.

78. Oral Lesson.

The teacher writes on the blackboard, "A horse runs," and asks "What does the horse do?" *Ans.*—A horse *runs.* What else may a horse do? *Ans.*—A horse *trots, walks, gallops, eats, drinks,* &c. Write these words on your slates. Are they the names of things? *Ans.*—They are not: they are the names of actions. What shall we call them? *Ans.*—*Action-words.* A very good name, but grammarians call them *Verbs.*

Write on your slates, "John studies." What is the subject of the sentence? *Ans.*—"John." What is the predicate? *Ans.*—"Studies." Does the sentence tell what John studies? *Ans.*—It does not. Write "grammar" after the verb "studies." The sentence now reads "John studies *grammar.*" In this sentence, the meaning of "studies" is *completed* by the word "grammar." What element is that word? *Ans.*—An objective element.

A verb which requires an objective element to complete its meaning, is called a *transitive* verb; a verb which does not require an objective element to complete its meaning is called an *intransitive* verb.

H. G. 6.

Why? *Ans.*—Because its meaning is completed by an objective element. What is "run," in the sentence "John runs?" *Ans.*— An intransitive verb. Why? *Ans.*—Because its meaning is not completed by an objective element.

Write this sentence on your slates: "The fields look green." What is the subject of this sentence? *Ans.*—"Fields." What is the predicate? *Ans.*—"Green." What is the office of the word "look"? *Ans.*—It asserts the predicate "green" of the subject "fields." Correctly answered: its use is *copulative;* and all copulative words, except the various forms of "be," are called *copulative verbs.* What is "look" in this sentence? *Ans.*—A copulative verb. What is "seems" in the sentence "He seems afraid?" *Ans.*—A copulative verb. Why? *Ans.*—Because it asserts the predicate of the subject.

79. Definition.

A **Verb** is a word which expresses being, action, or state; as, I *am;* George *writes;* The house *stands.*

Rem.—The *being, action,* or *state,* may be stated abstractly, or represented as belonging to a subject; as, "*To write;*" "Boys *write;*" "*To seem;*" "He *seems* discouraged."

80. Classes with Respect to Use.

1. With respect to their *use,* Verbs may be divided into *Copulative, Transitive,* and *Intransitive.*

2. A **Copulative Verb** is used to assert the predicate of a proposition of the subject; as, "Sugar *is* sweet;" "He *seems* honest."

Rem.—The copula *to be* is the only *pure* copulative. The verbs *become, seem, appear, stand, walk,* and other verbs of *motion, position,* and *condition,* together with the passive verbs *is named, is called, is styled, is elected, is appointed, is constituted, is made, is chosen, is esteemed,* and some others, are frequently used as copulatives.

Ex.—"The road *became* rough;" "The men *appeared* cheerful;" "He *is styled* the Czar of all the Russias;" "Sir Walter Scott *is called* the Wizard of the North;" "Gen. Washington *was elected* first President of the United States."

3. A **Transitive Verb** requires an object to complete its meaning; as, "The hunter *killed* a bear;" "The scholar *learned* his lesson;" "That house *has* seven gables."

4. An **Intransitive Verb** does not require an object to complete its meaning; as, "Flowers *bloom;*" "Grass *grows;*" "The wind *blows* furiously."

Rem. 1.—The action expressed by a *transitive* verb has reference to some object external to the subject, upon which it terminates: the action expressed by an *intransitive* verb has no such reference, but affects the subject only. If an object is required to complete its meaning, a verb is transitive, otherwise intransitive. A verb in the passive form is transitive, if its subject in the passive voice can be made its object in the active.

Ex.—"That boy *studies* algebra." The verb "studies" is transitive, because its meaning is completed by the object "algebra." "That boy *studies.*" The verb "studies" is transitive, because some word, as *lesson, grammar*, &c., is required to complete its meaning. "The winds *blow.*" The verb "blow" is intransitive, because the action expressed by it affects the subject only, and does not require the addition of an object to complete its meaning. "The letter *was written* by me," *i. e.*, I *wrote* the letter. The verb "was written" is transitive, because its subject in the passive voice becomes its object in the active.

Rem. 2.—Verbs which signify *to cause to do* what an intransitive verb expresses, are said to be used in a *causative* sense.

Ex.—"The *farmer* burns wood," *i. e.*, "The farmer *causes wood to burn.*" The verb "burns" is used in a causative sense.

Rem. 3.—Some verbs are transitive in one signification, and intransitive in another.

Ex.—"It *breaks* my chain;" "Glass *breaks* easily;" "He *returned* the book;" "I *returned* home;" "The vessel *ran* the blockade;" "The horses *ran.*"

Rem. 4.—A verb usually intransitive, sometimes becomes transitive. This generally occurs, in poetical expressions, when the object is like the verb in meaning, and when the verb is used in a causative sense.

Ex.—"He *lives* a noble *life;*" "And he *dreamed* yet another *dream;*" "Those men *are playing* a game of chess;" "*Grinned* horribly a ghastly smile;" "The pirate *sank* the ship;" "To equip and *march* armies requires money as well as forethought."

81. Classes with Respect to Nature.

1. With respect to their *nature*, Verbs may be divided into *Active*, *Passive*, and *Neuter*.

2. An **Active Verb** expresses action; as, "Horses *gallop;*" "The farmer *plows.*"

3. A **Passive Verb** represents its subject as acted upon; as, "The field *was plowed;*" "The soldier *was wounded.*"

· 4. A **Neuter Verb** implies being, or condition; as, "I *am;*" "Your hat *lies* on the stand;" "The child *sleeps* in its mother's arms."

82. Classes with Respect to Form.

1. With respect to their *form*, Verbs are either *Regular* or *Irregular*.

2. A **Regular Verb** forms its past indicative and perfect participle by adding *d* or *ed* to the present indicative, or simplest form of the verb; as, love, *love-d, love-d;* count, *count-ed, count-ed.*

3. An **Irregular Verb** does not form its past indicative and perfect participle by adding *d* or *ed* to the present indicative; as, see, *saw, seen;* go, *went, gone.*

83. Properties.

The **Properties** of Verbs are *Voice, Mode, Tense, Number,* and *Person.*

84. Voice.

1. **Voice** is that form of the *transitive* verb which shows whether the subject acts or is acted upon.

2. **Transitive Verbs** have two voices: an *Active* and a *Passive Voice*.

3. The **Active Voice** represents the subject as acting upon an object; as, "John *struck* James;" "The boy *was studying;*" "The cat *caught* the mouse."

4. The **Passive Voice** represents the subject as being acted upon; as, "James *was struck* by John;" "The mouse *was caught;*" "The lesson *was studied.*"

5. The Passive Voice is formed by prefixing some form of the neuter verb *to be* to the perfect participle of a transitive verb.

Rem. 1.—A verb in the active voice is changed into the passive, by making the direct object in the active the subject in the passive.

Ex.—"The boy *shut* the door," (*active;*) "The door *was shut* by the boy," (*passive.*) "He *saw* the comet;" "The comet *was seen* by the astronomer."

Rem. 2.—Certain verbs are sometimes used, with a passive signification, in the active voice. They then denote the capacity to receive an act, rather than its actual reception.

Ex.—"This stick *splits* easily;" "Butter *sells* for forty cents;" "This cloth *wears* well;" "This timber *saws* well;" "The bridge *is building;*" "I have nothing *to wear;*" "He has some ax *to grind;*" "He has no money *to spend* foolishly."

Rem. 3.—A few verbs sometimes assume the passive form, though used in an active sense.

Ex.—"The melancholy days *are come*," i. e., *have* come; "Babylon *is fallen*," i. e., *has* fallen; "She *is gone*," i. e., *has* gone; "The hour *is arrived*," i. e., *has* arrived.

Rem. 4.—The passive voice is used when the agent is unknown, or when we wish to conceal it and call attention to the act and its *object* alone; as, "The robbery *was committed* (by some person unknown, or known but not mentioned) in broad daylight." When we wish to make the agent prominent, the active voice should be used; as, "The escaped convict *committed* the robbery in broad daylight."

85. Exercises.

Tell which of the verbs, in the following sentences, are in the active voice, and which in the passive:

1. Sarah loves flowers.   2. John was astonished at the news. 3. William saw a meteor.   4. A meteor was seen.   5. I have written a letter.   6. That poem was written by Saxe.   7. He should have waited longer.   8. The heavens declare the glory of God. 9. He found the money.

86. The Participle.

1. A **Participle** is a word derived from a verb, partaking of the properties of a verb and of an adjective or a noun.

Rem.—The participle is so called from its partaking of the properties of a verb, and of an adjective and a noun. It is the attributive part of the verb, used without assertion. It is not a verb, consequently neither *mode* nor *tense* belongs to it. It simply denotes *continuance* or *completion* of action, being, or state, relatively to the time denoted by the principal verb of the sentence in which it is found.

2. There are three Participles: the *Present*, the *Perfect*, and the *Compound*. The present and the compound have both an active and a passive form and use. The perfect has an active and a passive use.

3. The **Present Participle** denotes the continuance of action, being, or state; as, *loving, being loved*.

Rem.—The *present active participle* always ends in *ing*. It may be used,

1st. As an adjective; as, *"Twinkling stars."*

2d. As a predicate; as, "The stars are *twinkling*."

3d. As a noun; as, "I am fond of *reading*."

4th. As a noun, with the modifications of a verb; as, *"Describing* a past event as present, has a fine effect in language."

4. The **Perfect Participle** denotes the *completion* of action, being, or state; as, *seen, appointed*.

Rem.—This participle generally, though not always, ends in *d* or *ed*. It is frequently used as an adjective, but never as a noun, and is usually found in compound forms of the verb.

Ex.—"He died, *loved* by all;" "Her promise, *made* cheerfully, was kept faithfully.

5. The **Compound Participle** denotes the *completion* of action, being, or state, at or before the time represented by the principal verb; as, "*Having written* the letter, he mailed it."

Rem.—This participle is formed by placing *having* or *having been* before the perfect participle, and may be used as a noun; as, "I am accused of *having plotted* treason;" "He is charged with *having been engaged* in the slave-trade." It is also formed by placing *having been* before the present participle; as, "*Having been loving.*"

87. Exercises.

Give the present, perfect, and compound participles of the following verbs:

Rely, find, help, study, recite, inquire, answer, plow, cultivate, join, emulate, spell, grow, paint, resemble, hope, suffer, sit, see, go, come, lay, arrive, exhaust, enjoy, write, read, learn, ventilate.

Form sentences, using any of the above participles as predicates.

Model.—"Mary *is studying* her lesson."

88. Auxiliaries.

1. **Auxiliary Verbs** are those which are used in the conjugation of other verbs.

2. They are *do, be, have, shall, will, may, can, must.*

Rem. 1.—*Do, be, have,* and *will* are often used as principal verbs; as, "He *does* well;" "I *am;*" "We *have* cares and anxieties;" "He *willed* me a thousand dollars."

Rem. 2.—The auxiliaries were originally used as principal verbs, followed by the infinitives of what are now called the principal verbs; as, "I *can* [to] read;" "You *may* [to] go;" "He *has* [to] come." The sign *to* is now dropped, and the infinitive is regarded as the principal verb; the auxiliaries being mere *form-words*, showing the relations of *mode* and *tense*.

Rem. 3.—The auxiliaries, when used as such, except *must*, which is used in the present tense only, have two tenses: the *present* and the *past*.

89. Conjugation of the Auxiliaries.

Present Tense.

	Singular.			Plural.	
1st Person.	*2d Person.*	*3d Person.*	*1st Person.*	*2d Person.*	*3d Person.*
I	*Thou*	*He*	*We*	*You*	*They*
Am,	art,	is,	Are,	are,	are,
Do,	dost,	does,	Do,	do,	do,
Have,	hast,	has,	Have,	have,	have,
Will,	wilt,	will,	Will,	will,	will,
Shall,	shalt,	shall,	Shall,	shall,	shall,
May,	mayst,	may,	May,	may,	may,
Can,	canst,	can,	Can,	can,	can,
Must,	must,	must,	Must,	must,	must.

Past Tense.

Was,	wast,	was,	Were,	were,	were,
Did,	didst,	did,	Did,	did,	did,
Had,	hadst,	had,	Had,	had,	had,
Would,	wouldst,	would,	Would,	would,	would,
Should,	shouldst,	should,	Should,	should,	should
Might,	mightst,	might,	Might,	might,	might,
Could,	couldst,	could,	Could,	could,	could.

MODE.

90. Definition.

1. **Mode** is the manner in which the action, being, or state is expressed.

2. There are five modes: the *Indicative*, *Subjunctive*, *Potential*, *Imperative*, and *Infinitive*.

91. Indicative Mode.

The **Indicative Mode** asserts a thing as a fact, or as actually existing; as, "The man *walks;*" "The house *was burned.*"

Rem.—The indicative mode may be used in interrogative and exclamatory sentences; also, in subordinate propositions, to denote what is actual, or what is assumed as actual; as, "*Is* he a merchant?" "The rascal *has stolen* my horse!" "I learn *that you have removed from town.*"

92. Subjunctive Mode.

The **Subjunctive Mode** asserts a thing as *doubtful,* as a *wish,* a *supposition,* or a *future contingency;* as, "If this *be* true, all will end well;" "*Had* I the wings of a dove;" "I shall leave, if you *remain.*"

Rem. 1.—The subjunctive mode is so called because it is used in *subjoined* or subordinate propositions only. It represents an ideal act, or a real act placed under a condition of more or less doubt, and is joined to the verb of the principal proposition by the subordinate connectives *if, though, except, lest, that, unless,* and some others. These connectives are called the *signs* of the subjunctive.

Rem. 2.—The sign is frequently omitted, in which case the auxiliary or copula precedes the subject; as, "*Had* I time," *i. e.,* If I had time; "*Were* I a king," *i. e.,* If I were a king.

Rem. 3.—The *present subjunctive* represents the thing supposed as possible, though doubtful; as, "If I *go:*" I may go or I may not. It implies future time; as, "If it *rain,* I *shall* not *go;*" "It is necessary that the dispatch *be sent* as soon as possible." "If it *rains*" is *indicative,* denoting present time; *i. e.,* it implies that the speaker does not know whether it is raining *now* or not.

Rem. 4.—The *past subjunctive* denotes indefinite or present time, and represents a supposition contrary to the fact, or unreal; as, "If he *were* honest, [implying that he is not,] he *would pay* me." "If he *was* honest" is *indicative,* implying that the speaker

H. G. 7.

does not know whether the person spoken of was honest, in time past, or not.

Rem. 5.—The *past perfect subjunctive* denotes past time, and represents a supposition contrary to the fact; as, "If I *had been* invited, [implying that I had not,] I *should have gone.*"

Rem. 6.—The subjunctive is very generally used in expressing suppositions and conclusions in reasoning; as, "If a regular hexagon *be inscribed* in a circle, any side will be equal to the radius of the circle;" "If the thankful *refrained*, it *would be* pain and grief to them."

93. Potential Mode.

The **Potential Mode** asserts the *power, necessity, liberty, duty,* or *liability* of acting, or being in a certain state; as, "You *can read;*" "He *must go;*" "You *may retire;*" "They *should be* more careful."

Rem. 1.—The potential mode, like the indicative, is used in interrogative and exclamatory sentences; also, in subordinate propositions, to represent what is assumed as actual, or what has not been realized; as, "I know that I *may be* disappointed;" "He says that I *may study* algebra."

Rem. 2.—The *signs* of the potential mode are the auxiliaries *may, can, must, might, could, would,* and *should.*

1. **Can** or **could** implies power or ability *within* one's self; as, "He *can* do it," *i. e.,* he has ability to do it without assistance from others.

2. **May** or **might** implies an agency *without* or *beyond* one's self; hence, *possibility, probability, permission, wishing*—the act being contingent on something beyond one's own will or power; as, "He *may* go," *i. e.,* all hindrances are removed: "You *may* all go to the picnic," denotes permission: "O, that he *might* return," denotes a wish that all hindrance to his return be removed.

3. **Must** denotes physical, mental, or moral necessity; as, "We *must* submit to the laws," *i. e.,* in the nature or fitness of things, there is a necessity for our doing so.

4. **Should** denotes that the act or state is not dependent upon the doer's will, but on that of another; hence, *duty* or *obligation;*

as, "He *should* pay his debts," *i. e.*, it is his duty, or he is under a moral obligation to pay his debts.

5. **Would** implies inclination, wish, or desire; as, "He *would* pay his debts, if he could," *i. e.*, he has the inclination or desire.

94. Imperative Mode.

The **Imperative Mode** expresses a *command,* an *exhortation,* an *entreaty,* or a *permission;* as, "*Charge,* Chester, *charge!*" "*Do come* to see us;" "*Lead* us not into temptation."

Rem. 1.—The imperative mode may usually be known by the omission of the subject; as, "*Write*" [*thou, you,* or *ye*]. It denotes a command, when a superior speaks to an inferior; an exhortation, when an equal speaks to an equal; a prayer or supplication, when an inferior addresses a superior. It is used mostly in principal propositions, and is made subordinate in direct quotations only; as, "He said, '*Be* silent.'"

Rem. 2.—The expressions "*Let* Ellen come," "*Let* him go," &c., are made up of the imperative of the verb *let,* and the objective case of a noun or pronoun, limited by an infinitive. They are equivalent to "*Permit* [thou] Ellen *to* go," &c.

Rem. 3.—These expressions are sometimes abridged by dropping the verb *let,* changing the infinitive to the imperative, and the objective case to the nominative; as, "*Come* one, *come* all," *i. e., Let* one come, *let* all come: "*Sing* we to our God above," *i. e., Let* us sing to our God above. In such cases, the noun or pronoun should be parsed as the subject of the proposition, the imperative agreeing with it in number and person. This use of the imperative, in the first or third person, is not uncommon.

Ex.—"*Ruin seize* thee, ruthless king."—*Gray.* "*Laugh* those who may, *weep* those who must."—*Scott.* "Then *turn* we to her latest tribune's name."—*Byron.* "*Proceed* we therefore to our subject."—*Pope.* "*Be* it enacted."—*Statutes of Ohio.* "*Be* it so."—*Webster.* "Somebody *call* my wife."—*Shakspeare.* "So *help* me God." "Hallowed *be* thy name."

Rem. 4.—The imperative mode is sometimes used to denote merely the intention or wish of the speaker, without special reference to any person addressed; as, "God said, *Let* there be light;"

"*Deliver* me from such friends." It may also be used to denote indifference or unconcern on the part of the speaker; as, "*Let* it rain;" "*Let* him sue me if he dare."

95. Infinitive Mode.

The **Infinitive Mode** expresses the action, being, or state, without affirming it; as, *to write; to have written;* "He rose *to speak.*"

Rem. 1.—The infinitive may usually be known by the sign *to* placed before it. This sign is omitted after the verbs *bid, dare, feel, hear, help, let, make, need, see,* and a few others; as, "*Bid* them *be* quiet;" "*Let* them *come* on;" "*See* him *run.*"

Rem. 2.—The infinitive, as an abstract noun, may be the subject or predicate of a sentence; may be in apposition with a noun; and may be the object of a transitive verb or preposition; as, "*To lie* is disgraceful;" "*To work* is *to pray;*" "Delightful task, *to rear* the tender thought;" "I love *to read;*" "Can save the son of Thetis from *to die.*"

Although the infinitive has the construction of a noun, it may govern an object, or be modified by an adverb. It is never limited by an adjective attribute, but may have a predicate adjective belonging to it; as, "*To converse* is *pleasant.*"

96. Exercises.

Tell the mode of the verbs in the following sentences:

1. A great storm is raging. 2. You may go or stay. 3. Bring me some flowers. 4. Hope thou in God. 5. If he study, he will excel. 6. If he studies, it is when he is alone. 7. Were I rich, I would purchase that property. 8. Who will go with me? 9. Do let me see your book.

10. I must not be tardy. 11. Lift up your heads, O ye gates! 12. Blessed are the poor in spirit; for theirs is the kingdom of heaven. 13. He should have told you. 14. They dare not puzzle us for their own sakes. 15. Let us not, I beseech you, deceive ourselves longer.

16. God help us! what a poor world this would be, if this were the true doctrine. 17. If a line is parallel to a line of a plane, it

is parallel to that plane. 18. If a plane intersect two parallel planes, the lines of intersection will be parallel. 19. Such a man were one for whom a woman's heart should beat constant while he breathes, and break when he dies.

> 20. Reign thou in hell, thy kingdom; let me serve
> In heaven, God ever blest.—*Milton*.

> 21. Place me on Sunium's marble steep,
> Where nothing, save the waves and I,
> May hear our mutual murmurs sweep;
> There, swan-like, let me sing and die.—*Byron*.

TENSE.

97. Definition.

1. **Tense** denotes the *time* of an action or event.

2. There are three divisions of time: *Past*, *Present*, and *Future*. Each division has two tenses: an **absolute** and a **relative**.

3. The **Absolute Tenses** are the *Present*, the *Past*, and the *Future*. They denote indefinite or incomplete action.

4. The **Relative Tenses** are the *Present Perfect*, the *Past Perfect*, and the *Future Perfect*. They denote completed action.

98. Present Tense.

The **Present Tense** denotes present time; as, " I *walk;*" " The army *is marching*."

Rem. 1.—The present tense is used in expressing a general truth, or what is habitual; as, "Perseverance *conquers* all things;" "The mail *arrives* at six P. M."

Rem. 2.—The *historical* present is the present used for the past, to describe more vividly what took place in past time; as, "Tacitus *describes* the manners and customs of the ancient Germans;"

"Ulysses *wakes*, not knowing where he was."—*Pope.* "Matthew *traces* the descent of Joseph; Luke *traces* that of Mary."

Rem. 3.—The *present subjunctive* implies future time; as, "If I *go*, I *shall* not *return.*"

The *present potential* implies either present or future time; as, "It *may be snowing*" (now); "I *may go*" (to-morrow).

The *present imperative* is future in regard to the act or state; as, "*Come* again," *i. e.,* at some future time.

Rem. 4.—The present of the speaker or hearer is what is meant by present time. The present of the reader may not be the same as that of the writer.

Rem. 5.—When preceded by a relative pronoun, or by conjunctive adverbs of time, the present tense is sometimes future in its reference; as, "He will please all who *employ* him;" "The flowers will bloom when spring *comes.*"

99. Present Perfect Tense.

The **Present Perfect Tense** represents an action or event as past, but connected with present time; as, "I *have learned* my lesson."

Rem. 1.—**Have**, the sign of the present perfect tense, originally denoted *possession.* It retains this meaning when used as a principal verb. As an auxiliary, it denotes *completion;* as, "The hunters *have killed* a wolf;" "A man *has fallen* from the bridge."

Rem. 2.—The *present perfect indicative* also expresses action completed in past time, but continued in itself. or in its effects, to the present; as, "He *has lived* here ten years," (and lives here now); "Cicero *has written* orations," (and still lives in his writings).

The *present perfect potential* usually denotes the present or future probability that an act relatively past was performed; as, "I *must have* paid that note," (a fact *now* probable); "In two years he *may have* outgrown you," (a fact *then* to be probable).

Rem. 3.—When preceded by a conjunctive adverb of time, the present perfect tense sometimes denotes future time; as, "He will forward the goods as soon as he *has received* them."

100. Past Tense.

The **Past Tense** expresses what took place in time wholly past; as, "I *wrote;*" "I *was sailing.*"

Rem.—The *past indicative* denotes what was habitual or customary; as, "We *lived* high in those days." In the progressive form, it denotes an act in past time, but not completed; as, "He *was driving* furiously when I saw him."

The *past subjunctive* generally expresses a supposition contrary to the fact, and represents present time; as, "If I *were* going [now], I would ride."

The *past potential* denotes (1) a duty or obligation, without reference to time; as, "Judges *should be* merciful:" (2) a habit or custom; as, "He *would be* absent a week at a time:" (3) ability possessed in past time; as, "He *could* walk yesterday:" (4) present possibility or power; as, "I *could* write [now] if I would:" (5) a future possibility; as, "If I *should* write to you [hereafter], you must answer immediately."

101. Past Perfect Tense.

The **Past Perfect Tense** represents an act as ended or completed in time fully past; as, "The cars *had started* before we reached the depot."

Rem. 1.—The past is frequently used instead of the past perfect, to denote the completion of an act at or before a certain past time mentioned; as, "The boat *left* before midnight."

Rem. 2.—The *past perfect subjunctive* and *past perfect potential* denote past time simply, and deny the action or event; as, "If I *had started* sooner, I *should have* overtaken you."

102. Future Tense.

The **Future Tense** expresses what will take place in future time; as, "I *shall return* soon;" "The lion *shall eat* straw like the ox."

Rem. 1.—**Shall** and **will** are the *signs* of the future tense. *Shall* expresses the action or event (1) as a duty commanded or authorized; as, "He *shall* pay you;" "Thou *shalt* not steal:" (2) as something unavoidable, unless a certain condition be complied with; as, "I *shall* suffer, if I do not take my overcoat:" (3) as future; as, "I *shall* leave at noon;" "You *shall* often find the richest men the meanest."

Will expresses the action or event (1) as something determined upon, or proceeding from the nature of things; as, "I *will* go: no power on earth can prevent me;" "The cause *will* raise up armies:" (2) as future; as, "You *will* feel better to-morrow."

Rem. 2.—*Shall*, in the first person, and *will*, in the second and third, are usually employed to denote futurity; as, "We *shall arrive* there by noon;" "You *will be* glad to see us;" "He *will be* with us."

Will is used, in the first person, to denote determination; and *shall*, in the second and third, to denote necessity; as, "I *will write* to you;" "Neither he nor you *shall go* without me."

103. Future Perfect Tense.

The **Future Perfect Tense** represents an action as finished or ended at or before a certain future time; as, "I *shall have finished* my task at three o'clock;" "We *shall have dined* before you arrive."

104. Tenses in all the Modes.

1. The Indicative Mode has the *six* tenses.

2. The Subjunctive Mode has *three* tenses: the *present, past,* and *past perfect.*

3. The Potential Mode has *four* tenses: the *present, present perfect, past,* and *past perfect.*

4. The Imperative Mode has *one* tense: the *present.*

5. The Infinitive Mode has *two* tenses: the *present* and *present perfect.*

Rem.—Tense does not properly belong to the infinitive mode. Its tenses are mere *forms,* without regard to time. The *present* tense denotes progressive or completed action or state, with reference to past, present, or future time; the *present perfect*, a completed action or state in an unlimited manner.

105. Signs of the Tenses: Active Voice.

Indicative Mode.

Present, . . . Simple form of the verb.
Past, ... When regular, add *ed* to the simple form.
Future, . . . Prefix *shall* or *will* to the simple form.
Present Perfect, " *have, hast*, or *has* to the perfect participle.
Past Perfect, . " *had* or *hadst* to the perfect participle.
Future Perfect, " *shall have* or *will have* to the perfect participle.

Subjunctive Mode.

If, though, except, unless, &c., placed before tense forms given in the Conjugation, are signs of the subjunctive mode.

Potential Mode.

Present, . . . Prefix *may, can*, or *must* to the simple form.
Past, ... " *might, could, would*, or *should* to the simple form.
Present Perfect, " *may, can*, or *must have* to the perfect participle.
Past Perfect, . " *might, could, would*, or *should have* to the perfect participle.

Imperative Mode.

Present, . . . *Let*, or a *command*.

Infinitive Mode.

Present, . . . Prefix *to* to the simple form.
Present Perfect, " *to have* to the perfect participle.

Participles.

Present, . . . Add *ing* to the simple form.
Perfect, . . . When regular, add *ed* or *d* to the simple form.
Compound, . . Prefix *having* to the perfect participle.

106. Forms of the Verb.

1. **Verbs** have five forms, which may be considered subdivisions of the tenses: the *Common*, the *Emphatic*, the *Progressive*, the *Passive*, and the *Ancient*, or *Solemn Style*.

2. The **Common Form** represents an act as a custom, or as completed without reference to its progress; as, "I *write;*" "I *shall write.*"

3. The **Emphatic Form** represents an act with emphasis; as, "I *do* write;" "He *did* go."

Rem.—This form is used in the *present* and *past* indicative and subjunctive, and in the *present* imperative. It is formed by prefixing the present and past tenses of *to do* to the simple form of the verb.

4. The **Progressive Form** is used to denote action or state in progress; as, "I *am writing;*" "He *had been singing.*"

Rem.—The progressive form may be used in all the modes and tenses, and is formed by prefixing the various modes and tenses of the neuter verb *to be* to the present participle of the principal verb.

5. The **Passive Form** denotes the reception of an act by its subject; as, "I *am struck;*" "John *was punished;*" "I *shall be loved.*"

Rem.—The passive form is used in all the modes and tenses, and is formed by prefixing the various modes and tenses of the neuter verb *to be* to the perfect participle of the principal verb.

6. The **Ancient Form**, or *Solemn Style*, is used in the Bible, in religious worship, and sometimes in poetry and burlesque; as, "Thou *art* the man;" "So *shalt* thou *rest;*" "Thou *art* a pretty fellow."

107. Person and Number.

1. The **Person** and **Number** of verbs are the changes which they undergo to mark their agreement with their subjects.

2. A subject in the *second person singular*, generally requires the verb, or its auxiliary, to end in *t*, *st*, or *est;*

as, "Thou *shalt* not steal;" "Thou *canst* read;" "Thou *runnest;*"

3. A subject in the *third person singular*, generally requires the verb, or its auxiliary, to end in *s*, *es*, or *eth*; as, " Julia *reads;*" "The horse *goes;*" "God *loveth* us."

4. The personal terminations in the plural are the same as the *first person singular*, except in the verb *to be.*

5. A verb must agree with its subject in person and number.

Rem. 1.—When two or more nominatives, differing in person, are taken collectively, the verb prefers the first to the second, and the second to the third. When they are connected by *or* or *nor*, or are taken separately, it prefers the person of the nominative next to it. Courtesy requires the first place to be given to the *second* person, and last place to the *first.*

Ex.—"*You, he*, and *I have* to remain;" "*You* and *he have* to learn that long lesson;" "*You* or *I am* mistaken;" "*Thou* and *thy friends are* to make reparation."

Rem. 2.—A verb must be in the singular number (1) when its nominative is in the singular; (2) when its nominative is a group of objects viewed as one thing; (3) when its nominative is an object conceived as a unit, though denoted by a plural nominative; (4) when its nominative is two or more objects taken singly, and denoted by different or by several nominatives.

Ex.—"Rain *falls;*" "The army *is marching;*" "*Dombey & Son was* written by Dickens;" "The *ten dollars was* duly paid;" "*Descent* and *fall* to us *is* adverse;" "For thine *is* the *kingdom*, and the *power*, and the *glory.*"

Rem. 3.—A verb must be in the plural number (1) when its nominative is a single object, or a group of objects conceived as to its individual parts; (2) when its nominative is plural; (3) when plural nominatives are used in connection with singular nominatives, taken separately, or connected by *or* or *nor;* (4) when it has two or more objects taken collectively.

Ex.—"The *rains descend;*" "The *multitude pursue* pleasure;" "Either the *magistrate* or the *laws are* at fault;" "*You, he*, and *I are* here."

108. Unipersonal Verbs.

A **Unipersonal Verb** is one by which an act or state is asserted independently of any particular subject; as, "It *snows;*" "It *cleared off;*" "It *behooves* us to be careful."

Rem.—*Meseems, meseemed, methinks, methought,* may be regarded as unipersonal verbs, equivalent to *it seems, it seemed to me, I think, I thought.*

109. Conjugation.

1. The **Conjugation** of a verb, is the correct expression, in regular order, of its *modes, tenses, voices, persons,* and *numbers.*

2. There are four forms of conjugation: the *Regular,* the *Emphatic,* the *Progressive,* and the *Interrogative.*

3. The **Principal Parts** of a verb are the *present indicative,* the *past indicative,* and the *perfect participle.*

4. The **Synopsis** of a verb is its variation in form, through the different modes and tenses, in a single number and person.

110. Conjugation of the Verb "To Be."

PRINCIPAL PARTS.

Present Tense.	Past Tense.	Perfect Participle.
Be, or am,	Was,	Been.

SYNOPSIS.

INDICATIVE MODE.

Present, . . .	I am.	Past Perfect, .	I had been.
Present Perfect,	I have been.	Future, . . .	I shall be.
Past, ...	I was.	Future Perfect,	I shall have been.

SUBJUNCTIVE MODE.

Present, . . . If I be. *Past,* . . . . If I were.

Past Perfect, ... If I had been.

POTENTIAL MODE.

Present, . . . I may, can, or must be.

Present Perfect, I may, can, or must have been.

Past, ... I might, could, would, or should be.

Past Perfect, . I might, could, would, or should have been.

REGULAR CONJUGATION.

Note.—*Shall,* in the first person, and *will,* in the second and third, future tenses, are used to denote futurity. When *will* is used in the first person, or *shall,* in the second or third, *determination* or *necessity* is represented.

INDICATIVE MODE.

PRESENT TENSE.

Singular.	*Plural.*
1. I am,	1. We are,
2. Thou art,	2. You are,
3. He is;	3. They are.

PRESENT PERFECT TENSE.

1. I have been,	1. We have been,
2. Thou hast been,	2. You have been,
3. He has been;	3. They have been.

PAST TENSE.

1. I was,	1. We were,
2. Thou wast,	2. You were,
3. He was;	3. They were.

PAST PERFECT TENSE.

1. I had been,	1. We had been,
2. Thou hadst been,	2. You had been,
3. He had been;	3. They had been.

FUTURE TENSE.

Singular.	*Plural.*
1. I shall be,	1. We shall be.
2. Thou wilt be,	2. You will be,
3. He will be;	3. They will be.

FUTURE PERFECT TENSE.

1. I shall have been,	1. We shall have been,
2. Thou wilt have been,	2. You will have been,
3. He will have been;	3. They will have been.

SUBJUNCTIVE MODE.

PRESENT TENSE.

1. If I be,	1. If we be,
2. If thou be,	2. If you be,
3. If he be;	3. If they be.

PAST TENSE.

1. If I were,	1. If we were,
2. If thou wert,	2. If you were,
3. If he were;	3. If they were.

PAST PERFECT TENSE.

1. If I had been,	1. If we had been,
2. If thou hadst been,	2. If you had been,
3. If he had been;	3. If they had been.

POTENTIAL MODE.

PRESENT TENSE.

1. I may be,	1. We may be,
2. Thou mayst be,	2. You may be,
3. He may be;	3. They may be.

PRESENT PERFECT TENSE.

1. I may have been,	1. We may have been,
2. Thou mayst have been,	2. You may have been,
3. He may have been;	3. They may have been.

PAST TENSE.

Singular.	Plural.
1. I might be,	1. We might be,
2. Thou mightst be,	2. You might be,
3. He might be;	3. They might be.

PAST PERFECT TENSE.

1. I might have been,	1. We might have been,
2. Thou mightst have been,	2. You might have been,
3. He might have been;	3. They might have been.

Note.—In reviews, use the auxiliary *can* or *must*.

IMPERATIVE MODE.

PRESENT TENSE.

2. Be, or do thou be;   2. Be, or do ye or you be.

INFINITIVE MODE.

Present, To be.   *Present Perfect,* To have been.

PARTICIPLES.

Present, Being.   *Perfect,* Been.   *Compound,* Having been.

---

111. Conjugation of the Verb "To Love."

ACTIVE VOICE.

PRINCIPAL PARTS.

Present Tense.	Past Tense.	Perfect Participle.
Love.	Loved.	Loved.

SYNOPSIS.

INDICATIVE MODE.

Present, . . . I love.	*Past Perfect,* . I had loved.
Present Perfect, I have loved.	*Future,* . . . I shall love.
Past, ... I loved.	*Future Perfect,* I shall have loved.

SUBJUNCTIVE MODE.

Present, . . . If I love.   *Past,* . . . If I loved.

Past Perfect, ... If I had loved.

POTENTIAL MODE.

Present, . . . I may, can, or must love.

Present Perfect, I may, can, or must have loved.

Past, ... I might, could, would, or should love.

Past Perfect, I might, could, would, or should have loved.

REGULAR CONJUGATION.

INDICATIVE MODE.

PRESENT TENSE.

Singular.	*Plural.*
1. I love,	1. We love,
2. Thou lovest,	2. You love,
3. He loves;	3. They love.

PRESENT PERFECT TENSE.

1. I have loved,	1. We have loved,
2. Thou hast loved,	2. You have loved,
3. He has loved;	3. They have loved.

PAST TENSE.

1. I loved,	1. We loved,
2. Thou lovedst,	2. You loved,
3. He loved;	3. They loved.

PAST PERFECT TENSE.

1. I had loved,	1. We had loved,
2. Thou hadst loved,	2. You had loved,
3. He had loved;	3. They had loved.

FUTURE TENSE.

1. I shall love,	1. We shall love,
2. Thou wilt love,	2. You will love,
3. He will love;	3. They will love.

FUTURE PERFECT TENSE.

Singular.

1. I shall have loved,
2. Thou wilt have loved,
3. He will have loved;

Plural.

1. We shall have loved,
2. You will have loved,
3. They will have loved.

SUBJUNCTIVE MODE.

PRESENT TENSE.

1. If I love,
2. If thou love,
3. If he love;

1. If we love,
2. If you love,
3. If they love.

PAST TENSE.

1. If I loved,
2. If thou loved,
3. If he loved;

1. If we loved,
2. If you loved,
3. If they loved.

PAST PERFECT TENSE.

1. If I had loved,
2. If thou hadst loved,
3. If he had loved;

1. If we had loved,
2. If you had loved,
3. If they had loved.

POTENTIAL MODE.

PRESENT TENSE.

1. I may love,
2. Thou mayst love,
3. He may love;

1. We may love,
2. You may love,
3. They may love.

PRESENT PERFECT TENSE.

1. I may have loved,
2. Thou mayst have loved,
3. He may have loved;

1. We may have loved,
2. You may have loved,
3. They may have loved

PAST TENSE.

1. I might love,
2. Thou mightst love,
3. He might love;

1. We might love,
2. You might love,
3. They might love.

H. G. 8

PAST PERFECT TENSE.

Singular.	*Plural.*
1. I might have loved,	1. We might have loved,
2. Thou mightst have loved,	2. You might have loved,
3. He might have loved;	3. They might have loved.

IMPERATIVE MODE.

PRESENT TENSE.

2. Love, or do thou love;　　2. Love, or do ye or you love.

INFINITIVE MODE.

Present, To love.　　*Present Perfect,* To have loved.

PARTICIPLES.

Present, Loving.　　*Perfect,* Loved.　　*Compound,* Having loved.

---

112. Conjugation of the Verb "To Love."

PASSIVE VOICE.

The **Passive Voice** is formed by prefixing, as an auxiliary, the various forms of the neuter verb *to be,* to the *perfect participle* of a transitive verb. The tense of the verb *to be* determines the tense in the Passive Voice.

SYNOPSIS.

INDICATIVE MODE.

Present, ...	I am loved.
Present Perfect, . . .	I have been loved.
Past, ...	I was loved.
Past Perfect, ...	I had been loved.
Future, ...	I shall be loved.
Future Perfect, . . .	I shall have been loved.

SUBJUNCTIVE MODE.

Present, . . If I be loved.　　*Past,* . . If I were loved.

Past Perfect, . . . If I had been loved.

POTENTIAL MODE.

Present, ...	I may be loved.
Present Perfect, . . .	I may have been loved.
Past, ...	I might be loved.
Past Perfect, ...	I might have been loved.

REGULAR CONJUGATION.

INDICATIVE MODE.

PRESENT TENSE.

Singular.	*Plural.*
1. I am loved,	1. We are loved,
2. Thou art loved,	2. You are loved,
3. He is loved;	3. They are loved.

PRESENT PERFECT TENSE.

1. I have been loved,	1. We have been loved,
2. Thou hast been loved.	2. You have been loved,
3. He has been loved;	3. They have been loved.

PAST TENSE.

1. I was loved,	1. We were loved,
2. Thou wast loved,	2. You were loved,
3. He was loved;	3. They were loved.

PAST PERFECT TENSE.

1. I had been loved,	1. We had been loved,
2. Thou hadst been loved,	2. You had been loved.
3. He had been loved;	3. They had been loved.

FUTURE TENSE.

1. I shall be loved,	1. We shall be loved,
2. Thou wilt be loved,	2. You will be loved,
3. He will be loved;	3. They will be loved.

FUTURE PERFECT TENSE.

1. I shall have been loved,	1. We shall have been loved,
2. Thou wilt have been loved,	2. You will have been loved,
3. He will have been loved;	3. They will have been loved.

SUBJUNCTIVE MODE.

PRESENT TENSE.

Singular.	*Plural.*
1. If I be loved,	1. If we be loved,
2. If thou be loved,	2. If you be loved,
3. If he be loved;	3. If they be loved.

PAST TENSE.

1. If I were loved,	1. Were I loved,	1. If we were loved,
2. If thou wert loved,	2. Wert thou loved,	2. If you were loved,
3. If he were loved;	3 Were he loved;	3. If they were loved.

Rem.—For the *Past Perfect Tense*, prefix *if* to the forms of the *past perfect indicative*.

POTENTIAL MODE.

PRESENT TENSE.

1. I may be loved,	1. We may be loved,
2. Thou mayst be loved,	2. You may be loved,
3. He may be loved;	3. They may be loved.

PRESENT PERFECT TENSE.

1. I may have been loved,	1. We may have been loved,
2. Thou mayst have been loved,	2. You may have been loved,
3. He may have been loved;	3. They may have been loved.

PAST TENSE.

1. I might be loved,	1. We might be loved,
2. Thou mightst be loved,	2. You might be loved,
3. He might be loved;	3. They might be loved.

PAST PERFECT TENSE.

1. I might have been loved,	1. We might have been loved,
2. Thou mightst have been loved,	2. You might have been loved,
3. He might have been loved;	3. They might have been loved.

Note.—In reviews, use the auxiliary *can* or *must*.

IMPERATIVE MODE.

PRESENT TENSE.

2. Be loved, or be thou loved;   2. Be loved, or be you loved

INFINITIVE MODE.

Present, To be loved.   *Pres. Perfect,* To have been loved.

PARTICIPLES.

Pres., Being loved.   *Perfect,* Loved.   *Compound* Having been loved.

---

113. Coördinate Forms of Conjugation.

The Progressive, the Emphatic, and the Interrogative are called the *Coördinate Forms of Conjugation.*

SYNOPSIS.

PROGRESSIVE FORM.

INDICATIVE MODE.

Present, ... I am loving.
Present Perfect, . . . I have been loving.
Past, ... I was loving.
Past Perfect, ... I had been loving.
Future, ... I shall be loving.
Future Perfect, . . . I shall have been loving.

SUBJUNCTIVE MODE.

Present, . . If I be loving.   *Past,* . . If I were loving.
Past Perfect, . . . If I had been loving.

POTENTIAL MODE.

Present, ... I may be loving.
Present Perfect, . . . I may have been loving.
Past, ... I might be loving.
Past Perfect, ... I might have been loving.

INFINITIVE MODE.

Present, To be loving.   *Present Perfect,* To have been loving.

IMPERATIVE MODE.

Present, ... Be thou loving.

PARTICIPLES.

Present, Loving.   *Compound,* Having been loving.

THE EMPHATIC FORM.

INDICATIVE MODE.

Present,   I do love.   *Past,*   I did love.

SUBJUNCTIVE MODE.

Present,   If I do love.   *Past,*   If I did love.

IMPERATIVE MODE.

Present, ...   Do thou love.

INTERROGATIVE FORM.

INDICATIVE MODE.

Present, . . . Love I? Do I love? Am I loving?
Present Perfect, Have I loved? Have I been loving?
Past, ... Loved I? Did I love? Was I loving?
Past Perfect, . Had I loved? Had I been loving?
Future, . . . Shall I love? Shall I be loving?
Future Perfect, Shall I have loved? Shall I have been loving?

POTENTIAL MODE.

Present, . . Must I love?   *Past,* . . . Might I love?
Pres. Perfect, Must I have loved? *Past Perfect,* Might I have loved?

114. Negative Forms.

1. To conjugate a verb *negatively*, place *not* after it, or after the first auxiliary; but before the infinitive and the participles.

Ex.—*Indicative,* I learn not, *or* I do not learn. I have not learned. I learned not, *or* did not learn, &c.

Infinitive.—Not to learn. Not to have learned.

Participle.—Not learning. Not learned. Not having learned.

2. To conjugate a verb *interrogatively* and *negatively*, in the indicative and potential modes, place the *subject* and *not* after the verb, or after the first auxiliary.

Ex.—Learn I not? *or,* Do I not learn? Have I not learned? Did I not learn? &c.

115. Exercises.

Write a synopsis of the transitive verbs *write, think, row, arouse, build, conquer, command, entreat, teach,* and *instruct,* in the Indicative, Subjunctive, and Potential Modes, Active and Passive Voices.

Tell the mode, tense, person, and number of each verb in the following sentences:

1. He has gone. 2. I might write. 3. We had gone. 4. He had been assured. 5. If I were loved. 6. They may have been left. 7. You were seen. 8. Thou wilt have loved. 9. She will have been invited. 10. He might have built. 11. You might have been seen. 12. The vessel will have sailed.

13. We might have written. 14. They were loved. 15. If I had been loved. 16. If he is loved. 17. Though he love. 18. Though he is loved. 19. If I may be seen. 20. We can go. 21. Go. 22. Remain. 23. If he return. 24. If he returns.

116. Irregular Verbs.

An **Irregular Verb** is one which does not form its past tense and perfect participle by adding *d* or *ed* to the present tense; as, *do, did, done; go, went, gone.*

The following list contains the *Principal Parts* of most of the Irregular verbs. Those marked R have also the regular forms.

Present.	Past.	Perfect Participle.	Present.	Past.	Perfect Participle.
Abide,	abode,	abode.	Become,	became,	become.
Am,	was,	been.	Befall,	befell,	befallen.
Awake,	awoke, R.	{ awaked, awoke.	Beget,	{ begat, begot.	begotten, begot.
Arise,	arose,	arisen.	Begin,	began,	begun.
Bear, (*bring forth,*)	{ bore, bare,	born.	Behold,	beheld,	beheld.
			Belay,	belaid, R.	belaid, R.
Bear, (*carry,*)	bore,	borne.	Bend,	bent, R.	bent, R.
Beat,	beat,	{ beaten, beat.	Bereave,	bereft, R.	bereft, R.
			Beseech,	besought,	besought.

Present.	Past.	Perfect Participle.	Present.	Past.	Perfect Participle.
Bet,	bet, R.	bet, R.	Dream,	dreamt, R	dreamt, R.
Betide,	{ betided, betid,	betided, betid.	Dress,	drest, R.	drest, R.
			Dwell,	dwelt, R.	dwelt, R.
Bid,	{ bid, bade,	bid, bidden.	Drive,	drove,	driven.
			Eat,	ate,	eaten.
Bite,	bit,	{ bitten, bit.	Fall,	fell,	fallen.
			Feed,	fed,	fed.
Bind,	bound,	bound.	Feel,	felt,	felt.
Bleed,	bled,	bled.	Fight,	fought,	fought.
Bless,	{ blessed, blest,	blessed, blest.	Find,	found,	found.
			Forbear,	forbore,	forborne.
Breed,	bred,	bred.	Forget,	forgot,	{ forgotten, forgot.
Break,	{ broke, brake,	broken, broke.	Forsake,	forsook,	forsaken.
Bring,	brought,	brought.	Flee,	fled,	fled.
Build,	built, R.	built, R.	Fling,	flung,	flung.
Burn,	burnt, R.	burnt, R.	Fly,	flew,	flown.
Burst,	burst,	burst.	Freeze,	froze,	frozen.
Buy,	bought,	bought.	Freight,	freighted,	fraught, R.
Cast,	cast,	cast.	Get,	got,	{ got, gotten.
Catch,	caught, R.	caught, R.			
Chide,	chid,	{ chidden, chid.	Give,	gave,	given.
			Gild,	gilt, R.	gilt, R.
Choose,	chose,	chosen.	Gird,	girt, R.	girt, R.
Cleave, (adhere,)	{ cleaved, clave,	cleaved.	Go,	went,	gone.
			Grave,	graved,	graven, R.
Cleave, (split,)	{ cleft, clove, clave,	cleft, cloven, cleaved.	Grind,	ground,	ground.
			Grow,	grew,	grown.
			Hang,	hung, R.	hung, R.
Cling,	clung,	clung.	Have,	had,	had.
Clothe,	{ clothed, clad,	clothed, clad.	Heave,	hove, R.	hoven, R.
			Hew,	hewed,	hewn, R.
Come,	came,	come.	Hear,	heard,	heard.
Cost,	cost,	cost.	Hide,	hid,	{ hidden, hid.
Creep,	crept,	crept.			
Crow,	crew, R.	crowed.	Hit,	hit,	hit.
Cut,	cut,	cut.	Hold,	held,	{ held, holden.
Dare,	durst, R.	dared.			
Deal,	dealt,	dealt.	Hurt,	hurt,	hurt.
Dig,	dug, R.	dug, R.	Keep,	kept,	kept.
Do,	did,	done.	Kneel,	knelt, R.	knelt.
Draw,	drew,	drawn.	Knit,	knit, R.	knit, R.

Present.	Past.	Perfect Participle.	Present.	Past.	Perfect Participle.
Know,	knew,	known.	Shake,	shook,	shaken.
Lay,	laid,	laid.	Shape,	shaped,	shapen, R.
Lead,	led,	led.	Shave,	shaved,	shaven, R.
Lean,	leant, R.	leant, R.	Shear,	shore, R.	shorn, R.
Leap,	leapt, R.	leapt, R.	Shed,	shed,	shed.
Learn,	learnt, R.	learnt, R.	Shine,	shone, R.	shone, R.
Leave,	left,	left.	Shoe,	shod,	shod.
Lend,	lent,	lent.	Shoot,	shot,	shot.
Let,	let,	let.	Show,	showed,	shown.
Lie, (recline,)	lay,	lain.	Shred,	shred,	shred.
Light,	lit, R.	lit, R.	Shut,	shut,	shut.
Lose,	lost,	lost.	Sit,	sat,	sat.
Load,	loaded,	laden, R.	Sing,	{ sang, sung,	sung.
Make,	made,	made.			
Mean,	meant,	meant.	Sink,	{ sank, sunk,	sunk.
Meet,	met,	met.			
Mow,	mowed,	mown, R.	Sow, (scatter,)	sowed,	sown, R.
Pay,	paid,	paid.	Slay,	slew,	slain.
Pass,	past, R.	past.	Sleep,	slept,	slept.
Pen, (inclose,)	pent, R.	pent, R.	Sling,	slung,	slung.
Plead,	{ plead, R. pled,	plead, R. pled.	Slink,	slunk,	slunk.
			Slit,	slit,	slit,
Put,	put,	put.	Smell,	smelt,	smelt, R.
Quit,	quit, R.	quit, R.	Smite,	smote,	{ smitten, smit.
Rap,	rapt, R.	rapt, R.			
Read,	read,	read.	Speak,	spoke,	spoken.
Reave,	reft,	reft.	Speed,	sped,	sped,
Rend,	rent,	rent.	Spell,	spelt, R.	spelt, R.
Rid,	rid,	rid.	Spend,	spent,	spent.
Ride,	rode,	{ ridden, rode.	Spill,	spilt, R.	spilt, R.
			Spin,	{ spun, span,	spun.
Ring,	{ rang, rung,	rung.	Spit,	{ spit, spat,	spit, spitten.
Rise,	rose,	risen.			
Rive,	rived,	riven, R.	Split,	split,	split.
Run,	ran,	run.	Spread,	spread,	spread.
Saw,	sawed,	sawn, R.	Spring,	{ sprang, sprung,	sprung.
Say,	said,	said.			
See,	saw,	seen.	Spoil,	spoilt, R.	spoilt, R.
Seethe,	sod, R.	sodden, R.	Stay,	staid, R.	staid, R.
Seek,	sought,	sought.	Stand,	stood,	stood.
Set,	set,	set.	Stave,	stove, R.	stove, R.

Present.	Past.	Perfect Participle.	Present.	Past.	Perfect Participle.
Steal,	stole,	stolen.	Tear,	tore,	torn.
Stick,	stuck,	stuck.	Tell,	told,	told.
Sting,	stung,	stung.	Think,	thought,	thought.
Stride,	{ strode, strid,	stridden, strid.	Thrive,	throve, R.	thriven, R.
			Throw,	threw,	thrown.
Strike,	struck,	{ struck, stricken.	Thrust,	thrust,	thrust.
			Tread,	trod,	{ trodden, trod.
String,	strung,	strung.			
Strive,	strove,	striven.	Wax,	waxed,	waxen, R.
Strow,	strowed,	{ strowed, strown.	Wear,	wore,	worn.
			Weave,	wove, R.	woven, R.
Swear,	{ swore, sware,	sworn.	Weep,	wept,	wept.
			Wake,	woke, R.	woke, R.
Sweat,	sweat, R.	sweat, R.	Wed,	wed, R.	wed, R.
Sweep,	swept,	swept.	Wet,	wet, R.	wet, R.
Swell,	swelled,	swollen, R.	Whet,	whet, R.	whet, R.
Swim,	{ swam, swum,	swum.	Win,	won,	won.
			Wind,	wound,	wound.
Swing,	swung,	swung.	Work,	wrought, R.	wrought, R.
Take,	took,	taken.	Wring,	wrung,	wrung.
Teach,	taught,	taught.	Write,	wrote,	written.

Rem.—The *auxiliaries* are all irregular verbs. Their forms may be found in the paradigm for their conjugation.

117. Defective and Redundant Verbs.

1. **Defective Verbs** are those which want some of the Principal Parts.

Ex.—**Beware**, from *be* and *aware*, used mostly in the imperative mode, but may be used wherever *be* would occur in the conjugation of the verb *to be;* as, "*Beware* the awful avalanche!" "If angels fell, why should not men *beware?*"

Ought, used in both present and past tenses; as, "I know I *ought* to go," (now); "I knew he *ought* to have gone," (then).

Quoth, used for *said;* as, "'Not I,' *quoth* Sancho." It always stands before its subject. **Quod** is also used in the same sense, by old authors.

Wit, in the sense of *know;* as, To wit, *i. e.*, namely. *Wot, wis, wert, wist, wote,* derived from *wit,* are found in old authors.

2. The **Auxiliaries** are also defective, wanting the perfect participle.

3. **Redundant Verbs** are those which have more than one form for their past tense or perfect participle.

Ex.—*Cleave; cleft, clove,* or *clave; cleft, cloven,* or *cleaved.*

118. Exercises.

Exercises to be corrected:

1. The cloth was weaved beautiful. 2. I seen him run when you come. 3. The boys fit 'most an hour. 4. I stringed the raspberries on a spear of grass. 5. Were the cattle drove to pasture? 6. She has took my pencil. 7. The ship which springed a leak has just hoved in sight. 8. The plastering has fell from the ceiling. 9. Charles winned the prize after he had strove many times.

10. I did not git my exercise wrote in time. 11. The wind has blowed the fence down. 12. He has went and brung some snow into the house. 13. Who learned you how to spell. 14. The stone smit him right in the face. 15. I laid down, and ris much refreshed. 16. The cars have ran off the track. 17. The bells ringed when we come into town.

18. He could have went. 19. I have saw some fine cattle to-day. 20. I and you is going to the concert, aint we? 21. Neither he nor she are good to me. 22. The steamboat come a puffing along. 23. His face has wore a sad expression for more 'n a week.

24. I'm in a quandary whether a horse or a grayhound run the fastest. 25. The man throwed a stone, and made the coon git. 26. John clumb the tree, and shaked the chestnuts down.

119. Order of Parsing.

1. A Verb, and why?
2. Regular or Irregular, and why?
3. Give its principal parts.
4. Copulative, transitive, or intransitive, and why?
5. Voice and form, and why?
6. Mode, and why?
7. Tense, and why? Inflect the tense.
8. Person and number, and why? Rule.

120. Models for Parsing.

I. "Mary *has recited* her lesson."

Has recited is a *verb;* it is a word which expresses being, action, or state: *regular;* it forms its past tense and perfect participle by adding *ed: principal parts* are pres., *recite,* past, *recited,* perfect participle, *recited: transitive;* it requires the addition of an object to complete its meaning: *active voice;* it represents the subject as acting: *common form;* it represents a customary act: *indicative mode;* it asserts a thing as actual: *present perfect tense;* it represents a past act as completed in present time: *third person, singular number;* to agree with its subject "Mary," according to Rule XIII: "A verb must agree with its subject in person and number."

II. "I *shall go* if you *stay.*"

Shall go . . . is a *verb;* (why?): *irregular;* it does not form its past tense and perfect participle by adding *ed: principal parts* are *go, went, gone: intransitive;* (why?): *common form;* (why?): *indicative mode;* (why?): *future tense;* (why?): *first person, singular number;* (why?): Rule XIII.

Stay . . . . is a *verb;* (why?): *regular;* (why?): *principal parts;* (give them): *intransitive;* (why?): *common form;* (why?): *subjunctive mode;* it represents an act as conditional: *present tense* in form, but denotes future time: *second person, singular* or *plural number;* (why?): Rule XIII.

III. "He *should have answered* my letter."

Should have answered is a *verb;* (why?): *regular;* (why?): *principal parts;* (give them): *transitive;* (why?): *active voice;* (why?): *common form;* (why?): *potential mode;* it represents an act as obligatory: *past perfect tense;* it is the form used to represent an act as completed at or before some other act: *third person, singular number;* (why?): Rule XIII.

IV. "*Bring* me a glass of water."

Bring . . . . . is a *verb;* (why?): *irregular;* (why?): *principal parts;* (give them): *transitive;* (why?): *active voice;* (why?):

common form; (why?): *imperative mode;* (why?): *present tense;* (why?): *second person, singular number,* to agree with its subject "thou" understood: Rule XIII.

V. "He attempted *to ascend* the mountain."

To ascend .. is a *verb;* (why?): *regular;* (why?): *principal parts;* (give them): *transitive;* (why?): *active voice;* (why?): *common form,* (why?): *infinitive mode;* (why?): *present tense;* (why?): object of "attempted": Rule VI.

VI. "The letter *was written* yesterday."

Was written is a *verb;* (why?): *irregular;* (why?): *principal parts;* (give them): *transitive;* (why?): *passive voice;* it represents the subject as being acted upon: *indicative mode;* (why?): *past tense;* (why?): *third person, singular number;* (why?): Rule XIII.

VII. "Liberty *is* sweet."

Is .... is a *verb;* (why?): *irregular;* (why?): *principal parts;* (give them): *neuter;* (why?): *copulative;* it is used to connect the predicate "sweet" to the subject "liberty": *indicative mode;* (why?): *present tense;* (why?): *third person, singular number,* to agree with its subject "liberty": Rule XIII.

VIII. "He *was considered* rich."

Was considered is a *verb;* (why?): *regular;* (why?): *principal parts;* (give them): *passive form;* (why?): *copulative;* (why?): *indicative mode;* (why?): *past tense;* (why?): *third person, singular number;* (why?): Rule XIII.

IX. "The fields *look* green."

Look ...... is a *verb;* (why?): *regular;* (why?): *principal parts;* (give them): *copulative;* it connects the predicate "green" to the subject "fields": *indicative mode;* (why?): *present tense;* (why?): *third person, plural number;* (why?): Rule XIII.

X. "John hastened *to assist* us."

To assist ... is a *verb;* (why?): *regular;* (why?): *principal parts;* (give them): *transitive;* (why?): *active voice;* (why?): *infinitive mode;* it expresses action without affirming it: it depends upon "hastened": Rule XVII.

XI. *"To lie is disgraceful."*

To lie...... is a *verb;* (why?): *regular;* (why?): *principal parts;*
(give them): *infinitive mode;* (why?): it is the subject
of the sentence "To lie is disgraceful," and is in the
nominative case; Rule I.

XII. "I heard the wolves *howling* in the forest."

Howling ... is a *participle;* it partakes of the properties of a verb
and of an adjective: it is derived from the verb
"howl": *present participle;* it denotes *continuance:* it
belongs to "wolves": Rule XII.

XIII. "Take this letter, *written* by myself."

Written.... is a *participle;* (why?): (from what word derived?):
perfect participle; it denotes *completion:* it belongs to
"letter": Rule XII.

XIV. "He *has been reading* Shakspeare."

Has been reading is a *verb;* (why?): *irregular;* (why?): *principal
parts;* (give them): *active voice;* (why?): *progressive
form;* it denotes continuance of action: *indicative mode;*
(why?): *present perfect tense;* (why?): *third person,
singular number;* (why?): Rule XIII.

XV. "That man *did buy* our house."

Did buy ... is a *verb;* (why?): *irregular;* (why?): *principal parts;*
(give them): *active voice;* (why?): *emphatic form;* it
denotes assertion with emphasis: *indicative mode;*
(why?): *past tense;* (why?): *third person, singular number;* (why?): Rule XIII.

121. Exercises.

*Parse the nouns, pronouns, adjectives, and verbs in the following
sentences:*

1. They commenced plowing yesterday.   2. I seldom write letters.   3. My father brought me some pine-apples when he came
from the city.   4. She had gone to walk.   5. When do you intend
to return my umbrella?   6. The workmen should have been more
careful.   7. Hallowed be thy name.   8. Respect the aged.   9. I
could not learn to do it.

10. The weather was unpleasant. 11. He should have been more industrious. 12. Shall I assist you? 13. How many regiments were mustered out? 14. Have all the gifts of healing? 15. Remember thy Creator in the days of thy youth. 16. The poor must work in their grief. 17. We were speedily convinced that his professions were insincere.

18. Hear, father, hear our prayer!
  Long hath thy goodness our footsteps attended.

19. That very law that molds a tear,
    And bids it trickle from its source,
  That law preserves the earth a sphere,
    And guides the planets in their course.—*Rogers.*

20. Why restless, why cast down, my soul?
    Hope still, and thou shalt sing
  The praise of Him who is thy God,
    Thy Savior, and thy King.

Passive Forms. 1. He was beaten with many stripes. 2. The sheep were destroyed by wolves. 3. Every crime should be punished. 4. You, he, and I were invited. 5. America was discovered by Christopher Columbus. 6. He has been elected mayor of our city. 7. This lake is said to be one hundred feet deep. 8. The work might have been finished yesterday.

Progressive, Emphatic, and Interrogative Forms. 1. He is writing a letter. 2. They should have been studying their lessons. 3. They were digging for gold. 4. I do wish you were here. 5. He did not commit forgery. 6. How do you learn so fast? 7. Why does he persist in denying it? 8. Where were you going when I met you?

Exercises to be corrected:

1. John didn't go to do any mischief. 2. He laid down to take a nap. 3. I reckon you are from the East. 4. You had not ought to have done so, for you knowed better. 5. Had I have known that, I should rather have not seen him. 6. The blacksmith shoed my horse. 7. I should not of known him. 8. He could have went as well as not.

9. I have saw a steam-boat to-day. 10. I never seen any thing like it. 11. He has gone and done it. 12. Mary was chose on my side. 13. The water has ran into our cellar. 14. He knew

nothing of what was being done.   15. Those trees will bear being
pruned more yet.   16. A new school-house is being built in our
district.   17. The boy had swam the river.

18. I will be drowned: nobody shall help me.   19. Would we
have a good time if we should go?   20. Was I to play truant, I
should get punished.   21. By following me, you shall get there
sooner.   22. We will receive our money to-morrow.   23. Writing
is to make letters with a pen or pencil.

24. The order served rather to exasperate instead of quieting the
people.   25. Money is scarce and times hard.   26. I never could,
and presume I never shall understand that passage.   27. Your in-
tentions might, and probably were, good.   28. No one ever worked
so hard as I have done to-day.   29. Any word that will compare
is an adjective.

30. Time and tide waits for no man.   31. Either Stephen or
Jonas have to stay at home.   32. What black despair, what horror
fill his mind?   33. That a belle should be vain, or a fop ignorant,
are not to be wondered at.   34. Our potatoes is all gone.

THE ADVERB.

122. Oral Lesson.

Write this sentence on your slates: "Jane sang a *song*." What
element is "song"?   *Ans.*—An objective element.   Why?   *Ans.*—
Because it completes the meaning of the predicate.   Write "Jane
sang a song *sweetly*."   Does "sweetly" complete the meaning of
the predicate?   *Ans.*—It does not.   What word is modified by it,
however?   *Ans.*—"Sang."   How does it modify "sang"?   *Ans.*—
It tells *how* Jane sang.

Write this sentence: "You are *very* kind."   What word is
modified by "very"?   *Ans.*—"Kind."   What part of speech is
"kind"?   *Ans.*—An adjective.   Write "A letter, *hastily* written,
was sent me yesterday."   What does "hastily" modify?   *Ans.*—
"Written."   What part of speech is "written?"   *Ans.*—A participle.   Write "The letter was written *very* hastily."   What does
"very" modify?   *Ans.*—"Hastily."   What does "hastily" modify?
Ans.—"Was written."

Those words, and all others used in a similar manner, are called
Adverbs.

123. Definition.

An **Adverb** is a word used to modify the meaning of a verb, adjective, participle, or an adverb; as, "She sings *sweetly;*" "The roads are *very* rough;" "The ranks were *quickly* broken;" "He reads *tolerably* well."

Rem. 1.—An adverb is equivalent to a phrase consisting of a preposition and its object, limited by an adjective.

Ex.—"He walks *rapidly*," i. e., He walks *in a rapid manner.* "He lives *there*," i. e., He lives *at that place.* "The work is *intensely* interesting," i. e., The work is interesting *in an intense degree.*

Rem. 2.—An adverb sometimes modifies a phrase or a clause.

Ex.—"He sailed *nearly* round the globe;" "The old man *likewise* came to the city." In the first sentence, *nearly* limits the phrase " round the globe;" and in the second, *likewise* modifies the entire proposition.

124. Classes.

1. With respect to their meaning and use, adverbs are divided into five classes: Adverbs of *Time, Place, Cause, Manner,* and *Degree.*

2. **Adverbs of Time** answer the questions, *When? How long? How often?*

Ex.—After, again, ago, always, anon, early, ever, never, forever, frequently, hereafter, hitherto, immediately, lately, now, often, seldom, soon, sometimes, then, when, while, weekly, until, yet, &c.

Rem.—*To-day, to-morrow, to-night, yesterday, yesternight,* (formerly written *yester day* and *yester night,*) are nouns, not adverbs. When used as modifiers, they should be parsed as nouns in the objective case, without a governing word. (See Rule VIII.)

Ex.—"He will come *to-day;*" "They all left *yesterday;*" "We had a severe storm *yesternight.*"

3. **Adverbs of Place** answer the questions, *Where? Whither? Whence?*

Ex.—Above, below, down, up, hither, thither, here, there, where, herein, therein, wherein, hence, thence, whence, every-where, nowhere, somewhere, far, yonder, back, forth, aloof, away, aboard, aloft, ashore, backwards, forwards, first, secondly, wherever, &c.

Rem.—*There* is sometimes used as an expletive to introduce a sentence; as, "*There* were giants in those days;" "Breathes *there* a man with soul so dead?"

4. Adverbs of Cause answer the questions, *Why? Wherefore?*

Ex.—Wherefore, therefore, then, why.

5. Adverbs of Manner answer the question, *How?*

Ex.—Amiss, asunder, anyhow, well, badly, easily, foolishly, sweetly, certainly, indeed, surely, verily, nay, no, not, nowise, haply, perhaps, perchance, peradventure, probably, &c.

Rem.—Most adverbs of *manner* are formed by adding *ly* to adjectives or participles; as, wise, *wisely;* united, *unitedly.*

6. Adverbs of Degree answer the questions, *How much? How little?*

Ex.—As, almost, altogether, enough, even, equally, much, more, most, little, less, least, wholly, partly, only, quite, scarcely, nearly, excellently, too, chiefly, somewhat, &c.

7. Adverbs which show the manner of the *assertion* are called **modal adverbs**; as, *verily, truly, not, no, yes,* &c.

8. *When, where, why,* &c., when used in asking questions, are called **interrogative adverbs**.

9. An **Adverbial Phrase** is a combination of words used as a single adverb.

Ex.—"In general;" "hand in hand;" "by and by;" "through and through;" "no more;" "for the most part;" "as usual," &c. Such combinations may be parsed as single adverbs.

10. **Conjunctive Adverbs** are those which connect two propositions, and modify a word in each.

Ex.—"I shall see you again *when* I return;" "Go *where* glory waits thee;" "I have been to Boston *since* I saw you last;" "Pay your bills *before* you leave;" "The book remained *where* I left it;" "I will go *as soon as* I have eaten my dinner."

Rem. 1.—Conjunctive adverbs are equivalent to two phrases; one containing a relative pronoun, the other the antecedent of the relative. In the sentence, "He defends himself *when* he is attacked," *when* = *at the time in which*. "At the time" modifies "defends," and "in which" modifies "attacked;" hence *when*, the equivalent of the two phrases, modifies both.

Rem. 2.—The principal conjunctive adverbs are *as, after, before, how, since, therefore, till, until, when, where, wherefore, while,* and *why.*

125. Comparison.

Many adverbs admit of comparison.

1. Derivatives ending in *ly* are usually compared by prefixing *more* and *most, less* and *least* to the simple form; as, *wisely, more wisely, most wisely; firmly, more firmly, most firmly.*

2. Three adverbs are compared by adding *er* and *est* to the simple form, viz.: *fast, faster, fastest; often, oftener, oftenest; soon, sooner, soonest.*

3. Some adverbs are compared irregularly; as, *well, better, best; ill, worse, worst; little, less, least; much, more, most,* &c.

GENERAL REMARKS.

1. Some adverbs seem to be used *independently;* as, *yes, no, why, well,* &c., in certain constructions. They may be parsed as modifying the entire proposition, the preceding sentence, something understood, or as independent.

Ex.—"Have you my book?—*No.*" "*Why,* that is strange." "*Well,* I am surprised." "*Yea,* the Lord sitteth King forever."

2. An adverb frequently denotes *manner* when it modifies a verb, and *degree* when it modifies an adjective or an adverb; as, "I think *so*" = *manner;* "I feel *so* lonely" = *degree.*

3. Adverbs frequently become adjectives after copulative and passive verbs; as, "He reads *better*" = *adverb;* "He seems *better*" = *adjective.* "It runs *well*" = *adverb;* "He looks *well*" = *adjective.*

4. The adjective form of a word, or the adjective mode of com-

parison, is allowed in poetry to a greater extent than in prose; as, "Breathe *soft*, ye winds;" "Drink *deep;*" "*Dry* clanked his harness."

5. Certain words are used sometimes as adverbs and sometimes as adjectives. They are adverbs when they modify verbs, adjectives, and other adverbs, and adjectives when they modify nouns or pronouns.

Ex.—"I can remain *no* longer;" "Let *no* man deceive you." In the first sentence, "no" is an adverb, modifying "longer"; in the second, it is an adjective, modifying "man."

6. In such expressions as "He works for hire *only*," "One man *only* was injured," "only" is an adjective, modifying the preceding noun. "He sells drugs and books *also*." Here "also" is an adverb, modifying "sells" understood. "He sells drugs, and he *also* sells books."

126. Order of Parsing.

1. An Adverb, and why?
2. Compare it.
3. Tell what it modifies.
4. Rule.

127. Models for Parsing.

I. "He acted *wisely*."

Wisely ...... is an *adverb;* it is used to modify the meaning of a verb: *compared,* wisely more wisely, most wisely: it is an adverb of *manner,* and modifies "acted": Rule XVIII: "Adverbs modify verbs, adjectives, participles, and adverbs."

II. "*Why* do you laugh?"

Why .... is an *adverb;* (why?): it is not compared: *interrogative adverb,* and modifies "do laugh": Rule XVIII.

III. "They walk *hand in hand*."

Hand in hand is an *adverbial phrase;* it is a combination of words used as a simple adverb: it modifies "walk": Rule XVIII.

IV. "I shall *certainly* recover."

Certainly . . . is an *adverb;* (why?): *modal;* it shows the manner in which the assertion is made: it modifies "shall recover": Rule XVIII.

V. "I will go *whenever* you wish."

Whenever . . . is an *adverb;* (why?): *conjunctive adverb;* it connects two clauses, and modifies a word in each: it modifies "will go" and "wish": Rule XVIII.

128. Exercises.

Parse the adverbs in the following sentences:

1. They lived very happily. 2. Why do you look so sad? 3. When spring comes, the flowers will bloom. 4. How rapidly the moments fly! 5. He signed it then and there. 6. I have read it again and again. 7. He will do so no more. 8. The mystery will be explained by and by. 9. Perchance you are the man.

10. Whither has he gone? 11. They were agreeably disappointed. 12. He lives just over the hill yonder. 13. Henceforth let no man fear that God will forsake us. 14. I saw him before he left. 15. I will not be unjust. 16. I have not seen him since I returned from New York. 17. Doubtless, ye are the people. 18. Perhaps I shall go.

THE PREPOSITION.

129. Oral Lesson.

Write this sentence on your slates: "Mr. Olds is a wealthy man." What element is "wealthy"? *Ans.*—An adjective element. What does it modify? *Ans.*—"Man." Write this sentence: "Mr. Olds is a man of wealth." You see that "of wealth," in this sentence, has the same meaning as "wealthy" in the other. What part of speech is "wealth"? *Ans.*—A noun. The word "of" connects "man" and "wealth," and shows the relation between the ideas expressed by them. In this case, the relation is that of possession: "man" possesses "wealth." Words used in this manner are called *Prepositions*, because they are usually *placed before* nouns.

In the sentence "We live in London," what words tell where

we live? *Ans.*—"In London." These words constitute what is called a *phrase*, and form an adverbial element. The word limited by the phrase is called the *antecedent* term of relation, and the noun following the preposition, the *subsequent* term, or *object*. The antecedent term may be any thing which can be modified, but the subsequent must be the objective case of a noun or something used as a noun.

In the sentence "I recite in the afternoon," what is the antecedent term of relation? *Ans.*—"Recite." Why? *Ans.*—Because it is the word which is modified by the phrase "in the afternoon." What is the subsequent term, or object? *Ans.*—"Afternoon." Why? *Ans.*—Because it is the object of the preposition "in."

130. Definition.

A **Preposition** is a word used to show the relation between its object and some other word; as, "The man *of* Uz;" "Ellen is walking *in* the garden."

Rem. 1.—A preposition and its object form a separable phrase, which modifies some word or combination of words, called the *antecedent* term of the relation expressed by the preposition; the object of the preposition being the *subsequent* term. In the sentence, "The house stands *on* a hill," *stands* is the antecedent term of relation, and *hill* the subsequent.

Rem. 2.—The object of a preposition may be a word, a phrase, or an entire proposition; as, "He lives in *Chicago;*" "The ship was about *to be launched;*" "Reason and Justice have been jurymen since before *Noah was a sailor.*"

Rem. 3.—Two prepositions are frequently combined and used as one; as, "He came *from over* the sea;" "The church stands *over against* the school-house." In such cases, parse the two prepositions as one, calling the combination a *complex preposition.*

Rem. 4.—Sometimes the object of a preposition is omitted; as, "The boys went *out;*" "The regiment marched *by.*" In such cases, parse the preposition as an adverb.

Rem. 5.—The antecedent term is sometimes omitted; as, "'*From* Vermont?' asked the landlord;" "'*As to* that,' said the dial-plate." In such cases, parse the preposition as showing the relation between its object and an antecedent term understood.

For, in the complex phrases, "*For* him to lie," "*For* you to deceive," &c., may be parsed as an *introductory* preposition.

Rem. 6.—When the relations between objects of thought are so obvious that they need no expression, the prepositions are usually omitted; as, "I came home *yesterday;*" "He is worth a *million;*" "The bridge is a *mile* long." In such cases, the subsequent term of relation is said to be in the objective case without a governing word.

131. List of Prepositions.

A = *at, on,* or *in;* "Be quiet, and go *a*-angling."
Aboard; "*Aboard* ships, dull shocks are sometimes felt."
About; "It was a day to be at home, crowding *about* the fire."
Above; "*Above* your voices sounds the wail of starving men."
According to; "Proceed *according to* law."
Across; "Their way was *across* a stretch of open meadow."
After; "*After* life's fitful fever, he sleeps well."
Against; "Uplift *against* the sky, your mighty shapes."
Along; "I hear the waves resounding *along* the shore."
Amid, amidst; "A lark reared her brood *amid* the corn."
Among, amongst; "He was always foremost *among* them."
Around; "I hear *around* me cries of fear."
As to; "*As to* the parts of the cargo, they were already made fast."
At; "She is *at* church;" "The bell rings *at* noon."
Athwart; "*Athwart* the waste the pleasant home-light shines."
Before; "Who shall go *before* them?" "I left *before* sunrise."
Behind; "We have seen the moon rising *behind* the eastern pines."
Below; "It was on the road to Kennebec, *below* the town of Bath."
Beneath; "The steps creaked *beneath* his noiseless tread."
Beside; "I sat *beside* her;" "He is *beside* himself."
Besides; "There is nothing at all *besides* this manna."
Between; "The town is situated *between* two mountains."
Betwixt; "The waters roll *betwixt* him and the wooded knoll."
Beyond; "His thoughts turned to his home *beyond* the sea."
But = *except;* "He had retained nothing *but* his father's belt."
By; "Strength came *by* working in the mines."
Concerning; "The Lord hath spoken good *concerning* Israel."
Down; "They wandered in throngs *down* the valley."
During; "He staid at home *during* the war."
Ere; "Nile flowed *ere* the wonted season."
Except; "Are they all gone *except* you?"
For; "I looked up *for* a moment;" "I sell *for* cash."

From; "He felt like a leaf torn *from* a romance."

In; "Late *in* life, he began life *in* earnest."

Into; "He gazed *into* the vast surrounding darkness."

Notwithstanding; "He is proud, *notwithstanding* his poverty."

Of; "'T is the middle watch *of* a summer's night."

Off; "The vessel was becalmed *off* Cuba."

On; "He sprang *on* a rock;" "I leave *on* Saturday."

Out of; "No one was moving, at least *out of* doors."

Over; "The billows had rolled *over* him;" "He rules *over* us."

Past; "He drove *past* our house this morning."

Round; "A shoreless ocean tumbled *round* the globe."

Save; "Silent is all *save* the dropping rain."

Since; "The Lord hath blessed thee *since* my coming."

Till, until; "Not *till* the next morning did the boys appear."

Through; "Then stept she down *through* town and field."

Throughout; "There was much anxiety felt *throughout* the land."

To; "Let the old tree go down *to* the earth."

Toward, towards; "He turned me *toward* the moonlight."

Under; "He stands erect *under* the curved roof."

Unto; "Verily, I say *unto* you."

Up; "He sailed *up* the river."

Upon; "They were walking *upon* the hurricane deck."

With; "The sky was red *with* flame."

Within; "Something of ambition and pride stirred *within* him."

Without; "The morning broke *without* a sun."

Rem. 1.—The following prepositions, less commonly used, may be added to the foregoing list:

Abaft, aloft, alongside, afore, adown, aloof, aneath, aslant, atween, atwixt, despite, inside, outside, maugre, minus, plus, per, sans, underneath, versus, via, as for, along with, despite of, from among, from before, from betwixt, from off, from under, off of, over against, round about, but for; and the participial forms *excepting, regarding, bating, touching, respecting,* &c., when followed by objects.

Rem. 2.—*But, for, since,* and some others, are sometimes used as conjunctions; as, "I must go, *for* it is late."

Rem. 3.—Care should be taken to select such prepositions as express the relations intended.

Ex.—*Among, amongst* are applicable to more than two objects; as, "He divided the estate *among* the four brothers:" *between, betwixt,* are applicable to two objects only; as, "He divided the estate *between* the two brothers."

During should be used when the event continues through all the period mentioned; as, "I have examined law papers *during* the day:" *in, at,* or *within,* when the event does not continue during the whole period; as, "I alluded to that *in* my remarks this morning;" "The principal must be paid *within* the year."

Of denotes possession of a quality or thing; as, "He is a friend *of* mine:" *to* denotes that the quality or thing is directed towards something else; as, "He has been a friend *to* me."

In or *at* is used before the names of countries, cities, and towns; as, "She lives *in* New York;" "They reside *at* Glendale;" "We stayed *in* London."

Into should be used after verbs denoting entrance; as, "He came *into* the office;" "He put the knife *into* his pocket."

At is generally used after *to be,* not followed by a predicate; as, "They are *at* home;" "She is *at* church." When a predicate is understood, or clearly implied, *to* should be used; as, "I have been *to* Cincinnati," *i. e.,* I have been (traveling) to Cincinnati.

Of, not *about,* should be used after *boast* and *brag;* as, "He boasts *of* his wealth;" "He brags *of* his strength."

Upon should follow *bestow* and *dependent;* as, "Many favors were bestowed *upon* me;" "He is dependent *upon* his friends."

From should follow *differ* and *dissent;* as, "I differ *from* you;" "I dissent *from* that decision."

Of should follow *diminution;* as, "Any diminution *of* expenses is impossible."

In should follow *confide;* as, "I confide *in* you."

Of should be used when we are disappointed in obtaining a thing; as, "I was disappointed *of* money:" *in,* when we are disappointed in the quality of a thing, or the character of a person; as, "I am disappointed *in* that mower;" "I am disappointed *in* Mr. Johnson."

With denotes an *instrument; by,* a *cause: with,* the immediate, *by,* the remoter means; as, "A man is killed *with* a sword, and dies *by* violence;" "He walks *with* a cane *by* moonlight."

132. Order of Parsing.

1. A Preposition, and why?
2. What relation does it show?
3. Rule.

H. G. 10.

133. Models for Parsing.

I. "The horse ran *over* the hill."

Over . . . . . . is a *preposition;* it is a word used to show the relation between its object and some other word: it shows the relation between "hill" and "ran:" Rule XIX: "A preposition shows the relation of its object to the word upon which the latter depends."

II. "He came out *from under* the bridge."

From under is a *complex preposition;* (why?): it shows the relation between "bridge" and "came": Rule XIX.

134. Exercises.

Parse the prepositions in the following sentences:

1. Will you go with me into the garden? 2. In my father's house are many mansions. 3. We went over the river, through the corn-fields, into the woods yonder. 4. I am not satisfied as to that affair. 5. All came but Mary. 6. The Rhone flows out from among the Alps. 7. He went from St. Louis, across the plains, to California. 8. Light moves in straight lines, and in all directions from the point of emission. 9. They went aboard the ship.

10. Night, sable goddess! from her ebon throne,
   In rayless majesty, now stretches forth
   Her leaden scepter o'er a slumbering world.— *Young.*

Exercises to be corrected:

1. Divide the peaches among the two children. 2. I will pay you during the year. 3. Washington was a friend of his country. 4. He took the book in his own hand. 5. There is the key to that piano. 6. He arrived in Cleveland on Friday. 7. It corresponds with the sample. 8. They differ with each other in opinion. 9. The book was left out in the package I sent you. 10. The still, sultry morning was followed with a hailstorm.

11. Never depart out of the straight path. 12. He put money in his pocket. 13. He came in my office yesterday. 14. What is my grief in comparison of that which she bears? 15. He was eager of making money. 16. He went out of a fine morning, with a bundle in his hand. 17. He is conversant with Italian. 18. He boasted

about the money he had made. 19. They are to church. 20. I wish you would stay to home. 21. He is dependent on his daily labor for his support.

22. I can make no diminution in my tuition rates. 23. He died with a fever. 24. He left the room accompanied with his wife. 25. Crossing the isthmus is not attended with many difficulties. 26. Do not interfere among your neighbors' concerns. 27. We ought to profit from the errors of others. 28. The scenery was different to what I had supposed. 29. He does business in No. 147 Canal Street. 30. The space between the three roads is intended for a parade ground.

THE CONJUNCTION.

135. Oral Lesson.

In the sentence "Emma *and* Eva study algebra," what is the subject? *Ans.*—"Emma and Eva." Why? *Ans.*—Because something is affirmed of them. That is right. They are both subjects of the same predicate; and to indicate that they both sustain the same relation to the rest of the sentence, they are joined by the word "and." This is called a *Conjunction*, because its use is to join words. It is a *copulative conjunction*, because it joins elements of the same rank or name.

In the sentence "Emma *or* Eva studies algebra," "or" is a conjunction, but it denotes opposition of meaning. If *Emma* studies algebra, *Eva* does not. Those words which connect other words, but denote opposition of meaning, are called *disjunctive conjunctions*.

In the sentence "*Both* Emma *and* Eva study algebra," "both" and "and" are called *correlative conjunctions*, because each answers or refers to the other.

136. Definition.

A **Conjunction** is a word used to connect words, sentences, and parts of sentences.

Ex.—"The horse *and* wagon were captured, *but* the driver escaped;" "He lives out of town, *and* on a farm." In the first sentence, *and* connects "horse" and "wagon," and *but* connects the two propositions, "the horse and wagon were captured" and "the driver escaped." In the second sentence, *and* connects the phrases "out of town" and "on a farm."

Rem.—Conjunctions sometimes merely introduce sentences; as, "*And* it came to pass in those days;" "*That* the times are hard, is undeniable."

137. Classes of Connectives.

1. Connectives are divided into two general classes: *Coördinate* and *Subordinate.*

2. Coördinate Connectives are those which join elements of the same rank or name.

3. Subordinate Connectives are those which join elements of different ranks or names.

Rem. 1.—Coördinate connectives are *pure conjunctions.* They form no part of the material of which a sentence is composed—their use being to unite the material into a single sentence.

Ex.—"The man *and* his wife were both drowned;" "Knowledge comes, *but* wisdom lingers;" "The air is damp, *and* hushed, *and* close;" "And love the offender, *yet* detest the offense."

Rem. 2.—Subordinate connectives are either *relative pronouns, conjunctions,* or *conjunctive adverbs.* Relative pronouns represent antecedents, and join those antecedents to clauses which describe them: conjunctions introduce limiting clauses: conjunctive adverbs connect clauses, and modify a word in each.

Ex.—"The man *whom* you saw is my father." *Whom* represents "man," and joins to it the limiting clause "whom you saw." "I know *that* my Redeemer liveth." *That* joins the objective clause "my Redeemer liveth" to the verb "know." "The wind bloweth *where* it listeth." *Where* connects the two sentences, and modifies "bloweth" and "listeth."

Rem. 3.—In parsing *pure conjunctions,* give the rule for *coördinate connectives.* In parsing conjunctions which introduce limiting clauses, give the rule for *subordinate connectives.* Conjunctive adverbs should be parsed (1) as subordinate connectives; (2) as adverbs. A relative pronoun should be parsed (1) as a subordinate connective; (2) as a relative.

138. Classes of Conjunctions.

1. **Conjunctions** are divided into three classes: *Copulative, Disjunctive,* and *Correlative.*

2. **Copulative Conjunctions** join on members denoting an addition, consequence, cause, or supposition. They are,

And; "Cold *and* hunger awake not her care."
Also; As used in an enumeration of particulars.
As; "Always speak *as* you think."
Because; "He learns, *because* he is studious."
Consequently; "I am sick, *consequently* I can not come."
Even; "It was very cold; *even* mercury was frozen."
For; "If any, speak: *for* him have I offended."
If; "I shall not go *if* it rain."
So; "For Brutus is an honorable man;
So are they all, all honorable men."
Since; "They submit, *since* they can not conquer."
Seeing; "Wherefore come ye to me, *seeing* ye hate me?"
Than; used after comparatives; "He is older *than* I."
That; "These things I say, *that* ye might be saved."
Then; "You know our rules: *then* obey them."
Moreover; sometimes used as an introductory word.
Therefore; "Wisdom is the principal thing, *therefore* get wisdom."
Wherefore; used like *therefore* in drawing inferences.

3. **Disjunctive Conjunctions** join on members denoting opposition of meaning. They are,

Although, though; "*Though* coarse, it is good."
But; "I go, *but* I return."
Either; "*Either* John or Charles will come."
Neither; "*Neither* John nor Charles will come."
Except; "*Except* it be because her method is so glib and easy."
Lest; "Ye shall not eat it, neither shall ye touch it, *lest* ye die."
Nor; "Simois *nor* Xanthus shall be wanting there."
Notwithstanding; "He is just, *notwithstanding* he is stern."
Or; "He may study medicine, *or* law, *or* divinity."
Provided; "He will go, *provided* his fare is paid."
Save; "When all slept sound, *save* she who bore them both."
Still; "He has many faults, *still* he is very popular."

Unless; "We can not thrive, *unless* we are industrious and frugal."

Whether; "I will ascertain *whether* he has come."

Whereas; "Are not those found to be the greatest zealots who are most notoriously ignorant? *whereas* true piety should always begin with true knowledge."

Yet; "Though he slay me, *yet* will I trust in him."

4. **Correlative Conjunctions** are copulatives or disjunctives used in pairs, one referring or answering to another. They are,

Both . . . . . **and;** "He is *both* learned *and* wise."

As . . . . **as;** "I am *as* tall *as* you."

As . . . . **so;** "*As* it was then, *so* it is now."

So . . . . **as;** "He is not *so* tall *as* I."

So . . . . . . **that;** "It was *so* cold *that* I nearly perished."

Either . . . . **or;** "I will *either* send it *or* bring it."

Neither . . . **nor;** "*Neither* hath this man sinned, *nor* his parents."

If . . . . **then;** "*If* he confessed it, *then* forgive him."

Though . . . **yet, nevertheless;** "*Though* deep, *yet* clear."

Not only . . **but also;** "He was *not only* rich, *but also* generous."

Whether . . . **or;** "I care not *whether* it rains *or* snows."

Or . . . . **or,** } sometimes used for *either* . . *or*, *neither* . . *nor*.
Nor . . . . . . **nor;** }

5. Certain combinations of words have the force of connectives, and should be parsed as conjunctions or conjunctive adverbs. They are,

As if, as though, as well as, as soon as, as far as, as many as, except that, forasmuch as, in so much that, but also, but likewise, notwithstanding that, not only, &c.

Ex.—"Facts may be transmitted by tradition *as well as* by history;" "He went *as far as* the first line of pickets;" "You talk *as if* you were an idiot."

139. Order of Parsing.

1. A Conjunction, and why?
2. Copulative, Disjunctive, or Correlative, and why?
3. What does it connect?
4. Rule.

140. Models for Parsing.

I. "He came *and* went like a pleasant thought."

And ...... is a *conjunction;* it connects words: *copulative;* it denotes addition: it connects "came" and "went." Rule XX: "Coördinate connectives join similar elements."

II. "He *or* I will assist you."

Or .... is a *conjunction;* (why?): *disjunctive;* it denotes opposition of meaning: it connects "he" and "I." Rule XX.

III. "*Neither* James *nor* John had his lesson."

Neither ... nor ... are *conjunctions;* (why?): *correlative;* one refers or answers to the other: *neither* introduces the sentence, and *nor* connects "James" and "John." Rule XX.

IV. "Unto us was the gospel preached *as well as* unto them."

As well as is a *conjunction;* (why?): *copulative;* (why?): it connects and emphatically distinguishes the two phrases, "unto us" and "unto them": Rule XX.

141. Exercises.

Parse all the words in the following sentences:

1. I am a poor man, and argue with you, and convince you. 2. He'd sooner die than ask you, or any man, for a shilling. 3. Talent is something, but tact is every thing. 4. Neither military nor civil pomp was wanting. 5. The truth is, that I am tired of ticking. 6. I remember a mass of things, but nothing distinctly.

7. I alone was solitary and idle. 8. Both the ties of nature and the dictates of policy demand this. 9. There was no reply, for a slight fear was upon every man. 10. No man more highly esteems or honors the British troops than I do. 11. The soldier marches on and on, inflicting and suffering, as before. 12. There may be wisdom without knowledge, and there may be knowledge without wisdom.

Exercises to be corrected:

1. The answer is the same with that I have. 2. I can not weather this storm without some one helps me. 3. You are too

stuck up, so as you can never be popular.   4. Some of my books, and for which I paid a large price, are good for nothing.   5. Neither borrow or lend umbrellas.   6. I could not see nor hear him.

7. The loafer seems to be created for no other purpose, but to keep up the ancient and honorable order of idleness.   8. They told us how that it happened.   9. This is the reason that I remained at home.   10. Silver is both mined in Mexico and Peru.   11. The court of chancery frequently mitigates and breaks the teeth of the common law.   12. I as well as my sister are going West in the spring.

THE INTERJECTION.

142. Definition.

An **Interjection** is a word used to denote some sudden or strong emotion; as, "*Hark!* some one comes." "*Pshaw!* that is ridiculous."

The principal interjections are the following:

Ah, aha, hurra, huzza; oh, alas, welladay, alack; ha, indeed, zounds; bravo; faugh, fie, fudge, pshaw; heigh-ho; ha, ha, ha, (*laughter*); avaunt, begone; hail, all-hail; adieu, farewell, good-by; hallo, ahoy, lo, hark; hist, whist, hush, tush; avast, hold; eh? hey?

Rem. 1.—Interjections have no definite meaning or grammatical construction. They occur frequently in colloquial or impassioned discourse; but are expressions of emotion only, and can not be used as signs of thought. As their name imports, they may be *thrown in between* connected parts of discourse, but are generally found at the commencement of sentences.

Rem. 2.—Other parts of speech, when used as exclamations, may be treated as interjections; as, "*What!* art thou mad?" "*My stars!* what can all this be?" "*Revenge! about,—seek,— burn,—fire,—kill,—slay!*—let not a traitor live!" In most cases, however, words thus used may be parsed otherwise; as, "'*Magnificent!*' cried all at once." "Magnificent" may be parsed as an adjective, the attribute of the sentence, "*It is magnificent.*" "*Behold!* your house is left unto you desolate!" "Behold" may be parsed as a verb in the imperative mode.

143. Order of Parsing.

1. An Interjection, and why?
2. Rule.

144. Model for Parsing.

I. "*O, let me live.*"

O . . . is an *interjection;* it denotes some strong emotion . Rule XXII: "An interjection has no dependence upon other words."

145. Exercises.

Parse all the words in the following sentences :

1. Ha! laughest thou? 2. Heigh! sirs, what a noise you make here. 3. Huzza! huzza! Long live lord Robin! 4. Hah! it is a sight to freeze one. 5. Let them be desolate for a reward of their shame which say unto me, Aha! aha!

6. Oh, that the salvation of Israel were come out of Zion! 7. Alas! all earthly good still blends itself with home! 8. Tush! tush! man, I made no reference to you. 9. Hark! what nearer war-drum shakes the gale? 10. Soft! I did but dream!

11. What! old acquaintance! could not all this flesh
    Keep in a little life? Poor Jack, farewell!
I could have better spared a better man.—*Shakspeare.*

146. Miscellaneous Exercises.

1. A mercenary informer knows no distinction. 2. I send you here a sort of allegory. 3. Our island home is far beyond the sea. 4. Love took up the harp of life, and smote on all the chords with might. 5. Your *If* is the only peace-maker: much virtue in *If*. 6. He is very prodigal of his *ohs* and *ahs*.

7. He looked upward at the rugged heights that towered above him in the gloom. 8. He possessed that rare union of reason, simplicity, and vehemence, which formed the prince of orators. 9. Mark well my fall, and that that ruined me. 10. The jingling of the guinea helps the hurt that honor feels.—*Tennyson.*

11. His qualities were so happily blended, that the result was a great and perfect whole. 12. There is no joy but calm. 13. I

    H. G. 11.

must be cruel, only to be kind.   14. Why are we weighed upon
with heaviness? 15.   Now blessings light on him that first invented
sleep: it covers a man all over, thoughts and all, like a cloak.—
Cervantes.

16. Many a morning on the moorlands did we hear the copses
ring.   17. He stretched out his right hand at these words, and laid
it gently on the boy's head. 18. He acted ever as if his country's
welfare, and that alone, was the moving spirit.   19. The great
contention of criticism is to find the faults of the moderns, and the
beauties of the ancients.   Whilst an author is yet living, we estimate his powers by his worst performance; and when he is dead,
we estimate them by his best.—*Johnson.*

20. I will work in my own sphere, nor wish it other than it is.
21. As his authority was undisputed, so it required no jealous pre-
cautions, no rigorous severity.   22. Like all men of genius, he de-
lighted to take refuge in poetry.   23. To know how to say what
other people only think, is what makes men poets and sages; and
to dare to say what others only dare to think, makes men martyrs
or reformers, or both.   24. That done, she turned to the old man
with a lovely smile upon her face,—such, they said, as they had
never seen, and never could forget,—and clung with both her arms
about his neck.—*Dickens.*

25. To live in hearts we leave behind,
    Is not to die.—*Campbell.*

26. But war's a game which, were their subjects wise,
    Kings would not play at.—*Cowper.*

27. Whoever thinks a faultless piece to see,
    Thinks what ne'er was, nor is, nor e'er shall be.—*Pope.*

28. The Niobe of nations, there she stands,
    Childless and crownless, in her voiceless woe;
An empty urn within her withered hands,
    Whose holy dust was scattered long ago.—*Byron.*

29. Can storied urn or animated bust
    Back to its mansion call the fleeting breath?
Can Honor's voice provoke the sleeping dust,
    Or Flattery soothe the dull, cold ear of death?—*Gray.*

30. A thing of beauty is a joy forever;
    Its loveliness increases; it will never
Pass into nothingness.—*Keats.*

31. Forth from his dark and lonely hiding-place,
    (Portentous sight!) the owlet Atheism,
    Sailing on obscure wings athwart the noon,
    Drops his blue-fringed lids, and holds them close,
    And hooting at the glorious sun in heaven,
    Cries out, " Where is it?"—*Coleridge.*

32. Dry clank'd his harness in the icy caves
    And barren chasms, and all to left and right
    The bare black cliff clang'd round him, as he based
    His feet on jets of slippery crag that rang
    Sharp-smitten with the dint of armed heels.—*Tennyson.*

33.   Then came wandering by
    A shadow, like an angel with bright hair
    Dabbled in blood; and he shriek'd out aloud:
    "Clarence is come! false, fleeting, perjur'd Clarence!
    That stabbed me in the field by Tewksbury:
    Seize on him, furies, take him to your torments!"—*Shakspeare.*

34. There are things of which I may not speak:
       There are dreams that can not die:
    There are thoughts that make the strong heart weak,
       And bring a pallor upon the cheek,
          And a mist before the eye.
          And the words of that fatal song
       Come over me like a chill:
    "A boy's will is the wind's will,
    And the thoughts of youth are long, long thoughts."
                                   Longfellow.

35. These ages have no memory—but they left
       A record in the desert—columns strown
    On the waste sands, and statues fallen and cleft,
       Heap'd like a host in battle overthrown;
    Vast ruins, where the mountain's ribs of stone
       Were hewn into a city: streets that spread
    In the dark earth, where never breath has blown
       Of heaven's sweet air, nor foot of man dares tread,
    The long and perilous ways—the Cities of the Dead.—*Bryant.*

PART III.

SYNTAX.

147. Preliminary Oral Lessons.

Note to Teachers.—The object of these lessons is (1) To exercise pupils in the construction of simple sentences: (2) To teach the uses and definitions of the elements of a sentence: (3) To teach the analysis of sentences containing elements of the first class.

Use Oral Lesson on page 24 as introductory to these.

LESSON I.

I hold in my hand a piece of chalk: what is its color? *Ans.*—It is *white*. It breaks easily: what else can be said of it? *Ans.*—It is *brittle*. It crumbles readily: hence, we say it is *friable*. Each of the words, *white, brittle, friable,* expresses some quality belonging to chalk: what shall we call them? *Ans.—Quality-words.* We will now unite these *quality-words* with "chalk," by the word "is," thus:

> Chalk is white;
> Chalk is brittle;
> Chalk is friable.

Each of these groups of words is called a *Sentence;* for

"A **Sentence** is an assemblage of words making complete sense."

Write the definition on your slates. Now repeat it in concert. Each group is also called a *Proposition;* for

"A **Proposition** is a thought expressed in words."

Write this definition on your slates. Repeat it in concert.

In the proposition "Chalk is white," the noun "chalk" is called the *Subject;* for

"The **Subject** of a proposition is that of which something is affirmed."

"White" is called the *Predicate;* for

"The **Predicate** of a proposition is that which is affirmed of the subject."

The word "is" is called the *Copula;* for

"The **Copula** is a word or group of words used to affirm or assert the predicate of the subject."

In this sentence, it affirms that the quality "white" belongs to "chalk."

Write these definitions on your slates. Repeat them in concert.

In the proposition "Chalk is brittle," what is the subject? *Ans.*—"Chalk." Why? *Ans.*—It is that of which something is affirmed. What is the predicate? *Ans.*—"Brittle." Why? *Ans.*—It is that which is affirmed of the subject.

Affirm **qualities** *of the following subjects:*

Iron, gold, silver, lead, ink, cork, sugar, vinegar, grass, books, lessons.

Model.—Iron is *heavy.*

Affirm the following qualities of appropriate **subjects:**

Transparent, opaque, hard, round, square, good, bad, bitter, heavy, rough, smooth, red, yellow, green.

Model.—*Glass* is transparent.

LESSON II.

In the sentence "Iron is a metal," is any quality affirmed of "iron"? *Ans.*—There is not. That is right. The predicate "metal" denotes *kind* or *class,* not *quality.* It is a predicate, however, because it is affirmed of the subject "iron." In the sentence "Horses are animals," what is the subject? *Ans.*—"Horses." Why? *Ans.*—Because it is that of which something is affirmed. What is the predicate? *Ans.*—"Animals." Why? *Ans.*—Because it is that which is affirmed of the subject. What is the copula? *Ans.*—The word "are."

Affirm **class** *of the following subjects:*

Horses, oxen, coal, wood, hay, oats, wheat, ax, hoe, locomotive, dogs, sheep, copper, gold, apples, trees, wagons, houses.

Model.—Wheat is a *vegetable.*

Affirm **qualities** *of the same subjects.*

LESSON III.

Write this sentence on your slates: "Horses run." You see that the predicate "run" is affirmed *directly* of the subject without the use of the copula. The copula and predicate are united in one word; for "Horses run" means the same as "Horses are running."

What is the subject in this sentence: "Boys learn"? *Ans.*— "Boys." What is the predicate? *Ans.*—"Learn." Why? *Ans.*—It is that which is affirmed of the subject. Words which affirm any thing of subjects are called Verbs. What are the words "run" and "learn"? *Ans.*—Verbs. Why? *Ans.*—Because they affirm something of their subjects.

Write sentences, using the following verbs as predicates:

Walk, sing, whistle, swim, wrestle, play, write, study, plow, reap, drive, neigh, cackle, whine, snarl, gobble, quarrel, fight.

Model.—Cattle *walk*.

LESSON IV.

Write on your slates, and then repeat in concert:

"An **Element** is one of the distinct parts of a sentence."

The *Subject* and *Predicate* are called *Principal Elements*, because no sentence can be formed without them.

The *Copula* is not an element: it is used merely to affirm the predicate of the subject.

Separating a sentence into its elements is called **Analysis.** We will now analyze some sentences according to the following

MODELS.

I. "Apples are ripe."

Apples . . . is the subject; it is that of which something is affirmed: **ripe** is the predicate; it is that which is affirmed of the subject; **are** is the copula.

II. "Birds fly."

Birds . . . . is the subject; (why?): **fly** is the predicate; (why?).

EXERCISES.

1. Ink is black. 2. Gold is yellow. 3. Lead is a metal. 4. Birds sing. 5. Vessels sail. 6. Trees are plants. 7. Fishes swim.

8. Elihu was tardy. 9. Mary was studious. 10. Enoch may be angry. 11. Snow falls. 12. Houses stand.

LESSON V.

Write this sentence on your slates: "Horses eat." While you were writing did you not think some word should be added, representing *what* horses eat? *Ans.*—We did. What word shall we add? *Ans.*—Oats. Write "oats" after the verb. This word *completes* the meaning of the verb, and is called an *Objective Element*, or *Object*. In the sentence "Pupils study arithmetic," what word completes the meaning of the predicate or verb? *Ans.*—"Arithmetic." What element is it? *Ans.*—An objective element. Why? *Ans.*—Because it completes the meaning of the verb.

Write ten sentences, each containing an objective element.

Model.—Indians hunt buffaloes.

Analyze the sentences you have written, using this model:

"Children love play."

Children is the subject; (why?): **love,** the predicate; (why?): the predicate is modified by **play,** an objective element.

Analyze also the following sentences:

1. Heat melts lead. 2. Men love money. 3. I study botany. 4. Haste makes waste. 5. Cats catch mice. 6. Mr. Jones sells calicoes. 7. Clouds bring rain.

LESSON VI.

Write this sentence on your slates: "Apples are ripe." What is the subject of the sentence? *Ans.*—"Apples." Why? *Ans.*— It is that of which something is affirmed. What is the word "apples"? *Ans.*—It is a noun. Why? *Ans.*—It is a name. What is the predicate? *Ans.*—"Ripe." Why? *Ans.*—It is that which is affirmed of the subject. Now write these words, "Ripe apples." Is this a sentence? *Ans.*—It is not. Why? *Ans.*— There is nothing affirmed. That is correct. The word "ripe" is here used to modify the meaning of "apples," as an *attribute*, not as a *predicate:* that is, it is *assumed*, or *taken for granted*, that it belongs to "apples." All words which modify the meaning of nouns in this manner, are called *Adjective Elements*.

Write this sentence: "Ripe apples are cheap." What is

"ripe"? *Ans.*—An adjective element. Why? *Ans.*—It modifies the meaning of a noun. "Samuel's hat is torn." What element is "Samuel's"? *Ans.*—An adjective element. Why? *Ans.*—It modifies the meaning of the noun "hat." "Mr. Smith the mason is sick." What is "mason"? *Ans.*—An adjective element. Why? *Ans.*—It modifies the meaning of "Mr. Smith," a noun. What are the words "Samuel's" and "mason"? *Ans.*—They are nouns. Nouns, then, are adjective elements when they modify nouns.

Write five sentences, limiting the subjects by adjective elements denoting quality.

Models.—*Cross* dogs bite. *Cold* winter comes.

Write five sentences, limiting their subjects by adjective elements denoting number.

Models.—*Two* boys fought. *Three* men left.

Write five sentences, limiting their subjects by words which merely point them out.

Models.—*That* boy is studious. *This* boy is lazy.

Write five sentences, limiting their subjects by nouns.

Models.—*Eli's* uncle is rich. Mr. Tod the *lawyer* is young.

Write five sentences, limiting both subjects and objects by adjective elements.

Model.—*Emma's* mother bought a *new* bonnet.

Analyze the following sentences, using these models:

I. "Milton the poet was blind."

Milton . is the subject; (why?): **blind** is the predicate; (why?): "Milton" is modified by **poet,** an adjective element, and "poet" by **the,** an adjective element: **was** is the copula.

II. "Evil communications corrupt good manners."

Communications is the subject; (why?): **corrupt,** the predicate; (why?): "communications" is modified by **evil,** an adjective element; "corrupt," by **manners,** an objective element; and "manners," by **good,** an adjective element.

EXERCISES.

1. Sarah's book is lost. 2. Mrs. Elkins the milliner found Sarah's book. 3. Old people love quiet. 4. Young children love play. 5. I like ripe cherries. 6. You have found my pencil.

LESSON VII.

Write this sentence on your slates: "Birds sing sweetly." Does "sweetly" denote *what* the birds sing? *Ans.*—It does not; it tells *how* they sing. That is right. "Sweetly" does not complete the meaning of "sing," like an objective element; but it modifies its meaning in another way. All words used in such a manner are called *Adverbial Elements.* Words which modify adjectives are called adverbial elements also. In this sentence, "The storm rages violently," what is the subject? *Ans.*—"Storm." What is the predicate? *Ans.*—"Rages." What is "violently"? *Ans.*— An adverbial element. Why? *Ans.*—It modifies a verb, but does not complete its meaning.

In the sentence "Very large vessels were seen," what is modified by "very"? *Ans.*—"Large." What is "large"? *Ans.*—An adjective. What element, then, is "very"? *Ans.*—An adverbial element. Why? *Ans.*—It modifies an adjective. Adverbial elements also modify other adverbial elements.

Write ten sentences, modifying the verbs by adverbial elements.

Model.—The wind blows *furiously.*

Write ten sentences, containing adjective elements modified by adverbial elements.

Model.—James recited a *very* long lesson.

Analyze the following sentences, using these models:

I. "The wind blows violently."

Wind . is the subject; (why?): **blows,** the predicate; (why?): "wind" is modified by **the,** an adjective element: "blows" is modified by **violently,** an adverbial element.

II. "Emma has a very severe headache."

Emma is the subject; (why?): **has,** the predicate; (why?): "has" is modified by **headache,** an objective element; "headache" by **a** and **severe,** adjective elements; and "severe," by **very,** an adverbial element.

EXERCISES.

1. A sluggard sleeps soundly.   2. The horses were much fatigued.
3. Very loud reports were heard.   4. That boy spends his money foolishly.   5. You may go now.   6. He then left the country.

148. Definitions.

1. **Syntax** treats of the construction of sentences.

2. A **Sentence** is an assemblage of words making complete sense.

Ex.—Birds fly. Man is mortal. "The great throat of the chimney laughed." "When the farmer came down in the morning, he declared that his watch had gained half an hour in the night."

3. A **Proposition** is a thought expressed in words.

Ex.—The weather is pleasant. Pupils should be studious. The boy seems frightened. Horses are animals.

Rem.—The term *sentence* is applied to any assemblage of words so arranged as to make complete sense; *proposition*, to the thought which those words express. The same assemblage of words, therefore, may be both a sentence and a proposition.

4. **Propositions** are either *Principal* or *Subordinate*.

5. A **Principal Proposition** is one which makes complete sense when standing alone.

6. A **Subordinate Proposition** is one which does not make complete sense when standing alone, but which must be connected with another proposition.

Ex.—"The man that does no good does harm." In this sentence, "*the man does harm*" is the principal proposition, for it makes complete sense when standing alone: "*that does no good*" is a subordinate proposition, for it does not make complete sense when standing alone.

7. A **Phrase** is an assemblage of words forming a single expression, but not making complete sense.

Ex.—Till lately; in haste; since then; year by year; little by little; to see; to have seen; to be seen.

8. A **Discourse** is a series of sentences on the same subject, arranged in logical order.

9. A **Paragraph** is a series of sentences on the same branch of a subject.

10. An **Element** is one of the component parts of a sentence.

11. **Analysis** is the separation of a sentence into its elements.

12. **Synthesis** is the construction of sentences from words.

SENTENCES.

149. Classification with Respect to Use.

1. With respect to *use,* sentences are divided into four classes: *Declarative, Interrogative, Imperative,* and *Exclamatory.*

2. A **Declarative Sentence** is one used to affirm or deny something.

Ex.—Fishes swim. Fishes do not walk.

Rem.—**Direct Discourse** is telling what somebody thinks or says, by using his own words; as, "Our teacher said, '*Be frank, honest, and truthful.*'"

Indirect Discourse is giving the substance of what somebody thinks or says, but not using his own words; as, "Our teacher said, *that we should be frank, honest, and truthful.*"

3. An **Interrogative Sentence** is one used to ask a question.

Ex.—Are you angry? Where does that man live?

Rem.—A **Direct Question** is one which can be answered by *yes* or *no ;* as, "Has the money been paid?"

An **Indirect Question** is one which can not be answered by *yes* or *no ;* as, "Who paid the money?"

4. An **Imperative Sentence** is one used to express a command or an entreaty.

Ex.—Bring me that book. Do not strike me.

5. An **Exclamatory Sentence** is one used in exclamations, or in the expression of strong emotion.

Ex.—Oh, how glad I am to see you!

150. Exercises.

Tell to which class each of the following sentences belongs:

Model.—"The dews bring their jewels."

This is a *declarative sentence;* it is used to affirm something.

1. The days are calm. 2. How many quarts are there in a gallon? 3. The winds bring perfumes. 4. Study diligently. 5. He waved his arm. 6. And the fellow calls himself a painter! 7. He deserved punishment rather than pity.

8. O, how careless you are! 9. What was the Rubicon? 10. How brightly the sun shines! 11. Alas for the man who has not learned to work! 12. Bring forth the prisoner now. 13. I had a dream which was not all a dream. 14. A plague of all cowards, still say I.

15. Attend to the duties I have assigned you. 16. Many fell by thy arm: they were consumed in the flame of thy wrath. 17. When shall it be morn in the grave, to bid the slumberer awake? 18. The commons, faithful to their system, remained in a wise and masterly inactivity.—*Mackintosh.*

151. Classification with Respect to Form.

1. With respect to *form*, sentences are divided into three classes: *Simple, Complex,* and *Compound.*

2. A **Simple Sentence** consists of a single proposition.

Ex.—Flowers bloom. Who is he? Tread lightly. How glad I am!

3. A **Complex Sentence** consists of a principal proposition, some part of which is modified by one or more subordinate propositions.

Ex.—Flowers bloom *when spring returns.* He *who is diligent* shall be rewarded. I hear *that you have sold your farm, and that you are going to California.*

Rem.—The propositions in complex sentences are called **Clauses.** They are named and numbered according to the order of their subordination.

Ex.—"I believe that he is honest." In this sentence, *"I believe"* is the *principal* clause, and *"that he is honest"* is the *subordinate.*

4. A **Compound Sentence** consists of two or more simple or complex sentences, joined by coördinate connectives.

Ex.—Spring comes, *and* the flowers bloom. "I go, *but* I return." "Though Truth is fearless and absolute, *yet* she is meek and modest."

Rem. 1.—The simple or complex sentences of which compound sentences are composed, are called **Members.** They are numbered according to their place in the sentence.

Ex.—"Every man desires to live long; but no man would be old." In this sentence, *"every man desires to live long"* is the *first* member, and *"no man would be old"* is the *second.*

Rem. 2.—The clauses of complex sentences are connected by *relative pronouns, conjunctions,* and *conjunctive adverbs.* The members of compound sentences are connected by conjunctions.

Rem. 3.—The connectives are sometimes omitted; as, "I thought [that] he was absent;" "Talent is power, [but] tact is skill."

152. Models for Classification.

I. "The nights are tranquil."

This is a *sentence;* it is an assemblage of words making complete sense: *declarative;* it is used to affirm something: *simple;* it consists of a single proposition.

II. "Shall I return the book which you lent me?"

This is a *sentence;* (why?): *interrogative;* it is used to ask a question: *complex;* it is composed of a principal and a subordinate proposition: *"Shall I return the book"* is the principal proposition, and *"which you lent me,"* the subordinate, limiting "book." "Which" is the connective.

III. "She counseled him, that when he arose in the morning, he should beat them without mercy."—*Bunyan*.

This is a *sentence;* (why?): *declarative;* (why?): *complex;* (why?): "*She counseled him*" is the principal proposition; "*that he should beat them without mercy*" the first subordinate, modifying "counseled"; and "*when he rose in the morning,*" the second subordinate, modifying "beat." "That" and "when" are connectives.

IV. "Pope had perhaps the judgment of Dryden: but Dryden certainly wanted the diligence of Pope."—*Johnson*.

This is a *sentence;* (why?): *declarative;* (why?): *compound;* it is composed of two propositions, joined by a coördinate connective: "*Pope had perhaps the judgment of Dryden*" is the first member, and "*Dryden certainly wanted the diligence of Pope*" is the second. "But" is the connective.

153. Exercises.

1. Thy feet are fetterless. 2. Level spread the lake before him. 3. He waved his broad felt hat for silence. 4. A soldier of the Legion lay dying in Algiers. 5. It sank from sight before it set. 6. Ye softening dews, ye tender showers, descend! 7. None will flatter the poor. 8. Ye are the things that tower. 9. The house was wrapped in flames.

10. Hope and fear are the bane of human life. 11. The village all declared how much he knew. 12. He that refuseth instruction despiseth his own soul. 13. Is it for thee the lark ascends and sings? 14. How dreadful is this place, for God is here! 15. He dares not touch a hair of Catiline. 16. What can compensate for the loss of character? 17. Lead us not into temptation, but deliver us from evil.

18. Time slept on flowers, and lent his glass to Hope. 19. All were sealed with the seal which is never to be broken till the great day. 20. O God, we are but leaves on thy stream, clouds in thy sky. 21. Talk to the point, and stop when you have reached it.

22. "It was now the Sabbath-day, and a small congregation, of about a hundred souls, had met for divine service, in a place more magnificent than any temple that human hands had ever built to Deity."— *Wilson*.

23. I know thou art gone where the weary are blest,
    And the mourner looks up and is glad.

24. What matter how the night behaved?
   What matter how the north wind raved?— *Whittier.*

25. Bird of the broad and sweeping wing,
   Thy home is high in heaven,
   Where the wide storms their banners fling,
   And the tempest-clouds are driven.—*Percival.*

ELEMENTS.

154. Principal Elements.

1. The **Principal Elements** of a proposition are those which are necessary to its construction. They are the *Subject* and the *Predicate.*

2. The **Subject** of a proposition is that of which something is affirmed.

Ex.—*"Time* is precious." "Time" is the *subject;* it is that of which *"precious"* is affirmed.

3. The **Predicate** of a proposition is that which is affirmed of the subject.

Ex.—"Time is *precious."* "Precious" is the *predicate;* it is that which is affirmed of the subject.

Rem.—In these definitions, the term "affirm" is meant to include *say, ask for, command, entreat,* or *exclaim.*

4. The Subject may be a *word,* a *phrase,* or a *clause.*

Ex.— *Winter* is coming. *H* is a letter. *To steal* is base. *"Pay as you go,"* is a good rule. *"Why will he persist?"* is often asked.

Rem.—The subject of a proposition may be known by its answering the question formed by using *Who?* or *What?* with the predicate.

Ex.—"John is careless." *Who* is careless? *Ans.*—"John." "John," therefore, is the subject. *"To be sick* is disagreeable." *What* is disagreeable? *Ans.*—"To be sick." "To be sick," therefore, is the subject.

5. The **Copula** is some form of the verb *to be,* (*is, was,*

has been, might be, &c.,) or a *copulative* verb. Its office is to affirm the predicate of the subject.

Ex.—"Silence *is* impressive." "Is" is the *copula,* and "impressive" the *predicate.* "Gold *is* a metal." "Is" is the *copula,* and "metal" the *predicate.* "He *may have been* injudicious." "May have been" is the *copula,* and "injudicious" the *predicate.* "The fields *look* green." "Look" is the *copula,* and "green" the *predicate.*

6. In affirming *action, being,* or *state,* the copula and predicate are generally united in one word, or one form, called a *verb.*

Ex.—Pupils *study.* I *am.* The house *stands.* Rain *is falling.* Letters *are written.*

7. The Predicate may be a *word,* a *phrase,* or a *clause.*

Ex.—Horses *gallop.* Wheat is a *vegetable.* The sun *was shining.* "To obey is *to enjoy.*" He seems *honest.* My desire is, *that you attend school.*

Rem.—The predicate is sometimes erroneously called the *attribute* of a proposition, and the copula and predicate, taken together, the *predicate.*

155. Models for Analysis.

I. "Birds sing."

This is a *sentence;* (why?): *declarative;* (why?): *simple;* (why?).

Birds is the subject; it is that of which something is affirmed; **sing** is the predicate; it is that which is affirmed of the subject.

II. "Scholars should be studious."

This is a *sentence;* (why?): *declarative;* (why?): *simple;* (why?).

Scholars is the subject; (why?): **studious** is the predicate; (why?): **should be** is the copula.

III. "Franklin was a philosopher."

This is a *sentence;* (why?): *declarative;* (why?): *simple;* (why?).

Franklin is the subject; (why?): **philosopher** is the predicate; (why?): **was** is the copula.

IV. "He was considered responsible."

This is a *sentence;* (why?): *declarative;* (why?): *simple;* (why?).

He is the subject; (why?): **responsible** is the predicate; (why?): **was considered** is the copula.

V. "Be truthful."

This is a *sentence;* (why?): *imperative;* (why?): *simple;* (why?).

Thou or **you,** understood, is the subject; (why?): **truthful** is the predicate; (why?): **be** is the copula.

156. Exercises in Analysis.

1. Children play. 2. Virtue ennobles. 3. Spring has come. 4. Winter has departed. 5. You may go. 6. Mary might have sung. 7. Horses can run. 8. Flowers are blooming. 9. Money may be loaned. 10. Books will be bought. 11. Stars were shining. 12. John should have been studying.

13. Glass is brittle. 14. Water is transparent. 15. Savages may be merciful. 16. Men should be just. 17. Samuel should have been obedient. 18. Geography is interesting. 19. Job was patient. 20. I will be industrious. 21. They have been successful.

22. Iron is a metal. 23. Flies are insects. 24. Napoleon was a general. 25. Ostriches are birds. 26. "Men would be angels; angels would be gods." 27. They may have been truants. 28. Howard was a philanthropist. 29. He might have been a lawyer. 30. George had been a captain.

31. John looks cold. 32. I feel aguish. 33. Ants appear industrious. 34. Washington was elected president. 35. Avarice has become his master. 36. He seems dejected. 37. He became wealthy. 38. It was deemed inexpedient.

157. Arrangement of Elements.

1. **Arrangement** is the correct *placing* of elements.

2. Elements are arranged in *Natural* or *Inverted* order.

3. The **Natural** order of arrangement is that which is most customary.

4. The **Inverted** order of arrangement is any departure from the natural order.

Rem.—In inverted order, the elements are said to be transposed.

5. The *Natural* order of arrangement is,

In **Declarative Sentences:**
1. *Subject* .... *Predicate ;* as "Winds blow."
2. *Subject* .... *Copula* .... *Predicate ;* as, "Chalk is white."
3. *Subject* .... *Auxiliary* .. *Predicate ;* as, "You may go."

In **Interrogative Sentences:**
1. *Copula* .... *Subject* .... *Predicate ;* as, "Is he wise?"
2. *Auxiliary* .. *Subject* .... *Predicate ;* as, "May I go?"
3. *Predicate* .. *Subject ;* as, "Say you so?"
4. *Subject* .... *Predicate ;* as, "Who remained?"

In **Imperative Sentences:**
1. *Predicate* .. *Subject ;* as, "Go thou."
2. *Copula* .... *Subject* .... *Predicate ;* as, "Be ye merciful."

In **Exclamatory Sentences,** the arrangement is the same as in *declarative, interrogative,* and *imperative* sentences.

6. The *Inverted* order is used when the predicate is made emphatic.

Rem.—**Inversion** occurs in declarative and exclamatory sentences. The usual order of arrangement is *Predicate* ... *Copula* ... *Subject ;* as, "Great was our wonder;" "Known unto God are all his works."

158. Exercises in Synthesis.

Affirm **actions** *of the following subjects :*

Winds, waters, stars, fire, light, acorns, sheep, rabbits, fishes, men, women, boys, girls, children, thunder, lightning, storms, nobles, kings, merchants.

Models.—Winds *blow.* Storms *rage.*

Affirm q   of the following subjects:

App   cherries, peaches, fruit, books, desks, winter, spring, summe   utumn, sugar, quinine, vinegar, grammar, writing, evenings, darkness, chemistry, geography.

Models.—Apples *are ripe.* Quinine *is bitter.*

Ascertain all the distinguishing properties of five substances. Affirm them of the substances to which they belong.

Models.—Chalk *is white;* chalk *is opaque;* chalk *is brittle;* chalk *is incombustible,* &c.

Affirm **class** *or* **kind** *of the following subjects:*

Oranges, horses, hens, flies, Henry, Washington, ships, gold, silver, sharks, water, air, table.

Models.—Oranges *are fruit.* Henry *is a clerk.*

159. Subordinate Elements.

1. A **Modifier** is a word, phrase, or clause joined to a term to limit or restrict its meaning or application.

Ex.—A *wealthy* man. Chairs *to mend.* A man *who is wealthy.*

2. **Subordinate Elements** are those which modify other elements. They are distinguished as *Objective, Adjective,* and *Adverbial.*

160. Objective Element.

An **Objective Element** is a word or group of words which completes the meaning of a transitive verb in the active voice, or of its participles. It is usually called the **object.**

Ex.—Heat melts *metals.* Men love *money.* I wish *to be quiet.* Alice knew *that we were not at home. Him* they sought.

Rem. 1.—The objective element answers the question formed by using *Whom?* or *What?* with the predicate, or with the subject and predicate.

Ex.—"John writes letters." Writes *what? Ans.*—"Letters"=the *object.* "Brutus killed Cæsar." Brutus killed *whom? Ans.*—"Cæsar"=the *object.*

Rem. 2.—By "completing the meaning of a verb" is meant restricting its application, by stating that on which its action terminates. In the sentence "John writes," the predicate "writes" is taken in its most general sense: *what* John writes is not mentioned. In the sentence "John writes letters," the application of the predicate is restricted to the single act of writing letters. "Letters" being the object on which the act of writing terminates, it is called the *objective element*.

Rem. 3.—Some verbs are followed by two objects: one denoting a person or thing; the other, the rank, office, occupation, or character of the person, or the species of the thing. See, also, ? 32, Rem. 2.

Ex.—They elected *Charles captain*. He called *him* a *scoundrel*. He makes the *sea* his *home*. They declared *self-government* a *delusion*.

Rem. 4.—Another class of verbs is followed by two objects: one denoting a person or thing; the other, that *to* or *from* which the act tends. The former is called the *direct*, the latter the *indirect* object.

Ex.—He taught *me arithmetic*. He sold *me* a *horse*. I gave *him money*. They sent *John* a *telegram*.

161. Models for Analysis.

VI. "Columbus discovered America."

This is a *sentence;* (why?): *declarative;* (why?): *simple;* (why?).

Columbus is the subject; (why?): **discovered** is the predicate: (why?). The predicate is modified by **America**, an objective element.

VII. "Whom did you see?"

This is a *sentence;* (why?): *interrogative;* (why?): *simple;* (why?).

You is the subject; (why?): **did see** is the predicate; (why?). The predicate is modified by **whom**, an objective element.

VIII. "Bring me flowers."

This is a *sentence;* (why?): *imperative;* (why?): *simple;* (why?).

Thou or **you**, understood, is the subject: (why?): **bring** is the predicate; (why?). The predicate is modified by **me**, an indirect, and by **flowers**, a direct object.

IX. "They have chosen Mr. Ames speaker."

This is a *sentence;* (why?): *declarative;* (why?): *simple;* (why?).

They is the subject; (why?): **have chosen** is the predicate; (why?). The predicate is modified by **Mr. Ames,** an objective element; and **Mr. Ames,** by **speaker,** an adjective element, denoting office.

162. Exercises in Analysis.

1. He examined the books. 2. Silas studied geology. 3. They watched the storm. 4. You must obey the laws. 5. We earn money. 6. Merchants sell goods. 7. Engineers run locomotives. 8. Blacksmiths shoe horses.

9. Farmers sow grain. 10. Give me music. 11. They chose him. 12. We have chosen him director. 13. Bring him a book. 14. Whom did you call?

163. Exercises in Synthesis.

Sentences containing objective elements are arranged as follows:

Declarative; *Subject . . Predicate . . Object;* as, "I found it."

Interrogative; 1. *Object . . Predicate . . Subject;* as, "What see you?"

2. *Object . . Auxiliary . . Subject . . Verb;* as, "What did you see?"

Imperative; *Predicate . . Object;* as, "Practice economy."

Rem. 1.—In inverted order, the arrangement of declarative sentences, is

Object . . Subject . . Predicate; as, "Him they found."

Write sentences containing an objective element, using the following words as subjects:

Men, boys, heat, lightning, horses, locomotives, scythe, knife, shears, clerks, merchants, blacksmith, tailor, mason, doctors, lion, oxen, eagles.

Models.—Men drive *horses.* Boys fly *kites.* Merchants sell *goods.*

Write sentences containing two objects, using the above or any other nouns :

Models.—Charles calls *doctors physicians.*   Frank calls a *sleigh* a *cutter.*   I consider *William* a *genius.*

Write sentences containing a direct and an indirect object, using the following verbs:

Ask, buy, bring, do, draw, deny, find, get, leave, make, pass, pour, promise, provide, present, sell, send, show, refuse, teach, tell, throw, write.

Models.—Emma asked *me* a *question.*   He bought *Charles* a *pony.*

Change each of the verbs, in sentences written last, into the passive voice, making either object the subject.

Models.—I *was asked* a question.   A *pony was bought* for Charles.

Analyze the sentences you have written.

164. Adjective Element.

An **Adjective Element** is a word or group of words which modifies a noun, or any expression used as a noun.

Ex.—A *good* man.   Mr. Myers the *banker.*   *Friend* Hiram. "If you can: a *sensible* if."   "Done gone," a *vulgarism,* is frequently heard.   *My* book is on *Ellen's* desk.   A letter, *written* in haste.   She came, *laughing.*

Rem. 1.—An adjective element is a definitive or descriptive term used to modify the meaning of a noun or its substitute. The relation which a *predicate attribute* sustains to the subject is *affirmed:* the relation which an *adjective element* sustains to the term it modifies is *assumed,* or *taken for granted.*

Ex.—"That man is *wealthy.*"   The predicate "wealthy" is *affirmed* to belong to "man."   "A *wealthy* man."   The attribute "wealthy" is here *assumed* to belong to "man," and is an *adjective element.*

Rem. 2.—An adjective element containing a single word may be,

1. An **Adjective;** as, "*Ripe* apples."
2. A **Participle;** as, "Hats *made* to order."
3. A **Noun in Apposition;** as, "Powers the *sculptor.*"
4. A **Possessive;** as, "*Eli's* pen."   "*His* hat."

165. Models for Analysis.

X. "Small lakes are abundant."

This is a *sentence;* (why?): *declarative;* (why?): *simple;* (why?).

Lakes is the subject: (why?): **abundant** is the predicate; (why?): **are** is the copula. The subject is modified by **small,** an adjective element.

XI. "The steamship Hibernia has arrived."

This is a *sentence;* (why?): *declarative:* (why?): *simple;* (why?).

Steamship is the subject; (why?): **has arrived** is the predicate; (why?). The subject is modified by **the** and **Hibernia,** both adjective elements.

XII. "My brother broke Stephen's slate."

This is a *sentence;* (why?): *declarative;* (why?): *simple;* (why?).

Brother is the subject; (why?): **broke** is the predicate; (why?). The subject is modified by **my,** an adjective element. The predicate is modified by **slate,** an objective element, and "slate" is modified by **Stephen's,** an adjective element.

XIII. "The old man, laughing, said 'Yes.'"

This is a *sentence;* (why?): *declarative;* (why?): *simple;* (why?).

Man is the subject; (why?): **said** is the predicate; (why?). The subject is modified by **the, old,** and **laughing,** adjective elements. The predicate is modified by **Yes,** an objective element.

166. Exercises in Analysis.

1. A large house was burned. 2. I wrote a long letter. 3. This land is government property. 4. Many hands make quick work. 5. A wise son maketh a glad father. 6. Man's necessity is God's opportunity. 7. Mr. Hodge the farmer hired Mr. Olds the mason. 8. Great wits jump.

9. He is a vain, conceited blockhead. 10. I want the largest apple. 11. Mary has chosen the better part. 12. Carlo's barking wakened the family. 13. I saw six swans. 14. This is my fortieth birthday. 15. Every man received a penny.

167. Exercises in Synthesis.

Adjectives and possessives are usually placed before, and participles and nouns in apposition, after the nouns they modify.

Write seven sentences, limiting the subject by one of the following adjectives:

Round, square, oval, rough, smooth, transparent, translucent, white, green, sour, sweet, old, young, new, wise, foolish, lucky, unlucky, careful, careless.

Models.—A *round* table was purchased. A *square* box was found.

Write seven sentences, limiting both subject and object by an adjective.

Model.—A *stout* horse draws *heavy* loads.

Write seven sentences, limiting the subject or object by the possessive case of one of the following nouns:

Elephant, swan, hawk, sparrow, summer, winter, father, mother, uncle, aunt, John, Samuel, Celia, Harriet, Jackson, teacher, doctor, pupil, merchant.

Models.—An *elephant's* tusks are white. A *swan's* movements are graceful.

Write seven sentences, limiting the subject or object, or both, by a noun in apposition.

Models.—Mr. Sledge the *blacksmith* is sick. Wilson the *burglar* robbed Wilson the *banker*.

Analyze the sentences you have written.

168. Adverbial Element.

An **Adverbial Element** is a word or group of words used to modify a verb, participle, adjective, or adverb.

Ex.—The stranger was *very* kind. The wind blows *fiercely*. Come *here*. Who goes *there?*

Rem. 1.—Adverbial elements, when they modify the meaning of verbs, usually denote some circumstance of *time, place, cause, degree,* or *manner.*

Ex.—He calls *frequently.* There is no night *there. Why* are you angry? The teacher labored *faithfully.*

Rem. 2.—Adverbial elements which modify the manner of the assertion, and not the predicate itself, are called *modal adverbs.*

Ex.—He has *not* come. *Perhaps* I shall go. He was absent, *probably.* He will *certainly* resign.

169. Models for Analysis.

XIV. "He is strictly honest."

This is a *sentence;* (why?): *declarative;* (why?): *simple;* (why?).

He is the subject: (why?): **honest** is the predicate: (why?). The predicate is modified by **strictly,** an adverbial element.

XV. "The sun shines brightly."

This is a *sentence;* (why?): *declarative;* (why?): *simple;* (why?).

Sun is the subject; (why?): **shines** is the predicate; (why?). The subject is modified by **the,** an adjective element; the predicate by **brightly,** an adverbial element.

XVI. "He is not handsome."

This is a *sentence;* (why?): *declarative;* (why?): *simple;* (why?).

He is the subject; (why?): **handsome** is the predicate; (why?). The copula **is** is modified by **not,** an adverbial element.

170. Exercises in Analysis.

1. The birds sing sweetly. 2. We struck the vessel just amidships. 3. I now demand your votes. 4. He formerly lived here. 5. The fire went out. 6. He seems very sad. 7. The boy wrote the letter carelessly. 8. They have been long absent. 9. I shall certainly defend you.

171. Exercises in Synthesis.

In the natural order of arrangement, the adverbial element is placed after the word or group of words, it limits.

Ex.—He denied the charge *vehemently.*
H. G. 13.

Rem.—In inverted order, the adverbial element is placed between the subject and predicate, or at the head of the sentence.

Ex.—He *vehemently* denied the charge. *Vehemently* did he deny the charge.

Write seven sentences, limiting the predicates by an adverbial element of **manner.**

Models.—She writes *rapidly.* He does his work *thoroughly.*

Write seven sentences, limiting the predicates by an adverbial element of **place.**

Models.—He lives *there.* *Where* do you live?

Write seven sentences, limiting the predicates by an adverbial element of **time.**

Models.—I was very happy *then.* *When* will you come?

Write seven sentences, limiting the predicates by an adverbial element of **cause** *or* **degree.**

Models.—*Why* are you sad? The work is *scarcely* commenced.

Write seven sentences, limiting the copulas by a **modal** *adverb.*

Models.—He is *certainly* insane. James is *not* a truant.

Write seven sentences, containing adjectives modified by adverbial elements.

Models.—That tree is *very* tall. It is a *remarkably* fine gem.

Analyze the sentences you have written.

172. Attendant Elements.

Attendant or **Independent Elements** are words or expressions not used as principal or subordinate elements of the sentences in which they are found. They are,

1. Nouns and pronouns in the absolute case; as, "*Children,* obey your parents;" "*Rome,* her glory has departed;" "*He* having arrived, we returned."

2. Interjections and nouns used in broken exclamations; as "*Pshaw,* what *nonsense!*" "Wretched *man* that I am!"

3. Expletives, and words used to introduce sentences in a peculiar way; as, "*Now*, Barabbas was a robber;" "*There* is no report of any disaster;" "*It* is a shameful thing to tell a lie."

4. Words used for emphasis merely; as, "You *yourself* told me so;" "*Either* he or I will come."

5. All phrases and clauses which have no perceptible connection with the rest of the sentence.

Rem.—Attendant elements should be omitted in the analysis of the sentences containing them. They have no grammatical connection with other words, except in certain constructions in which they are used as antecedents of pronouns. Sometimes the entire group of words of which they form a part has the force of an adverbial element.

Ex.—"*Gad*, a troop shall overcome him." The attendant element "Gad," is the antecedent of the pronoun "him." "*They* having left, order was restored." The attendant element "they," is connected with "having left," and the combination has the force of the adverbial clause "after they left."

173. Words, Phrases, and Clauses.

1. Elements are divided into three classes: *Words*, *Phrases*, and *Clauses*.

2. An element consisting of a word, is an element of the **first class.**

Ex.—"A careless boy seldom learns his lesson." In this sentence, all the elements are single words, therefore of the *first class.*

3. A *phrase* consisting of an infinitive, or of a preposition and its object, is an element of the **second class.**

Rem.—There are two kinds of phrases: *Separable* and *Inseparable.*

A **Separable Phrase** is one whose words should always be parsed separately; "He rode *in a wagon.*" The three words composing the phrase "in a wagon," should be parsed separately—"in" as a preposition; "a" as an adjective; "wagon" as a noun.

An **Inseparable Phrase** is one whose words need not be separated in parsing; as, "I will come *by and by;*" "He labors *in* *vain.*" The phrases "by and by" and "in vain" may be parsed as single words. All the forms of the infinitive mode are *inseparable* phrases.

4. A *clause*, or subordinate proposition, is an element of the **third class.**

Ex.—"A man *who is indolent* will not prosper;" "I learn *that you are out of employment.*" The clauses "who is indolent" and "that you are out of employment" are elements of the *third class.*

174. Models for Analysis.

XVII. "Tumultuous murder shook the midnight air."

This is a *sentence;* (why?): *declarative;* (why?): *simple;* (why?).

Murder is the subject; (why?): **shook** is the predicate; (why?). The subject, "murder," is modified by **tumultuous,** an adjective element of the first class: the predicate "shook" is modified by **air,** an objective element of the first class: "air" is modified by **the** and **midnight,** adjective elements of the first class.

XVIII. "A life of prayer is a life of heaven."

This is a *sentence;* (why?): *declarative;* (why?): *simple:* (why?).

Life is the subject; (why?): **life** is the predicate; (why?): **is** is the copula. The subject, "life," is modified by **a,** an adjective element of the first class, and by **of prayer,** an adjective element of the second class. The predicate, "life," is modified by **a,** an adjective element of the first class, and by **of heaven,** an adjective element of the second class.

XIX. "He sold me a farm."

This is a *sentence;* (why?): *declarative;* (why?): *simple;* (why?).

He is the subject; (why?): **sold** is the predicate; (why?). The predicate, "sold," is modified by **me,** an indirect objective element of the first class, and by **farm,** a direct objective element of the first class: "farm" is modified by **a,** an adjective element of the first class.

XX. "To love is to obey."

This is a *sentence;* (why?): *declarative;* (why?): *simple;* (why?).

To love is the subject; (why?): it is an element of the second class: **to obey** is the predicate; (why?): it is an element of the second class: **is** is the copula.

XXI. "Many actions apt to procure fame, are not conducive to our ultimate happiness."

This is a *sentence;* (why?): *declarative;* (why?); *simple;* (why?).

Actions is the subject; (why?): **conducive** is the predicate; (why?): **are** is the copula. The subject, "actions," is modified by **many** and **apt,** adjective elements of the first class: "apt" is modified by **to procure,** an adverbial element of the second class, and "to procure," by **fame,** an objective element of the first class. The copula, "are," is modified by **not,** a modal adverbial element of the first class; and the predicate, "conducive," by **to happiness,** an adverbial element of the second class, and "happiness," by **our** and **ultimate,** adjective elements of the first class.

XXII. "The credulity which has faith in goodness, is a sign of goodness."

This is a *sentence;* (why?): *declarative;* (why?): *complex;* (why?). *"Credulity is a sign of goodness"* is the principal proposition, and *"which has faith in goodness,"* the subordinate.

Credulity is the subject of the principal proposition; (why?): **sign** is the predicate; (why?): **is** is the copula. The subject, "credulity," is modified by **the,** an adjective element of the first class, and by **which has faith in goodness,** an adjective element of the third class: "sign," the predicate, is modified by **a,** an adjective element of the first class, and by **of goodness,** an adjective element of the second class. **Which** is the subject of the subordinate proposition; (why?): **has** is the predicate; (why?). The predicate, "has," is modified by **faith,** an objective element of the first class, and by **in goodness,** an adverbial element of the second class.

XXIII. "I thought, when I saw you last, that I should never see you again."

This is a *sentence;* (why?): *declarative;* (why?): *complex;* (why?). *"I thought"* is the principal proposition: *"when I saw you last"* and *"that I should never see you again,"* are subordinate propositions.

I is the subject of the principal proposition; (why?): **thought** is the predicate; (why?). The predicate, "thought," is modified by **when I saw you last,** an adverbial element of the third class, and by **that I should never see you again,** an objective element of the third class. **I** is the subject of the objective clause; (why?): **should see** is the predicate; (why?): "should see" is modified by **you,** an objective element of the first class, and by **never** and **again,** adverbial elements of the first class. **I** is the subject of the adverbial clause; (why?): **saw** is the predicate; (why?): "saw" is modified by **you,** an objective element of the first class, and by **when** and **last,** adverbial elements of the first class. **When** and **that** are connectives, joining the clauses they introduce to "thought."

175. Exercises in Analysis.

1. Thou hast uttered cruel words. 2. I bow reverently to thy dictates. 3. He shakes the woods on the mountain side. 4. He builds a palace of ice where the torrents fall. 5. The panther's track is fresh in the snow. 6. Black crags behind thee pierce the clear blue sky. 7. Soon rested those who fought. 8. His home lay low in the valley. 9. He had a remarkably good view of their features. 10. All said that Love had suffered wrong. 11. Heaven burns with the descending sun. 12. I will go to-morrow.

13. How pleasant it is to see the sun! 14. To doubt the promise of a friend is a sin. 15. He wishes to go to the house. 16. It was now a matter of curiosity, who the old gentleman was. 17. The fires of the bivouac complete what the fires kindled by the battle have not consumed. 18. In my daily walks in the country, I was accustomed to pass a certain cottage. 19. Toward night, the school-master walked over to the cottage where his little friend lay sick.

20. I am now at liberty to confess that much which I have heard objected to my late friend's writings, was well founded. 21. One of his favorite maxims was, that the only way to keep a secret is never to let any one suspect that you have one. 22. How his essays will *read*, now they are brought together, is a question for the publishers, who have thus ventured to draw out into one piece his "weaved-up follies."—*Lamb.*

23. Examples may be heaped until they hide
 The rules that they were made to render plain.

24. Merciful wind, sing me a hoarse, rough song,
 For there is other music made to-night
 That I would fain not hear.

25. Woe worth the chase! woe worth the day!
 That cost thy life, my gallant gray.—*Scott.*

176. Exercises in Synthesis.

Write seven sentences, limiting their subjects by an adjective element of the second class.

Models.—Love *of display* is a sin. Greed *of gain* is wrong.

Write seven sentences, limiting their subjects by an adjective element of the third class.

Model.—The house *which you see yonder*, belongs to my father.

Write seven sentences, limiting their predicates by an objective element of the second or third class.

Models.—I wish *to remain*. He says *that he can not walk*.

Write seven sentences, limiting their predicates by an adverbial element of the second or third class.

Models.—I study *to learn*. I will come *when you call me*.

Write seven sentences, introducing attendant elements.

Model.—I think, *my dear friend*, that you are mistaken.

Analyze the sentences you have written.

KINDS OF ELEMENTS.

177. Simple Elements.

1. A **Simple Element** is one which is not restricted by a modifier.

Ex.—"A *rich* man;" "A man *of wealth;*" "A man *who is wealthy.*" The word *rich*, the phrase *of wealth*, and the clause *who is wealthy*, are *simple* adjective elements.

2. The **Grammatical Subject** is the *simple* subject.

3. The **Grammatical Predicate** is the *simple* predicate.

Rem.—The same distinction may be made in the other elements.

178. Models for Complete Analysis.

XXIV. "To err is human."

This is a *sentence;* (why?): *declarative;* (why?): *simple;* (why?).

To err is the grammatical subject; (why?): **human** is the grammatical predicate; (why?): **is** is the copula.

XXV. "I am in haste."

This is a *sentence;* (why?): *declarative;* (why?): *simple;* (why?).

I is the grammatical subject; (why?): **in haste** is the grammatical predicate; (why?): **am** is the copula.

179. Exercises.

1. Banners were waving. 2. To forgive is divine. 3. It is pleasant to read. 4. Stars have been shining. 5. Weapons were procured. 6. To covet is sinful. 7. To quarrel is disgraceful. 8. To rob is to plunder. 9. Vessels are in sight.

180. Complex Elements.

1. A **Complex Element** is one which contains a leading element, restricted in meaning by one or more modifiers.

2. The leading element is called the **basis.**

Rem.—The *basis* determines the class of a complex element. If it be of the first, second, or third class, the entire element is said to be of the first, second, or third class.

Ex.—"A *very rich* man." *Very rich* is a *complex* adjective element of the first class, modifying "man": *rich* is the basis, and is modified by *very*, an adverbial element.

"A man *faithful when others were faithless.*" The words in italics form a *complex* adjective element of the first class, modifying "man": *faithful* is the *basis*, and is modified by the clause *when others were faithless*, an adverbial element of the third class.

"He wishes *to know who you are.*" The words in italics form a *complex* objective element of the second class; *to know* is the *basis*, and is modified by the clause *who you are*, an objective element of the third class.

"I like people *that listen when I talk.*" The words in italics form a *complex* adjective element of the third class: *that listen* is the *basis;* and *listen*, the predicate, is modified by the clause *when I talk,* an adverbial element of the third class.

3. The **Complex** or **Logical Subject** is the simple subject taken with all its modifiers.

Rem. 1.—The simple subject, when a noun, may be modified,

1. By an *adjective;* as, "*Loud* reports followed."
2. By a *participle;* as, "The hour *appointed* has come."
3. By a *possessive;* as, "*George's* plan succeeded."
4. By a *noun in the same case;* as, "Gay the *poet* is dead."
5. By a *phrase;* as, "A storm *of applause* followed."
6. By a *clause;* as, "Money *which I earn* is my own."

Rem. 2.—A subject may have all the preceding modifications in the same sentence.

Rem. 3.—When the simple subject is a pronoun, it may have all the modifications of a noun, except that made by a noun or pronoun in the possessive case.

Rem. 4.—An infinitive or participial noun, used as a subject, may be modified (1) *as a noun*, by a word, phrase, or clause in the nominative case, in apposition with it; (2) *as a verb*, by the modifiers of a verb.

4. The **Complex** or **Logical Predicate** is the simple predicate taken with all its modifiers.

Rem. 1.—The simple predicate, when a verb, may be modified,

1. If transitive, by an *object;* as, "He saves *money.*"
2. By an *adverb;* as, "The horse runs *swiftly.*"
3. By a *phrase;* as, "He lives *in Troy;*" "He studies *to learn.*"
4. By a *clause;* as, "He knows *where the mushrooms grow.*"

Rem. 2.—When the predicate is an adjective, a participle, a noun, or any thing used as a noun, it may have all the modifications of the part of speech with which it is classed.

Rem. 3.—The copula is modified by modal adverbs and adverbs of time only.

Rem. 4.—A predicate may have all the modifications given above in the same sentence.

5. A **Complex Objective Element** is the simple object taken with all its modifiers.

Rem.—A complex objective element may be,

1. A **word,** modified by words, phrases, or clauses; as, "We found *much gold;*" "He owns the *house on the hill;*" "I love *those who are frank.*"

2. A **phrase,** modified by single words, phrases, or clauses; as, "He desires *to learn rapidly;*" "He desires *to learn to write;*" "He desires *to repeat what he has heard.*"

3. A **clause,** some part of which is modified by another clause; as, "I said *that he was present when the assault was made.*"

6. A **Complex Adjective Element** is the simple adjective element taken with all its modifiers.

Rem.—A complex adjective element may be,

1. An **adjective,** modified by an adverb; as, "A *very large* lot."

2. A **participle,** with all the modifiers of a verb; as, "The young man was seen *clandestinely entering a dram-shop.*"

3. A **noun** or **pronoun,** with the modifications of a noun or pronoun; as, "*Mr. Elder's* house;" "Thompson, *the faithful guardian of our cousins;*" "*Our own* dear native land."

4. A **phrase,** modified by a word, phrase, or clause; as, "A time *to make friends;*" "A time *to learn to write;*" "A time *to repeat what you have learned.*"

5. A **clause,** some part of which is modified by another clause; as, "A man *who is angry whenever his views are controverted.*"

7. A **Complex Adverbial Element** is the simple adverbial element taken with all its modifiers.

Rem.—A complex adverbial element may be,

1. An **adverb,** modified by a single word, phrase, or clause; as, "We rode *very rapidly;*" "It is too *badly* done *to last;*" "He spoke so *indistinctly that we could not understand him.*"

2. A **phrase,** modified by a single word, phrase, or clause; as, "I am ready *to begin* the *work;*" "I shall be ready *to commence* work *by daylight;*" "I am ready *to go wherever duty calls me.*"

3. A **clause,** some part of which is modified by another clause; as, "He is afraid *that you will not return before he leaves.*"

181. Models for Complete Analysis.

XXVI. "A lad, made orphan by a winter shipwreck, played among the waste."

This is a *sentence;* (why?): *declarative;* (why?): *simple;* (why?).

"*A lad, made orphan by a winter shipwreck,*" is the logical subject, and "*played among the waste*" is the logical predicate.

Lad is the grammatical subject; (why?): **played** is the grammatical predicate; (why?). The subject, "lad," is modified by **a**, a simple adjective element of the first class, and by **made orphan by a winter shipwreck,** a complex adjective element of the first class. "Made orphan," the basis, is modified by **by a winter shipwreck,** an adverbial element of the second class: "shipwreck" is modified by **a** and **winter,** adjective elements of the first class.

The predicate, "played," is modified by **among the waste,** an adverbial element of the second class; and "waste" by **the,** an adjective element of the first class. "Made orphan" is an abridged proposition, equivalent to "that was made an orphan."

XXVII. "He who does as he lists, without regard to the wishes of others, will soon cease to do well."

This is a *sentence;* (why?): *declarative;* (why?): *complex;* (why?).

"*He will soon cease to do well*" is the principal proposition: "*who does as he lists, without regard to the wishes of others,*" the complex subordinate proposition.

"*He who does as he lists, without regard to the wishes of others,*" is the logical subject, and "*will soon cease to do well,*" the logical predicate.

He is the grammatical subject of the principal proposition; (why?): **will cease** is the predicate. The subject "he," is modified by **who does as he lists,** &c., a complex adjective element of the third class.

Who is the subject of this dependent proposition; (why?): **does** is the predicate; (why?): "does" is modified by **as he lists,** an adverbial element of the third class; of which **as** is the connective, **he** is the subject, and **lists** is the predicate; also by **without regard to the wishes of others**, a complex adverbial element of the second class, of which **regard** is modified by **to the wishes of others**, a complex adjective element of the second class. **Wishes** is modified by **the**, an adjective element of the first class, and by **of others**, an adjective element of the second class.

"Will cease," the predicate, is modified by **soon**, an adverbial element of the first class, and by **to do well**, a complex objective element of the second class; of which, **to do**, the basis, is modified by **well**, an adverbial element of the first class.

182. Exercises.

1. God's balance, watched by angels, is hung across the sky. 2. My eyes pursued him far away among the honest shoulders of the crowd. 3. Nothing is law that is not reason. 4. Vice itself lost half its evil by losing all its grossness. 5. There is a limit at which forbearance ceases to be a virtue. 6. If ye love me, keep my commandments. 7. Were I not Diogenes, I would be Alexander. 8. Unless he reforms soon, he is a ruined man. 9. Except ye repent, ye shall all likewise perish.

10. Withdraw thy foot from thy neighbor's house, lest he weary of thee, and so hate thee. 11. I am quite sure that Mr. Hutchins rode through the village this morning. 12. Seest thou a man wise in his own conceit? There is more hope of a fool than of him. 13. He spake as one having authority. 14. He never has a lesson, because he is too lazy to study. 15. Not many generations ago, where you now sit, the rank thistle nodded in the wind. 16. Do not forget to write when you reach home. 17. Even by means of our sorrows, we belong to the eternal plan.

18. The gentleman who was dressed in brown-once-black, had a sort of medico-theological exterior, which we afterward found to be representative of the inward man.

19.   Multitudes of little floating clouds,
    Ere we, who saw, of change, were conscious, pierced
    Through their ethereal texture, had become
    Vivid as fire.— *Wordsworth*.

20. Honest work for the day, honest hope for the morrow:
    Are these worth nothing more than the hand they make weary,
    The heart they have saddened, the life they leave dreary?

183. Compound Elements.

A **Compound Element** consists of two or more independent simple or complex elements, joined by coördinate connectives.

Ex.—The *moon* and *stars* are shining. You may *go* or *stay*.

Rem.—All the elements of a sentence may be compound.

184. Models for Complete Analysis.

XXVIII. "Industry, honesty, and economy generally insure success."

This is a *sentence;* (why?): *declarative;* (why?): *simple;* (why?).

"Industry, honesty, and economy" is the logical subject: *"generally insure success"* is the logical predicate.

Industry, honesty, and economy is the compound grammatical subject; (why?): **insure** is the grammatical predicate; (why?). The subject is not modified. The predicate, "insure," is modified by **generally,** an adverbial element of the first class, and by **success,** an objective element of the first class.

XXIX. "The charities that soothe, and heal, and bless,
    Are scattered at the feet of man like flowers."

This is a *sentence;* (why?): *declarative;* (why?): *complex;* (why?). Name the principal and the subordinate clause.

"The charities that soothe, and heal, and bless" is the logical subject: *"Are scattered at the feet of man like flowers"* is the logical predicate.

Charities is the grammatical subject of the principal proposition; (why?): **are scattered** is the grammatical predicate; (why?). The subject, "charities," is modified by **the,** an adjective element of the first class, and by **that soothe, and heal, and bless,** an adjective element of the third class; of which **that** is the subject, and **soothe, and heal, and bless** is the compound predicate; **and** being the connective.

The predicate, "scattered," is modified (1) by **at the feet of man,** a complex adverbial element of the second class; of which "feet," is modified by **the,** an adjective element of the first class, and by **of man,** an adjective element of the second class; (2) by **like flowers,** an adverbial element of the second class.

185. Exercises.

1. Exercise and temperance strengthen the constitution. 2. Youth is bright and lovely. 3. He is neither old nor infirm. 4. He is not angry, but excited. 5. They wash, iron, cook, eat, and sleep in the same room. 6. I want to be quiet, and to be let alone. 7. The book which I loaned you, and which you lost, was a present from my father. 8. To live in a fine house and drive fast horses is the height of his ambition.

9. All the girls were in tears and white muslins, except a select two or three, who were being honored with a private view of the bride and bridesmaids, up stairs.

10. There was another tap at the door—a smart, potential tap, which seemed to say, " Here I am, and in I'm coming."

11. Not a truth has to art or to science been given,
But brows have ached for it, and souls toiled and striven.

Lytton.

186. Classification of Phrases.

1. Complex elements of the first and second classes, and abridged propositions, are sometimes called **phrases.**

Rem.—The basis of the element, the manner in which it modifies, the connective, or the leading word, determines the name of the phrase.

2. Phrases may be,

1. **Appositive;** as, " Washington, *the father of his country.*"
2. **Adjective;** as, " A man, *tenacious of principle.*"
3. **Adverbial;** as, " He lives *just round the corner.*"
4. **Prepositional;** as, " We walked *on the bank of the river.*"
5. **Infinitive;** as, " He hoped *to receive a telegram.*"
6. **Participial;** as, "*Being unwell,* he remained at home."
7. **Absolute;** as, "*He being sick,* I remained."
8. **Independent;** as, "*O my ducats!*"

Rem. 1.—The infinitive, or participial phrase, when used as subject, is called the *Subject Phrase:* when used as predicate, the *Predicate Phrase.*

Rem. 2.—The absolute phrase is an abridged proposition. It usually modifies the predicate of the sentence of which it forms a part, but may modify the subject and predicate combined.

187. Classification of Clauses.

Clauses are classified with reference to their use or position in sentences. They are,

1. The **Subject Clause:** a proposition used as the subject of a sentence; as, "*How the accident occurred,* is not known."

2. The **Predicate Clause:** a proposition used as the predicate of a sentence; as, "The question is, *How did he obtain the money?*"

3. The **Relative Clause:** a dependent proposition introduced by a relative pronoun; as, "The vessel *which you see yonder,* is a sloop."

4. The **Appositive Clause:** a proposition put in apposition with a noun; as, "The question, *Are we a nation?* is now answered."

5. The **Interrogative Clause:** a proposition introduced by an interrogative word; as, "*Who* said so?" "*What* vessel is that?" "*Where* do you live?"

6. The **Objective Clause:** a proposition used as an objective element; as, "The chairman declared *that the motion was lost.*"

7. The **Adverbial Clause:** a proposition used as an adverbial element; as, "I will pay you *when I receive my week's wages.*"

Rem. 1.—*Subject, predicate,* and *objective* clauses are used as nouns.

Rem. 2.—*Relative* clauses are either *restrictive* or *explanatory.* If restrictive, the antecedent is usually modified by *a, the,* or *that;* as, "*The* vessel *which capsized,* was a bark." If explanatory, the antecedent is not so modified; as, "Steamships, *which are a modern invention,* make quick voyages."

A proposition introduced by a compound relative is frequently equivalent to an adverbial element; as, "He will succeed, *whoever may oppose him.*"

Rem. 3.—*Interrogative* clauses may be introduced by interrogative pronouns, interrogative adjectives, or interrogative adverbs.

Direct and **indirect** questions are asked by means of principal propositions; as, "Is he honest?" "Whose book is that?"

Indefinite questions are asked by means of subordinate propositions; as, "I do not know *whose book that is.*"

The disjunctive *or,* correlative with *whether,* connects the parts of a double indirect question; as, "I do not know *whether I shall go or stay.*"

Rem. 4.—*Adverbial* clauses may be classified as follows:

1. **Temporal:** dependent clauses denoting *time;* as, "I was absent *when the accident occurred.*"

2. **Local:** dependent clauses denoting *place;* as, "Go *where duty calls thee.*"

3. **Causal:** dependent clauses denoting *cause;* as, "He is beloved, *for he is good.*"

4. **Final:** dependent clauses denoting a *purpose* or a *result;* as, "We came *that we might assist you;*" "Love not sleep, *lest thou come to poverty.*"

5. **Comparative:** dependent clauses, expressing *comparison;* as, "He is older *than I* [am];" "Men generally die *as they live.*"

6. **Conditional:** dependent clauses modifying propositions containing *deductions* or *conclusions;* as, "He will be ruined, *unless he reform;*" "I would pay you, *if I could.*"

7. **Concessive:** dependent clauses denoting a *concession* or *admission;* as, "*Though he slay me,* yet will I trust in him."

Rem. 5.—Two clauses which mutually qualify are called **correlative;** as, "The deeper the well, the cooler the water."

188. Exercises.

Classify the phrases and clauses in the following sentences:

1. No one came to his assistance. 2. He were no lion, were not Romans hinds. 3. I would that ye all spake with tongues. 4. Thou shalt love thy neighbor as thyself. 5. Launch thy bark, mariner! 6. He made them give up their spoils. 7. Go quickly, that you may meet them.

8. Voltaire, who might have seen him, speaks repeatedly of his

majestic stature. 9. The French, a mighty people, combined for the regeneration of Europe. 10. Not many generations ago, where you now sit, circled with all that exalts and embellishes civilized life, the rank thistle nodded in the wind, and the wild fox dug his hole unscared.

11. Very few men, properly speaking, live at present: most are preparing to live another time. 12. I lisped in numbers, for the numbers came. 13. While the bridegroom tarried, they all slumbered and slept. 14. Study nature, whose laws and phenomena are all deeply interesting. 15. Its qualities exist, since they are known, and are known because they exist. 16. At ten o'clock, my task being finished, I went down to the river.

17. Some say, that ever 'gainst that season comes
Wherein our Savior's birth is celebrated,
This bird of warning singeth all night long:
And then no spirit dares stir abroad;
The nights are wholesome: then no planets strike,
No fairy takes, nor witch hath power to charm,
So hallowed and so gracious is the time.—*Shakspeare.*

CONTRACTED SENTENCES.

Sentences are contracted by ellipsis, abridgment, or by substituting a different expression.

Rem.—The object of contraction is to secure conciseness of expression by means of brevity in the construction of sentences.

189. Ellipsis.

1. **Ellipsis** is the omission of one or more words of a sentence. The words omitted are said to be *understood.*

Rem.—If required in analysis or parsing, the words omitted must be supplied.

2. A **Simple Sentence** is contracted by omitting all, or nearly all, but the most important part.

1. The *subject* may be omitted; as, "Come" = Come *thou*, or *do thou* come.

H. G. 14.

2. The *predicate* may be omitted; as, "Who will go? He [*will go*]." "I'll [*go*] hence to London;" "Ye are Christ's [*disciples*]."

3. Both *subject* and *predicate* may be omitted; as, "Water!" = *Give me some* water; "Forward!" = *March ye* forward.

4. The *object* may be omitted; as, "Whose book have you? John's" = *I have* John's *book*.

5. The neuter verb *to be*, in all its forms, may be omitted; as, "Where now [*are*] her glittering towers?" "A professed Catholic, he imprisoned the Pope" = *Being* a professed Catholic, &c.; "England's friend, Ireland's foe" = *To be* England's friend *is to be* Ireland's foe.

6. *Prepositions* and *conjunctions* may be omitted; as, "Build [*for*] me here seven altars;" "Woe is [*to*] me;" "I know [*that*] you are honest;" "Each officer, [*and*] each private did his duty."

7. A simple sentence, whose subject or predicate is a proposition, may be contracted by changing the proposition to an infinitive or participial phrase; as, "*That I may remain here*, is my desire" = *To remain here* is my desire; "My desire is, *that I may remain here*" = My desire is, *to remain here*.

3. A Compound Sentence may be contracted by uniting the parts not common to all its members, and using the common parts but once.

Ex.—"Exercise strengthens the constitution, and temperance strengthens the constitution" = Exercise and temperance strengthen the constitution. "Behold my mother and behold my brethren" = Behold my mother and my brethren.

190. Exercises.

Tell what parts are omitted in the following sentences:

1. Advance. 2. Up, comrades, up. 3. Quick, quick, or we are lost. 4. Honest, my lord? 5. Impossible! 6. This done, we instantly departed. 7. Thou denied a grave! 8. What would content you? Talent? 9. How, now, Jenkinson? 10. A rope to the side! 11. Rather he, than I. 12. The orphan of St. Louis, he became the adopted child of the Republic.

Compound Subjects.—1. Wisdom, judgment, prudence, and firmness, were his predominant traits. 2. To love God and to do good to men are the leading purposes of every Christian. 3. That the climate of the northern hemisphere has changed, and that its mean temperature nearly resembled that of the tropics, is the opinion of many naturalists.

Compound Predicates.—1. Rural employments are certainly natural, amusing, and healthy. 2. Education expands and elevates the mind. 3. His excuse was, that the roads were very bad, that the supply train could not be brought up, and that the army was not well enough equipped for offensive operations.

Compound Objective Elements.—1. He had a good mind, a sound judgment, and a vivid imagination. 2. Learn to labor and to wait. 3. The writings of the sages show that the best empire is self-government, and that subduing our passions is the noblest of conquests.

Compound Adjective Elements.—1. He is a good, faithful, and generous boy. 2. I am not the advocate of indolence and improvidence. 3. The chastity of honor, which felt a stain like a wound, which inspired courage while it mitigated ferocity, which ennobled whatever it touched, and under which vice itself lost half its evil by losing its grossness, is gone.

Compound Adverbial Elements.—1. Man is fearfully and wonderfully made. 2. During our voyage, we whiled away our time in reading, in writing a journal, and in studying navigation. 3. When public bodies are to be addressed on momentous occasions, when great interests are at stake, and strong passions excited, nothing is valuable in speech further than it is connected with high intellectual and moral endowments.

191. Abridgment.

1. **Complex Sentences** are often changed into simple sentences by abridging their subordinate clauses.

2. Contracted clauses are called *abridged propositions.*

Ex.—"We came *that we might assist you*" = We came *to assist you.* "I believe *that he is honest*" = I believe *him to be honest.*

Rem.—There is an essential difference between a sentence shortened by ellipsis and an abridged proposition. In the former, the omitted words are clearly implied, and must be restored before the sentence can be analyzed or parsed: in the latter, an equivalent expression is substituted for an entire proposition. The predicate is always retained, but is used as an *assumed* attribute, the *assertion* being wholly omitted.

3. To abridge a subordinate clause,

1st. Drop the subject, if it be already expressed in the principal clause: if not, retain it changing its case to the possessive, objective, or absolute.

2d. Drop the connective, and change the copula or verbal predicate to a participle or an infinitive.

Rem. 1.—The abridged form of an *adjective clause* is a participial, infinitive, or prepositional phrase.

Ex.—"Our friends *who live in the city*" = Our friends *living in the city* = Our friends *in the city*. "A book *that may amuse you*" = A book *to amuse you*.

Rem. 2.—The abridged form of an *adverbial clause* is a participial, infinitive, prepositional, or absolute phrase.

Ex.—"*When we heard the explosion*, we hastened to the spot" = *Hearing the explosion*, we hastened, &c.; "I attend school *that I may learn*" = I attend school *to learn;* "*If he be economical*, he will become rich" = He will become rich *by being economical;* "*When the soldiers arrived*, the mob dispersed"=*The soldiers having arrived*, &c.

Rem. 3.—The abridged form of an *objective clause* is an infinitive phrase.

Ex.—"We wish *that you would stay*" = We wish you *to stay*. "I thought *that he was a merchant*" = I thought *him to be a merchant*.

Rem. 4.—Abridged propositions retain the logical construction of the clauses which they represent: *i. e.*, abridged adjective, adverbial, or objective clauses become, respectively, adjective, adverbial, or objective phrases.

192. Model for Analysis.

XXX. "The shower having passed, we resumed our journey."

This is a *sentence;* (why?): *declarative;* (why?): *simple;* (why?).

We is the subject; (why?): **resumed** is the grammatical, and **resumed our journey, the shower having passed,** is the logical predicate. "Resumed" is modified by **journey,** an objective element of the first class, which is modified by **our**, an adjective element of the first class. "Resumed" is also modified by the absolute phrase, **the shower having passed**, an abridged proposition, equivalent to "when the shower had passed." "Shower" is modified by **the** and **having passed**, adjective elements of the first class.

193. Exercises.

Analyze the following sentences, giving equivalent clauses for the abridged propositions:

1. Cæsar having crossed the Rubicon, Pompey prepared for battle. 2. Having accumulated a large fortune, he retired from business. 3. Being but dust, be humble and wise. 4. Judging from his dress, I should pronounce him an artisan.

5. I believe him to be an honest man. 6. There is no hope of his recovering his health. 7. There is no prospect of the storm's abating. 8. Having been detained by this accident, he lost the opportunity of seeing them.

194. Directions for Analysis.

SENTENCES.

I.—In analyzing,

1. Read the sentence.

2. Determine from its form and use, whether it is *declarative, interrogative, imperative,* or *exclamatory.*

3. Determine whether it is *simple, complex,* or *compound.*

4. Arrange all the parts in natural order.

5. If necessary for analysis or parsing, supply all ellipses.

II.—If it is a *simple* sentence,

1. Point out the logical subject and logical predicate.

2. Point out the grammatical subject and grammatical predicate.

3. Determine whether the subject is *simple, complex,* or *compound;* and when complex, point out and classify its modifiers with their qualifications.

4. Determine whether the predicate is *simple, complex,* or *compound;* and when complex, point out and classify (1) its objective modifiers, (2) its adverbial modifiers, with their qualifications.

5. Point out the attendant elements, and all the connectives.

III.—If it is a *complex* sentence,

1. Analyze the principal clause as in (II).

2. Analyze the subordinate clause or clauses as in (II).

IV.—If it is a *compound* sentence, each member should be analyzed as a simple or complex sentence, as in (II) or (III).

ELEMENTS.

V.—1. If an element is a *single word*, it is completely reduced.

2. If an element is a phrase or a clause, determine,

a. The *connective*, and the parts it joins.

b. In a *phrase*, determine the antecedent and subsequent terms of relation of the preposition.

c. In a *clause*, point out the subject and predicate.

3. If an element is *complex*,

a. Reduce it to simple elements.

b. First point out the *basis* of each complex element, then the others in their order.

4. If an element is *compound*,

a. Separate it into its component simple elements.

b. Point out and classify the connective which joins them.

c. Dispose of each element separately, as in (1) and (2) above.

Rem.—The sentence being reduced by analysis to the parts of speech of which it is composed, let the teacher select such words as should be parsed, and instruct his pupils how to dispose of them according to the "models for parsing."

195. Model for Complete Analysis.

XXXI. "The patriot, whom the corrupt tremble to see arise, may well feel a grateful satisfaction in the mighty power which heaven has delegated to him, when he thinks that he has used it for those purposes only which heaven approves."

This is a *sentence;* (why?): *declarative;* (why?): *complex;* (why?). It is composed of six clauses. The *principal clause* is,

The patriot may well feel a grateful satisfaction in the mighty power.

The *subordinate clauses* are,

1. *Whom the corrupt tremble to see arise;*
2. *Which heaven has delegated to him;*
3. *When he thinks;*
4. *That he has used it for those purposes only;*
5. *Which heaven approves.*

"*Patriot*" is the subject of the principal clause; "*may feel*" is the predicate.

The subject, "*patriot*," is modified (1) by "*the*," an adjective element of the first class, and (2) by "*whom the corrupt tremble to see arise*," an adjective element of the third class; of which "*whom*" is the connective, "*corrupt*" is the subject, and "*tremble*" is the predicate. "*Corrupt*" is modified by "*the*," an adjective element of the first class: "*tremble*" is modified by "*to see*," an adverbial element of the second class; which is modified by "*whom*," an objective element of the first class, and "*whom*" is modified by "*[to] arise*," an adjective element of the second class.

The predicate, "*may feel*," is modified (1) by "*well*," an adverbial element of the first class: (2) by "*satisfaction*," an objective element of the first class; which is modified by "*a*" and "*grateful*," adjective elements of the first class: and (3) by "*in the mighty power which heaven has delegated to him*," an adverbial element of the second class; of which "*in power*" is the basis, "*in*" is the connective, and "*power*" is the object. "*Power*" is modified (1) by "*the*" and "*mighty*," adjective elements of the first class: (2) by "*which heaven has delegated to him*," an adjective element of the third class; of which "*which*" is the connective, "*heaven*" is the subject, and "*has delegated*" is the predicate: "*has delegated*" is modified (1) by "*which*," an objective element of the first class: (2) by "*to him*," an adverbial element of the second class; of which "*to*" is the connective, and "*him*" is the object.

"*May feel*" is modified (4) by "*when he thinks*," &c., an adverbial element of the third class; of which "*when*" is the connective, "*he*" is the subject, and "*thinks*" is the predicate. "*Thinks*" is modified by "*that he has used it*," &c., an objective element of the third class; of which "*that*" is the connective, "*he*" is the subject, and "*has used*" is the predicate. "*Has used*" is modified (1) by "*it*," an objective element of the first class: (2) by "*for those purposes only*," &c., an adverbial element of the second class; of which "*for purposes*" is the basis, "*for*" is the connective, and "*purposes*" is the object. "*Purposes*" is modified (1) by "*those*" and "*only*," adjective elements of the first class: and (2) by "*which heaven approves*," an adjective element of the third class; of which "*which*" is the connective, "*heaven*" is the subject, and "*approves*" is the predicate. "*Approves*" is modified by "*which*," an objective element of the first class.

196. Brief Method of Analysis.

"*Patriot*" is the subject; "*may feel*" is the predicate.

The subject, "*patriot*," is modified (1) by "*the*," an adjective element of the first class, and (2) by "*whom the corrupt tremble to see arise*," an adjective element of the third class.

The predicate, "*may feel*," is modified (1) by "*well*," an adverbial element of the first class, denoting *manner:* (2) by "*a grateful satisfaction*," a complex objective element of the first class: (3) by "*in the mighty power which . . . . him*," a complex adverbial element of the second class: and (4) by "*when he thinks . . . . approves*," a complex adverbial element of the third class, denoting *time*.

197. Miscellaneous Examples.

1. Hypocrisy is a sort of homage that vice pays to virtue. 2. The gods have set a price on every real and noble pleasure. 3. He was a very young boy; quite a little child. 4. It has all the contortions of the sibyl, without the inspiration.—*Burke*.

5. "Well, what is it?" said my lady Brook. 6. Suddenly the watch gave the alarm of "A sail ahead!" 7. He saw a star shoot from heaven, and glittering in its fall, vanish upon the earth. 8. Sweet are thy murmurs, O stream!—*Ossian*.

9. Their slumbers are sound, and their wakings cheerful. 10. We one day descried some shapeless object floating at a distance. 11. And behold there came a voice unto him, and said, What dost thou here, Elijah?—*Bible*.

12. I passed the house many successive days. 13. He wore an ample cloak of black sheep's wool, which, having faded into a dull brown, had been refreshed by an enormous patch of the original color. His countenance was that of the faded part of his cloak.—*Bryant*.

14. The line which bisects the vertical angle of a triangle, divides the base into segments proportional to the adjacent sides. 15. He is so good, he is good for nothing. 16. The clouds are divided in heaven: over the green hills flies the inconstant sun: red, through the stony vale, comes down the stream of the hills.—*Ossian*.

17. The accusing angel flew up to Heaven's chancery with the oath, and blushed as he gave it in. And the recording angel, as he wrote it down, dropped a tear on the word, and blotted it out forever.—*Sterne.*

18. In the awful mystery of human life, it is a consolation sometimes to believe that our mistakes, perhaps even our sins, are permitted to be instruments of our education for immortality. 19. Even if his criticisms had been uniformly indulgent, the position of the nobles and leading citizens, thus subjected to a constant, but secret superintendence, would have been too galling to be tolerated.—*Motley.*

20. No ax had leveled the giant progeny of the crowded groves, in which the fantastic forms of withered limbs, that had been blasted and riven by lightning, contrasted strangely with the verdant freshness of a younger growth of branches.—*Bancroft.*

21. The sun was now resting his huge disk upon the edge of the level ocean, and gilding the accumulation of clouds through which he had traveled the livelong day; and which now assembled on all sides, like misfortunes and disasters around a sinking empire and falling monarch.—*Scott.*

22. It is, therefore, a certain and a very curious fact, that the representative, at this time, of any great whig family, who probably imagines that he is treading in the footsteps of his forefathers, in reality, while adhering to their party names, is acting against almost every one of their party principles.—*Lord Mahon.*

23. Rivers will always have one shingly shore to play over, where they may be shallow, and foolish, and childlike; and another steep shore, under which they can pause, and purify themselves, and get their strength of waves fully together for due occasion.—*Ruskin.*

24. I seem to have been only like a boy playing on the sea-shore, and diverting myself in now and then finding a smoother pebble or a prettier shell than ordinary, whilst the great ocean of truth lay all undiscovered before me.—*Newton.*

25.   We're nettles, some of us,
    And give offense by the act of springing up.—*Browning.*

26. The twilight deepened round us. Still and black
    The great woods climbed the mountain at our back.

27. May God forgive the child of dust
    Who seeks to *know* where Faith should *trust.*— *Whittier.*
    H. G. 15.

28.   Better far
   Pursue a frivolous trade by serious means,
   Than a sublime art frivolously.

29.   With grave
   Aspect he rose, and in his rising seemed
   A pillar of state; deep on his front engraven,
   Deliberation sat, and public care;
   And princely counsel in his face yet shone,
   Majestic, though in ruin.—*Milton.*

30. Summer's dun cloud, that, slowly rising, holds
    The sweeping tempest in its rising folds,
    Though o'er the ridges of its thundering breast,
    The King of Terrors lifts his lightning crest,
    Pleased we behold, when those dark folds we find
    Fringed with the golden light that glows behind.—*Pierpont.*

31. Near yonder copse, where once the garden smiled,
    And still where many a garden flower grows wild,
    There, where a few torn shrubs the place disclose,
    The village preacher's modest mansion rose,
    A man he was to all the country dear,
    And passing rich with forty pounds a year.—*Goldsmith.*

32. As when upon a trancéd summer night
    Those green-robed senators of mighty woods,
    Tall oaks, branch-charméd by the earnest stars,
    Dream, and so dream all night without a stir,
    Save from one gradual, solitary gust,
    Which comes upon the silence, and dies off,
    As if the ebbing air had but one wave:
    So came these words, and went.—*Keats.*

33. When Freedom, from her mountain height,
        Unfurled her standard to the air,
    She tore the azure robe of night
        And set the stars of glory there.
    She mingled with its gorgeous dyes
    The milky baldric of the skies,
    And striped its pure, celestial white,
    With streakings of the morning light.—*Drake.*

RULES OF SYNTAX.

Rule I.—The subject of a proposition is in the nominative case.

Rule II.—A noun or pronoun, used as the predicate of a proposition, is in the nominative case.

Rule III.—A noun or pronoun, used to limit the meaning of a noun denoting a different person or thing, is in the possessive case.

Rule IV.—A noun or pronoun, used to limit the meaning of a noun or pronoun denoting the same person or thing, is in the same case.

Rule V.—A noun or pronoun, used independently, is in the absolute case.

Rule VI.—The object of a transitive verb, in the active voice, or of its participles, is in the objective case.

Rule VII.—The object of a preposition is in the objective case.

Rule VIII.—Nouns denoting time, distance, measure, or value, after verbs and adjectives, are in the objective case without a governing word.

Rule IX.—Pronouns must agree with their antecedents in person, gender, and number.

Rule X.—A pronoun, with two or more antecedents in the singular, connected by *and*, must be plural.

Rule XI.—A pronoun, with two or more antecedents in the singular, connected by *or* or *nor*, must be singular.

Rule XII.—An adjective or participle belongs to some noun or pronoun.

Rule XIII.—A verb must agree with its subject in person and number.

Rule XIV.—A verb, with two or more subjects in the singular, connected by *and*, must be plural.

Rule XV.—A verb, with two or more subjects in the singular, connected by *or* or *nor*, must be singular.

Rule XVI.—An infinitive may be used as a noun in any case except the possessive.

Rule XVII.—An infinitive not used as a noun, depends upon the word it limits, or which leads to its use.

Rule XVIII.—Adverbs modify verbs, adjectives, participles, and adverbs.

Rule XIX.—A preposition shows the relation of its object to the word upon which the latter depends.

Rule XX.—Coördinate connectives join similar elements.

Rule XXI.—Subordinate connectives join dissimilar elements.

Rule XXII.—An interjection has no dependence upon other words.

198. Subject-Nominative.

Rule I.—The subject of a proposition is in the nominative case.

Rem. 1.—Any thing that may be used as a noun may be the subject; as, "*A* is a vowel;" "*To lie* is base;" "*What time he took orders* doth not appear."

Rem. 2.—The subject generally precedes the predicate, but is placed after it, or the first auxiliary, (1) When a wish is expressed by the potential; as, "May *you* prosper:" (2) When *if* or *though*, denoting a supposition, is suppressed; as, "Had *they* been wise, they would have listened to me:" (3) When the verb is in the imperative mode, or is used interrogatively; as, "Rest *ye;*" "Why do *you* persist?"

Rem. 3.—The subject of the imperative mode is usually omitted; as, "*Depart!*" "*Shut* the door." It is also omitted after *while, when, if, though,* or *than,* when the verb is made one of the terms of a comparison; as, "He talks *while* [he is] writing;" "He is kind *when* [he is] sober;" "I will come, *if* [it be] possible;" "They are honest, *though* [they are] poor;" "He has more knowledge *than* [he has] wisdom."

EXERCISES.
To be corrected and parsed.

1. Him and me study grammar. 2. I never saw larger horses than them are. 3. Me and John sit together. 4. I knowed it as well as him or her. 5. Whom besides I do you suppose got a prize? 6. I am as tall as he, but she is taller than him. 7. Whom do you suppose has come to visit us? 8. We sorrow not as them that have no hope.

9. Thrice is he armed who hath his quarrel just; and him but naked, though locked up in steel, whose conscience with injustice is corrupted. 10. Them are the fellows that stoled your apples. 11. Who wants an orange?—Me. 12. No other pupil is so studious as her. 13. He is older than me. 14. I know not whom else are expected. 15. None of his companions is more beloved than him.

199. Predicate-Nominative.

Rule II.—A noun or pronoun, used as the predicate of a proposition, is in the nominative case.

Rem. 1.—The predicate-nominative denotes the same person or thing as the subject; and must agree with it in case, and usually in gender and number. It may be any thing that may be used as a noun; as, "That letter is *B;*" "To work is *to pray;*" "The command was, '*Storm the fort at daybreak.*'"

Rem. 2.—In questions, and when the predicate is emphatically distinguished, the subject and predicate change places; as, "*Who* is that *man?*" "Are *you* the ticket *agent?*" "His *pavilion* round about him were dark *waters* and thick *clouds* of the sky."

Rem. 3.—The neuter pronoun *it*, as subject, may represent a noun or pronoun of any person, number, or gender, as predicate; as, "*It* is *I*;" "*It* was *you*;" "*It* is *Sarah*."

EXERCISES.

To be corrected and parsed.

1. It is me. 2. It was her and him who you saw. 3. If I were him, I would go to Europe. 4. Whom do you say they were? 5. I do not know whom they are.

6. It was not me nor him who played truant. 7. It is not them who are to blame. 8. I disbelieve it to be he. 9. I have no doubt of its being them.

200. Possessive Case.

Rule III.—A noun or pronoun, used to limit the meaning of a noun denoting a different person or thing, is in the possessive case.

Rem. 1.—The possessive term is always an adjective element. It may limit a noun of any class or form, or a participial phrase; as, "*Our* houses;" "O *my* ducats!" "*Our* country's welfare;" "All *their* dearest hopes were blasted;" "*His* being a foreigner should not induce us to underrate him."

Rem. 2.—The relation of possession may be expressed by the preposition *of*, with the objective; as, "My friend's house" = The house *of* my friend. This form should be used when two or more nouns in the possessive would otherwise come together; as, "My *friend's father's* house" = The house *of my friend's father*.

Rem. 3.—The limited noun is sometimes omitted; as, "This house is the doctor's [house]." "We visited St. Paul's [church]." "This is a farm of my father's [farms]."

Rem. 4.—The limited noun need not be plural because the possessive is plural; as, "Their *judgment* is good;" "Our *decision* is made;" "The women's *hope* failed."

Rem. 5.—When a noun is put in apposition with a noun or pronoun in the possessive case, the sign may be omitted; as, "This was *Webster's* opinion, the most eminent *lawyer* in the country."

Rem. 6.—In some compound words, formed from the possessive and the word limited by it, both the hyphen and sign of possession are omitted; as, *hogshead, catshead,* &c.

EXERCISES.

To be corrected and parsed.

1. The boys story was believed. 2. He wore the knight's templar's costume. 3. The goods were sent by the Merchants Union Express. 4. That book is his'n. 5. The Bishop's of Dublin's palace. 6. My fathers health is not good. 7. My book is larger than your's. 8. The mistake was the teacher, not the pupil's.

9. The general's aids horse was killed. 10. No one could prevent him escaping. 11. I purchased this at Penfields', the bookseller's. 12. Some people regret the King of France's, Louis XVI, being beheaded. 13. He bought a hog's head of sugar. 14. William's and Mary's reign was prosperous. 15. It was John, not Emma's fault.

201. Apposition.

Rule IV.—A noun or pronoun, used to limit the meaning of a noun or pronoun denoting the same person or thing, is in the same case.

Rem. 1.—A noun may be in apposition with a sentence, and a sentence with a noun; as, "*I resolved to practice temperance—a resolution* I have ever kept." "Remember Franklin's *maxim: 'God helps them that help themselves.'*"

Rem. 2.—A noun in apposition sometimes precedes the noun it identifies; as, "*Child* of the Sun, refulgent *Summer,* comes."

Rem. 3.—Though a noun or pronoun usually agrees with the noun it identifies, in *number* and *gender,* it is not necessary that it agree with it in any thing else than *case;* as, "My *lunch—fried oysters* and *crackers*—was soon eaten."

Rem. 4.—When possessives are in apposition, the sign of possession is used only with the one next to the noun limited by the entire possessive term; as, "Peter the *Hermit's* eloquence."

Rem. 5.—Sometimes the noun in apposition is separated from the limited noun by *as,* denoting *rank, office,* or *capacity;* as, "Mr.

Jones, as my *attorney*, sold the land;" "My son sails as *supercargo*." Equivalent terms are sometimes introduced by *or;* as, "The *puma*, or American *lion*, is found in South America."

EXERCISES.

To be corrected and parsed.

1. Will you discard me; I who have always been your friend? 2. What was the General; him you wished to see? 3. I bought it of Mrs. Wilson; she who keeps the milliner's shop. 4. Ira Jacobs, him who you punished, was not to be blamed. 5. Whom shall we praise?—They who do their duty. 6. My watch was lost near Wilkins's the blacksmith's.

7. They are the lovely, them in whom unite
Youth's fleeting charms, with virtue's lovely light.

202. Absolute Case.

Rule V.—A noun or pronoun, used independently, is in the absolute case.

Rem. 1.—For the four forms of the absolute case, see §33.

Rem. 2.—The case absolute with a participle is generally equivalent to an adverbial element of the third class, commencing with *if, because, since, when,* or *while;* as, "*He being rich,* they feared his influence" = They feared his influence *because he was rich.* "*The sun being risen,* we pursued our journey" = *When the sun had risen,* we pursued our journey.

Rem. 3.—In mottoes and abbreviated sayings, and frequently in exclamations, nouns seem to have relation to something understood; as, "Laird's Bloom of Youth" = *Use* Laird's Bloom of Youth; "Confidence" (a motto) = *This is a token of* confidence; "A rat! a rat!" = *There is* a rat. It is better, however, to recognize the absolute case as a distinct use of a noun, than to destroy the force of an expression by supplying an awkward ellipsis.

EXERCISES.

Examples to be parsed.

1. Soldier, rest! thy warfare o'er. 2. "Stop! the hat!" he exclaims. 3. Our fathers, where are they? 4. I being a child, was a plea for my admission. 5. The north and the south, thou hast

created them. 6. John, James, and Henry, they are my scholars. 7. O Nelly Gray! O Nelly Gray! 8. "The Moon and the Stars—A Fable." 9. PROBLEM III.—To construct a mean proportional between two given lines.

203. Objective Case.

Rule VI.—The object of a transitive verb, in the active voice, or of its participles, is in the objective case.

Rem. 1.—The natural order of arrangement is, *subject—verb—object;* but in poetry, or when it is made emphatic, the object precedes the subject; as, "*Myself* I can not save;" "*Silver* and *gold* have I none." To avoid ambiguity, the natural order should be observed when the subject and object are both nouns. Say, "Alexander conquered Darius," not "Alexander *Darius* conquered." A relative or interrogative pronoun is placed at the head of its clause; as, "I am he *whom* ye seek;" "*Whom* shall I invite?"

Rem. 2.—The object may be a participial noun, a phrase, or a clause; as, "I like *running* and *jumping* better than *studying;*" "He hopes *to succeed;*" "'*Our armies swore terribly in Flanders,*' cried my Uncle Toby."

Rem. 3.—A phrase beginning with a noun or pronoun, may be the object of a transitive verb; as, "I want *books to read;*" "The merchant ordered *the goods to be shipped;*" "I heard the *water lapping on the crag;*" "I want *him to go.*" In such cases, the entire phrase is the object of the verb; but it is best to apply Rule VI in parsing the noun or pronoun beginning the phrase, Rule XVII in parsing the infinitive, and Rule XII in parsing the participle.

Rem. 4.—Some verbs used as copulatives in the passive voice, have two objects, one representing a person or thing, the other a thing; as, "They made *him* their *leader;*" "They chose him *chairman.*" When such verbs are made passive, either object may be taken as the subject, but the other, if retained, becomes a predicate-nominative. If the *thing* is made nominative, the *person* is governed by a preposition, expressed or understood: if the *person* is made nominative, the *thing* may be parsed by Rule II.

Rem. 5.—A transitive verb may have several objects connected by conjunctions; as, "He owns *houses, lands,* and *bank-stock.*"

Rem. 6.—Participial or verbal nouns may be limited by objective elements; as, "*Writing notes* is forbidden;" "I like *hunting buffaloes.*"

EXERCISES.

Examples to be corrected.

1. Who did you write to? 2. Please let him and I sit together. 3. I do not know who to trust. 4. He who did the mischief you should punish, not I. 5. I saw she and him at the concert last evening. 6. And me, what shall I do?

7. We will go at once, him and me. 8. Every one can master a grief but he that hath it. 9. He was presented a gold watch by his employers. 10. Who are you looking for?

Examples to be parsed.

1. We will rear new homes. 2. The parting words shall pass my lips no more. 3. I said that at sea all is vacancy. 4. They have left unstained what there they found. 5. Bring forth this counterfeit model. 6. Mad frenzy fires him now.

7. Reading makes a full man, conference a ready man, and writing an exact man. 8. Thou hast left no son—but thy song shall preserve thy name. 9. His disciples said, Who, then, can be saved? 10. I was forbidden the premises. 11. They were debarred the privilege of walking in the park.

> 12. "But what good came of it at last?"
>   Quoth little Peterkin.
> "Why, that I can not tell," said he;
> "But 't was a famous victory."—*Southey.*

204. Objective after Prepositions.

Rule VII.—The object of a preposition is in the objective case.

Rem. 1.—A preposition usually precedes its object; but in poetry this order is sometimes reversed; as, "From crag to crag, *the rattling peaks among*" = among the rattling peaks; "Come walk with me the jungle *through.*"

Rem. 2.—Interrogative pronouns frequently precede the prepositions which govern them; as, "*What* are you laughing *at?*"

Such expressions as "Whom are you talking to?" "Which house do you live in?" are inelegant, if not ungrammatical. The proper construction is, "To whom are you talking?" "In which house do you live?"

Rem. 3.—Some phrases consist of a preposition, followed by an adjective or an adverb; as, *in vain, at once, in secret, from below, on high, from above, till now, till lately,* &c. In such phrases, an object may be understood; the word following the preposition, parsed as an adjective or adverb *used as a noun;* or the entire expression may be regarded as an *inseparable phrase.*

Rem. 4.—A preposition should never be placed between a verb and its object; as, "He does not want *for* any thing." Say "He does not *want* any thing."

Rem. 5.—A noun or pronoun which is the object of two or more prepositions, or of a preposition and a transitive verb, should be placed after the first verb or preposition, and be represented by a pronoun following each of the others. "He came *into* and passed *through* the cars," should be "He came *into* the *cars,* and passed *through them.*" "He first *called,* and then *sent for,* the *sergeant,*" should be "He first *called* the *sergeant,* and then *sent for* him."

EXERCISES.

To be corrected.

1. The army shall not want for supplies. 2. Which school do you go to? 3. What firm are you agent for? 4. What country are you a native of? 5. I will not permit of such conduct.

6. It is our duty to assist and sympathize with those in distress. 7. The convicts are hired by and employed for the benefit of a few speculators. 8. He lives in and came from Pittsburgh.

To be parsed.

1. We cruised about for several hours in the dense fog. 2. He has a touch of our family. 3. Here rests his head upon the lap of earth. 4. He will steal, sir, an egg out of a cloister. 5. The pile sank down into the opening earth.

6. The ground lifts like a sea. 7. The clouds are driven about in the sky, like squadrons of combatants rushing to the conflict. 8. In vain does the old dragon rage. 9. I had supposed till lately that you were my friend. 10. A shoreless ocean tumbled round the globe. 11. The morning broke without a sun.

Rule VIII.—Nouns denoting *time, distance, measure,* or *value,* after verbs and adjectives, are in the objective case without a governing word.

Rem. 1.—The names of *things,* following the passive forms of the verbs *ask, lend, teach, refuse, provide,* and some others, are in the objective case without a governing word; as, "He was asked a *question;*" "John was refused *admittance;*" "I was taught *grammar.*"

Rem. 2.—The following expressions are elliptical: "Wilson, Hinkle & Co., No. 137 Walnut St., Cincinnati, O." = *To* Wilson, Hinkle & Co., No. 137 *on* Walnut St., *in* Cincinnati, *in* Ohio. "July 4, 1776" = *On the* 4th *day of* July, *in the year* 1776.

EXERCISES.
To be parsed.

1. The horse ran a mile. 2. I do not care a straw. 3. He is worth a million of dollars. 4. The child is nine years old. 5. They marched Indian file. 6. He wore his coat cloak-fashion. 7. Spring has already covered thy grave, twelve times, with flowers. 8. The ship sailed four knots an hour.

9. This is worth remembering. 10. The tower is 250 feet high. 11. How many square yards of plastering in a room 21 feet long, 15 feet wide, and 10 feet high? 12. The poor, dissipated student was refused his diploma.

205. Pronouns.

Rule IX.—Pronouns must agree with their antecedents in person, gender, and number.

Rem. 1.—The person, gender, and number of an interrogative pronoun are indeterminate when no answer is given to the question in which it is found; as, "*Who* owns that vessel?" The answer may be, "*Mr. Gordon* owns it," "*Jones & Smith* own it," "*I* own it," "*He* and *I* own it," or "*You yourself* own it." When an answer is given, or when one can be inferred from well-known facts, these properties are determinate; as, "*Who* owns that vessel?—*I* own it." "Who" is in the first person, common gender, singular number, agreeing with "I." "*Who* commanded the allied forces at the battle of Waterloo?" "Who" is in the third person, masculine gender, singular number—the answer, though not given, being well known.

Rem. 2.—There being no pronoun of the third person singular, denoting either sex, in the English language, the masculine forms, *he, his, him,* are used in its place. Do not say, "Each pupil should learn *his* or *her* lesson:" use *his* alone. Say, "Should any one desire to consult me, let *him* call at my office," even though the invitation be intended for both sexes. Should the gender of the person referred to, be known, use a masculine or feminine pronoun, as the case requires.

Rem. 3.—Things personified should be represented as masculine or feminine by the pronouns referring to them; as, "Night, sable goddess, from *her* ebon throne;" "Grim-visaged War has smoothed *his* wrinkled front."

Rem. 4.—A pronoun sometimes precedes its antecedent; as, "*Thy* chosen temple, Lord, how fair!" "Hark! *they* whisper, angels say."

Rem. 5.—The relative pronoun is frequently omitted; as, "That is the house [*which*] we live in;" "This is the book [*which*] you inquired for."

Rem. 6.—*That,* as a relative, should generally be used after *a, all, every, same,* and *very;* after *who,* used interrogatively; after an adjective in the superlative degree; and when both persons and things are referred to.

Ex.—"He is *a* man *that* all respect;" "I gave him *all that* I had;" "Is this the *same* book *that* I lent you?" "It is the *very* book *that* you lent me;" "He is the *wisest that* says the least;" "*Who that* has once heard him does not wish to hear him once again;" "Here are the *persons* and *things that* were sent for."

Rem. 7.—Unless great emphasis is required, a noun or pronoun should not be used in the absolute case by pleonasm. Say "The horse ran away," not "The horse, *it* ran away;" "Many words darken speech," not "Many words, *they* darken speech."

Rem. 8.—To avoid ambiguity, a relative pronoun should be placed as near as possible to its antecedent.

Ex.—"A purse was lost in the street, *which* contained a large sum of money." The clause introduced by "which," should be placed immediately after "purse."

Rem. 9.—A pronoun whose antecedent is a collective noun conveying the idea of unity, should be in the neuter singular: one whose antecedent is a collective noun conveying the idea of plurality, should be plural, taking the gender of the individuals composing the collection.

Rem. 10.—*It* is used to represent (1) a noun or pronoun in any person, in either number, or of any gender; (2) a sentence, or a part of a sentence; or (3) it may be used without representing any person or thing.

Ex.—"*It* is *I;*" "*It* was *land-warrants* that I purchased;" "*It* was *Milton* who wrote Paradise Lost;" "*You have wronged me,* and will repent of *it;*" "*It* snows;" "We roughed *it* in the woods."

EXERCISES.

To be corrected.

1. James, he has been whispering.   2. Whom, when they had washed, they laid her in an upper chamber.   3. The names I called you, I am now sorry for them.   4. If any one has not paid their fare, let them call at the captain's office.   5. Every one should have his or her life insured.

6. Every one should have their lives insured.   7. That book is in the book-case, which contains pictures.   8. This is the dog whom my father bought.   9. These are the men and the guns which we captured.   10. That is the same pen which I sold you.   11. He is the wisest which lives the most nobly.

12. The moon took its station still higher.   13. The jury could not agree in its verdict.   14. The news came of defeat, but no one believed them.   15. If you see an error or a fault in my conduct, remind me of them.

To be parsed.

1. The hand that governs in April, governed in January.   2. I perish by this people which I made.   3. Many a man shall envy him who henceforth limps.   4. I venerate the man whose heart is warm.   5. Your sorrows are our gladness.   6. The blooming morning oped her dewy eyes.

7. Men are like birds that build their nests in trees that hang over rivers.   8. He was followed by another worthless rogue, who flung away his modesty instead of his ignorance.   9. A bird is placed in a bell-glass, A, which stands over the mercury.

10.   Remorseless Time !
Fierce spirit of the glass and scythe !   What power
Can stay him in his silent course, or melt
His iron heart to pity?—*Prentice*.

11. "Banished from Rome!" what's banished, but set free
From daily contact of the things I loathe?
"Tried and convicted traitor!"   Who says this?
Who'll prove it, at his peril, on my head?—*Croly*.

206. Antecedents connected by "And."

Rule X.—A pronoun, with two or more antecedents in the singular, connected by *and*, must be plural.

Rem. 1.—When the antecedents are but different names for the same person or thing, the pronoun must be singular; as, "The eminent lawyer and statesman has resigned *his* office."

Rem. 2.—When the antecedents are emphatically distinguished, the pronoun should be singular; as, "The mind *as well as* the body has *its* diseases;" "The country and not the government has *its* admirers."

Rem. 3.—When the antecedents are limited by *each*, *every*, or *no*, the pronoun must be singular; as, "Each man and each boy did *his* duty;" "Every hill and every mountain has *its* echo;" "No land and no clime possesses all earth's blessings."

Rem. 4.—When the antecedents taken together are regarded as a single thing, the pronoun must be singular; as, "The horse and wagon is in *its* place."

EXERCISES.
To be parsed.

1. Charles and Henry are flying their kites.   2. You and I should study our lessons.   3. The child wants some bread and milk: will you get it?.   4. The good man, and the sinner, too, shall have his reward.   5. The great philosopher and statesman is laid in his grave.   6. He bought a horse and a wagon, and sold them at a profit.   7. Every house and lot has its price set opposite its number.

207. Antecedents Connected by "Or" or "Nor."

Rule XI.—A pronoun, with two or more antecedents in the singular, connected by *or* or *nor*, must be singular.

Rem. 1.—When the two antecedents are of different genders, the use of a singular masculine pronoun to represent them is improper. In such cases,

1. Use a plural pronoun that may represent both genders; as, "Not on outward charms could *he* or *she* build *their* pretensions to please:"

2. Use different pronouns; as, "No boy or girl should whisper to *his* or *her* neighbor:"

3. Substitute a general term, including both, for the two antecedents, and represent this general term by a singular masculine pronoun; as, "No *pupil* (boy or girl) should whisper to *his* neighbor."

Rem. 2.—When one of the antecedents is plural, it should be placed last, and the pronoun should be plural; as, "Neither the farmer nor his sons were aware of *their* danger."

EXERCISES.

To be corrected.

1. No father or mother lives that does not love his or her children.   2. George or Charles are diligent in their business.   3. If an Aristotle. a Pythagoras, or a Galileo, suffer for their opinions, they are martyrs.   4. If you see my horse or mule, turn them into your pasture.   5. Poverty or wealth have their own temptations.

To be parsed.

1. Henry or Samuel will lend you his book.   2. If thy hand or thy foot offend thee, cut it off, and cast it from thee.   3. Neither James nor John has gained much credit for himself.

4. Either Mary or Sarah will recite her lesson.   5. Even a rugged rock, or a barren heath, though in itself disagreeable, contributes by contrast to the beauty of the whole.

6. Beginning with Latin or Greek hexameter, which is the same.   7. Either James or his father was mistaken in his opinion.   8. Neither the teacher nor the scholars used their books in the class.

208. Adjectives and Participles.

Rule XII.—An adjective or participle belongs to some noun or pronoun.

Rem. 1.—An adjective used as the predicate of a sentence, may modify an infinitive or a substantive clause, used as the subject; as, "To lie is *sinful*;" "That all men are created equal, is *self-evident.*"

Rem. 2.—An adjective may modify a noun and another adjective, taken together; as, "A *rich* old miser;" "A *large* bay horse."

Rem. 3.—After infinitives and participles, adjectives are frequently used which do not belong to any particular noun or pronoun; as, "To be *good* is to be *happy*;" "The main secret of being *sublime*, is to say great things in few and plain words."

Rem. 4.—An adjective should agree in number with the noun to which it belongs; as, *that* kind, *those* kinds; *one* man, *two* men. To denote a collective number, a singular adjective may precede a plural noun; as, "*One* thousand dollars;" "The census is taken *every* ten years." To denote plurality, *many a* is used instead of *many;* as, "*Many* a time;" "*Many* a morning."

Rem. 5.—In poetry, an adjective relating to a noun or pronoun is sometimes used instead of an adverb modifying a verb or a participle; as, "*Incessant* still you flow;" "*Swift* on his downy pinions flies from woe."

Rem. 6.—Adjectives are sometimes used as nouns; as, "The *rich* and the *poor* here meet together;" "*One* said, 'Let us go;' *another*, 'No, let us remain.'"

Rem. 7.—Two adjectives are frequently connected by a hyphen, forming a compound adjective; as, "A *sweet-faced* girl."

Rem. 8.—Numeral and pronominal adjectives precede another adjective which modifies the same noun; as, "The *seven* wise men;" "*That* old house."

EXERCISES.
To be parsed.

1. His spirit was so bird-like and so pure. 2. Dim, cheerless, is the scene my path around. 3. This life of ours is a wild Æolian harp of many a joyous strain. 4. Every tree-top has its shadow.

H. G. 16.

5. With fleecy clouds the sky is blanched. 6. Still stands the forest primeval. 7. 'Tis impious in a good man to be sad. 8. To hope the best is pious, brave, and wise. 9. Time wasted is existence; used, is life.

10.   Thoughts shut up, want air,
  And spoil, like bales unopened to the sun.

11. Tell me not in mournful numbers,
    Life is but an empty dream.

12. Pray for the living, in whose breast
    The struggle between right and wrong
    Is raging terrible and strong.

13. Petulant she spoke, and at herself she laughed;
    A rose-bud set with little willful thorns,
    And sweet as English air could make her.

14. The hills are dearest which our childish feet
    Have climbed the earliest, and the streams most sweet
    Are ever those at which our young lips drank,
    Stoop'd to their waters o'er the grassy bank.

15. Sometimes her narrow kitchen walls
    Stretched away into stately halls.— *Whittier.*

209. Verbs.

Rule XIII.—A verb must agree with its subject in person and number.

Rem. 1.—When the subject is a collective noun, conveying plurality of idea, the verb should be plural; as, "In France, the peasantry *go* barefooted, while the middle class *wear* wooden shoes."

Rem. 2.—When a subject, plural in form, represents a single thing, the verb must be singular; as, "The '*Pleasures of Memory*' was published in 1792;" "*Politics* is his trade;" "The *news* is confirmed."

Rem. 3.—When the subject is a mere word or sign, an infinitive, or a substantive clause, the verb should be in the third person singular; as, "*They* is a personal pronoun;" " + is the sign of addition;" "*To deceive* is wrong;" "'*Who comes there?*' was heard from within."

Rem. 4.—A verb in the imperative mode usually agrees with *thou, you,* or *ye,* expressed or understood; as, "*Look* [*ye*] to your hearths, my lords!" "*Smooth* [*thou*] thy brow."

EXERCISES.

To be corrected.

1. You and I was walking together. 2. The horses has been fed. 3. I called, but you was not at home. 4. Thou can assist me if thou will. 5. There was mountains where I came from. 6. A committee were appointed to report resolutions. 7. The fleet were seen off Hatteras.

8. The legislature have adjourned. 9. The corporation is individually responsible. 10. The Pleasures of Hope are a fine poem. 11. The scissors is dull. 12. *We* are a personal pronoun. 13. The derivation of these words are uncertain. 14. The board of trustees have a meeting to-night.

To be parsed.

1. Thus many a sad to-morrow came and went. 2. Return, O beautiful days of youth! 3. I alone was solitary and idle. 4. This well deserves meditating. 5. At an early hour, arrive the diligences. 6. He waved his arm.

7. Every rational creature has all nature for his dowry and estate. 8. The present needs us. 9. The jury were not unanimous. 10. Generation after generation passes away. 11. The public are respectfully invited to attend.

12.   Every age
Bequeathes the next for heritage,
No lazy luxury or delight.

13. There's not a beggar in the street
Makes such a sorry sight.

14. He that attends to his interior self,
That has a heart, and keeps it—has a mind
That hungers and supplies it, and who seeks
A social, not a dissipated life,
Has business.

15. Between Nose and Eyes a strange contest arose
    The spectacles set them unhappily wrong;
The point in dispute was, as all the world knows,
    To which the said spectacles ought to belong.—*Cowper.*

210. Subjects Connected by "And."

Rule XIV.—A verb, with two or more subjects in the singular, connected by *and*, must be plural.

Rem. 1.—When two or more subjects in the singular, connected by *and*, are but different names for the same person or thing, or, when taken together, they represent a single idea, the verb should be singular; as, "*Descent* and *fall* to us *is* adverse;" "A *hue* and *cry* was raised."

Rem. 2.—When two or more singular subjects are emphatically distinguished, or are preceded by *each, every,* or *no*, the verb should be singular; as, "The father, *as well as* the son, *was* in fault;" "All work and no play, *makes* Jack a dull boy;" "*Every* bird and beast *cowers* before the wild blast."

Rem. 3.—When two or more subjects, of different numbers, are emphatically distinguished, the verb agrees with the first; as, "Diligent industry, *and not* mean savings, *constitutes* honorable competence."

Rem. 4.—Two or more singular subjects, connected by *with, in company with, together with,* &c., require a singular verb; as, "Mr. Brown, *in company with* Mr. Shriver, *is* opening a new coal mine;" "The general, *with* all his army, *was* captured."

EXERCISES.

To be corrected.

1. Mr. Johnson and his brother was at the meeting. 2. Time and tide waits for no man. 3. Bread and milk are good food. 4. Each man, each child, and each woman know the hour. 5. The boy's mother, but not his father, deserve great praise.

6. Patience and diligence removes mountains. 7. I, together with my sister, are intending to make you a visit. 8. The salmon, as well as the trout, have become scarce in these waters. 9. A number of horses, together with a large amount of other property, were stolen last night.

To be parsed.

1. Her beauty, and not her talents, attracts attention. 2. No wife and no mother was there to comfort him. 3. Out of the same mouth proceed blessing and cursing. 4. You and I look alike.

5. My uncle, with his wife, is in town. 6. Charles and Emma are good scholars. 7. Charles, together with his sister Emma, is studying botany. 8. The crime, not the scaffold, makes the shame. 9. The ambition and avarice of man are the sources of his unhappiness.

10. Fire of imagination, strength of mind, and firmness of soul are gifts of nature. 11. Each battle sees the other's umbered face. 12. A coach and six is, in our time, never seen, except as a part of some pageant.

211. Subjects Connected by "Or" or "Nor."

Rule XV.—A verb, with two or more subjects in the singular, connected by *or* or *nor*, must be singular.

Rem. 1.—When the subjects are of different persons or numbers, the verb must agree with the nearest, unless another be the principal term; as, "Neither you nor I *am* to blame;" "Neither you nor he *is* in his place."

Rem. 2.—When two or more infinitives, or substantive clauses, are connected by *or* or *nor*, the verb must be singular, and a predicate nominative, following the verb, must be singular also; as, "Why we are thus detained, or why we receive no intelligence from home, *is* mysterious;" "To be, or not to be, that *is* the question."

Rem. 3.—When the subjects are singular, but of different genders, the verb is singular, relating to them taken separately; but a pronoun may be plural, relating to them taken conjointly; as, "Mary or her sister *has* lost *their* umbrella"—the umbrella being theirs by joint ownership.

EXERCISES.
To be corrected.

1. Has the horses or the cattle been found? 2. Were the boy or the girl badly bruised? 3. The ax or the hammer were lost. 4. Poverty or misfortune have been his lot. 5. Neither the horse nor the wagon are worth much. 6. Either you or I are to blame. 7. Neither the mule nor the horses is found. 8. He comes—nor want nor cold his course delay. 9. Neither avarice nor pleasure move me. 10. A lucky anecdote, or an enlivening tale, relieve the folio page.

11. Not the Mogul, or Czar of Muscovy,
    Not Prester John, or Cham of Tartary,
    Are in their houses monarchs more than I.

To be parsed.

1. To give an affront, or to take one tamely, is no mark of a great mind. 2. Neither he nor she has spoken to him. 3. To reveal secrets, or to betray one's friends, is contemptible perfidy. 4. Either ability or inclination was wanting.

5. Hatred or revenge deserves censure. 6. Neither poverty nor riches is desirable. 7. The vanity, the ambition, or the pride of some men keeps them always in trouble. 8. Emma or Jane has lost her dictionary.

9. The breezy call of incense-breathing morn,
    The swallow twittering from the straw-built shed,
    The cock's shrill clarion, or the echoing horn,
    No more shall rouse them from their lowly bed.—*Gray.*

10.   From the high host
    Of stars to the lulled lake, and mountain coast,
        All is concentered in a life intense,
    Where not a beam, nor air, nor leaf is lost.—*Byron.*

11. Time, nor Eternity, hath seen
        A repetition of delight
    In all its phases; ne'er hath been
    For men or angels that which *is.*

212. Infinitives.

Rule XVI.—An infinitive may be used as a noun in any case except the possessive.

Rem. 1.—An infinitive represents being, action, or state abstractly. It is the mere verb, without limitation. As such, it may be used,

1. As the *subject* of a proposition; as, "*To err* is human."

2. As the *predicate* of a proposition; as, "To obey is *to enjoy.*"

3. As the *object* of a transitive verb or of its participles; as, "He loves *to play;*" "He is trying *to learn.*"

4. In *apposition with a noun;* as, "Time *to come* is called future."

5. *Abstractly,* or *independently;* as, "*To tell* the truth, I was inattentive."

Rem. 2.—The infinitive always retains its verbal signification. Hence, *as a noun,* it may be limited by a predicate adjective or predicate nominative, and, *as a verb,* be followed by an object, or modified by an adverb; as, "*To spend* money recklessly is criminal."

Rem. 3.—The sign *to* should never be separated from the rest of the infinitive. "*To correctly report* a speech is difficult," should be "*To report* a speech *correctly* is difficult."

Rem. 4.—The preposition *for* should not be used immediately before the infinitive. "I study *for to learn,*" should be "I study *to learn.*"

Rem. 5.—The sign *to* should never be used alone. "I never told a lie, and never intend *to,*" should be "I never told a lie, and never intend *to do so.*"

Rem. 6.—After the verbs *bid, dare* (venture), *hear, feel, let, make, need, see,* in the active voice, and *let,* in the passive, the sign *to* is generally omitted; as, "He bade him *depart;*" "I saw him *fall.*" The sign *to* is sometimes omitted after several other verbs.

Rem. 7.—Verbs expressing *hope, expectation, command, intention,* &c., require the present infinitive after them; as, "I hoped *to see* you;" "I *intended to call* for you;" "He *expected to see* you yesterday."

EXERCISES.
To be corrected.

1. What came ye out for to see? 2. I never voted that ticket, and never intend to. 3. To greedily eat one's dinner is ill-mannered. 4. I dared him come to me. 5. He durst not to leave his room. 6. I saw him to write on his slate.

7. I have known him to frequently be tardy. 8. He made his horses to go very fast. 9. He needs study more carefully. 10. He need not to remain long. 11. He intended to have written to you. 12. They had hoped to have seen you before they left.

To be parsed.

1. To do right, is to do that which is ordered to be done. 2. To

die is to be banished from myself. 3. To do justice and judgment is more acceptable to the Lord than sacrifice. 4. It is our duty to try, and our determination to succeed. 5. He had dared to think for himself. 6. She shall rejoice in time to come.

> 7. It is the curse of kings to be attended
> By slaves that take their humors for a warrant
> To break within the bloody house of life,
> And on the winking of authority,
> To understand a law.—*Shakspeare.*

> 8. Have ye brave sons? Look in the next fierce brawl
> To see them die. Have ye fair daughters? Look
> To see them live, torn from your arms, distained,
> Dishonored, and if ye dare call for justice,
> Be answered by the lash.—*Mitford.*

213. Infinitives not used as Nouns.

Rule XVII.—An infinitive not used as a noun, depends upon the word it limits, or which leads to its use.

Rem. 1.—An infinitive may depend upon,

1. A *noun;* as, "Flee from the *wrath to come.*"
2. A *pronoun;* as, "I heard *him* declaim."
3. A *verb;* as, "He *went to see* the show."
4. An *adjective;* as, "The gods are *hard to reconcile.*"
5. A *participle;* as, "The rain *threatening to fall,* we left."
6. An *adverb;* as, "He told me *when to come.*"

Rem. 2.—The sign *to* is sometimes improperly omitted; as, "Please *excuse* James for absence." Supply *to* before "excuse."

Rem. 3.—The infinitive is often understood; as, "I considered him [*to be*] honest."

Rem. 4.—The sign *to* may be omitted before all but the first of two or more infinitives in the same construction; as, "They tried *to cheat, rob,* and *murder* me."

EXERCISES.
To be parsed.

1. I come not here to talk. 2. I can not see to spin my flax. 3. In sooth, deceit maketh no mortal gay. 4. I saw along the

winter snow a spectral column pour. 5. Let the great world spin forever down the ringing grooves of change.

6. He lived to die, and died to live. 7. It is a brave thing to understand something of what we see. 8. It is better to fight for the good than to rail at the ill.

9.   Let us be content in work,
  To do the thing we can, and not presume
  To fret because it's little.

10. One day with life and heart,
  Is more than time enough to find a world.

11. Needful auxiliars are our friends, to give
  To social man true relish of himself.

12. Learn well to know how much need not be known,
  And what that knowledge which impairs your sense.

13. Let him not violate kind nature's laws,
  But own man born to live as well as die.

14.   The blood more stirs
  To rouse a lion than to start a hare.

15. He that lacks time to mourn lacks time to mend.
  Eternity mourns that.

214. Adverbs.

Rule XVIII.—Adverbs modify verbs, adjectives, participles, and adverbs.

Rem. 1.—Adverbs sometimes modify phrases and entire propositions; as, "He lives *just* over the hill;" "*Verily*, ye are the people."

Rem. 2.—Adverbs are frequently used as expletives; as, "*Well*, that is a strange story;" "*There, now*, you have said enough."

Rem. 3.—The adverbs *yes, no, aye, yea*, and *nay*, are generally answers to questions, and are equivalent to a whole sentence. They are then used independently, or modify the sentences preceding or following them.

Ex.—"Are you angry?—*No*." "*Yea*, they shall sing in the ways of the Lord;" "*Nay;* but it is really true."

Rem. 4.—Two contradictory negatives in the same clause are equivalent to an affirmative; as, "I can *not* write *no* more" = I can write more. Hence, two negatives should never be employed to express a negation. Say "I want *no* assistance," not "I *do n't* want *no* assistance." Two or more negatives, not contradictory, do not destroy the negative character of a sentence; as, "He will *never* consent, *no, never, not* he, *nor* I *neither*."

Rem. 5.—When the quality of an object, and not the manner of an action, is to be expressed, an adjective should be used as predicate; as, "He arrived *safe*," not "*safely;*" "She looks *beautiful*," not "*beautifully*."

Rem. 6.—Though sanctioned by good authority, the use of *from* before *whence, hence,* and *thence* should be avoided. Say, "*Whence* came you?" not "*From whence* came you?"

Rem. 7.—The word modified by an adverb is sometimes omitted; as, "*Down,* royal state!" Supply "fall." "*Up* in the morning early." Supply "get" or "rise." "I 'll *hence* to London." Supply "go." In some cases, adverbs thus used seem to have the force of verbs in the imperative mode, but not always. *Up* and *out,* followed by the preposition *with,* take the place of verbs in declarative sentences; as, "She *up with* her fist, and took him on the face."

Rem. 8.—*There* is frequently used as an expletive to introduce a sentence; as, "*There* was no grass there;" "*There* were three of us."

Rem. 9.—An adverbial phrase should not be parsed as a single word when its parts can be parsed separately; as, "They walked *hand in hand*." Place "with" before the phrase.

Rem. 10.—The comparative and superlative forms of adjectives, preceded by the definite article, are often used as adverbs; as, "*The longer* I study, *the better* I like it;" "He lives *best* who acts *the noblest*."

Rem. 11.—Adverbs should be so placed as to render the sentence clear, correct, and elegant. The sense intended to be conveyed depends on their position. Compare "He is thought to be *generally* honest," with "He is *generally* thought to be honest."

EXERCISES.

To be corrected.

1. He won't give me no satisfaction. 2. We did n't find nobody at home. 3. Nobody never saw such a crowd of people. 4. The

nation never was more prosperous, nor never was more ungrateful.
5. Neither he, nor nobody else who don't do no work, can have
my vote.

6. The velvet feels smoothly. 7. He speaks slow and distinct.
8. The children all looked beautifully. 9. You did splendid last
examination. 10. I am tolerable well, I thank you. 11. Sure,
you don't mean to humbug me. 12. I scarce know what I am
saying.

13. He did handsomer than he promised. 14. He out with his
knife, and slashed right and left, (*See Rem.* 7.) 15. The dog
grabbed him by the throat, and downed him. 16. I only want
to borrow your umbrella.

17. The dog wanted in, but he now wants out. 18. There is
nothing better pleases me than to see boys truthful. 19. There is
still a wider field for enterprise in California. 20. It rains most
every day. 21. I would not have believed no tongue but Hu-
bert's.

To be parsed.

1. All the world was ours once more. 2. Up goes my grave
Impudence to the maid. 3. I saw the blue Rhine sweep along.
4. Death erects his batteries right over against our homes. 5.
Slowly the throng moves o'er the tomb-paved ground. 6. The
complication of a town is often happily unraveled by starting from
a main trunk.

7. Man desires not only to be loved, but to be lovely. 8. West-
ward the course of empire takes its way. 9. Your menaces move
me not. 10. We see but dimly through the mists and vapors.
11. Man by man, and foot by foot, did the soldiers proceed over
the Alps. 12. Finally, the war is already begun, and we must
either conquer or perish. 13. He heaped up great riches, but
passed his time miserably.

14. Night's candles are burnt out, and jocund Day,
    Stands tiptoe on the misty mountain's top.—*Shakspeare.*

15.   I'll look no more,—
    Lest my brain turn, and the deficient sight
    Topple down headlong.

16. Not a word to each other; we kept the great pace—
    Neck by neck, stride by stride, never changing our place.
                    Browning.

17. Who does the best his circumstance allows,
  Does well, acts nobly, angels could no more.
  Our outward act indeed admits restraint;
  'T is not in things o'er thought to domineer.
  Guard well thy thought, our thoughts are heard in heaven.
  Young.

215. Prepositions.

Rule XIX.—A preposition shows the relation of its object to the word upon which the latter depends.

Rem. 1.—The object of a preposition, as well as the preceding term of relation, often determines what preposition should be used; as, "He read *to* me *about* the war, *with* much feeling;" "He wrote *to* me *in* great haste *concerning* his losses."

Rem. 2.—Prepositions are frequently omitted; as, "He lives opposite [*to*] the court-house;" "Lend [*to*] me a pencil;" "His house is near [*to*] the river."

EXERCISES.

To be corrected and parsed.

1. The man is dependent on his relatives. 2. I differ with you on that point. 3. The man was killed by a sword and died with violence. 4. The two thieves divided the money among them. 5. During his life-time, he was twice shipwrecked.

6. Above the clouds and tempests' rage,
  Across yon blue and radiant arch,
  Upon their long, high pilgrimage,
  I watched their glittering armies march.

216. Coördinate Connectives.

Rule XX.—Coördinate connectives join similar elements.

Rem. 1.—Elements placed in the same relation or rank are similar; as, nouns or pronouns in the same case, verbs in the same construction, words, phrases, and clauses limiting the same term, &c.

Rem. 2.—Conjunctions are sometimes omitted; as, "Had I the means, I would buy that farm" = *If* I had the means, &c. "He is rich, noble, wise, [*and*] generous."

Rem. 3.—In a series of similar terms, the conjunction is usually omitted, except between the last two; as, "Henry, Horace, *and* Samuel are my pupils." When great emphasis is required, the conjunction should be supplied; as, "You have been an honest, *and* a bold, *and* a faithful hound."

Rem. 4.—Dissimilar or disproportionate terms should never be joined by conjunctions; as, "I always *have* [been] and always *shall be* of this opinion."

Rem. 5.—Conjunctions are sometimes used as introductory words, either to awaken expectation, or to make the introduction of a sentence less abrupt; as, "*And* it came to pass in those days," &c.; "*So* you are going to New Orleans, it seems."

EXERCISES.

To be corrected and parsed.

1. We moved along silently and with caution. 2. To play is more pleasant than working. 3. They either could not, nor desired to learn. 4. He can brag, but is not able to do much. 5. That lot is preferable and cheaper than yours. 6. He looks as though he was hungry. 7. He has no love nor veneration for him.

8. I can not tell whether he has returned or not. 9. All were drowned save me. 10. Neither James or John came home yesterday. 11. I always desire and always wished for your society. 12. The boy would and did have his own way. 13. The parliament addressed the king, and has been prorogued the same day.

217. Subordinate Connectives.

Rule XXI.—Subordinate connectives join dissimilar elements.

Rem. 1.—A clause introduced by a subordinate connective performs the office of a noun, an adjective, or an adverb. The connective always unites the clause which it introduces to the word or phrase which is modified; as, "He said *that* he would come;" "The man *whom* you saw is the sheriff;" "Do you know *where* I live?"

Rem. 2.—A subordinate connective is almost invariably placed at the beginning of the clause which it introduces. When this clause is used as the subject of a sentence, or is put in apposition with a noun in any case, the connective is a mere introductory word; as, "*That* you have deceived me doth appear from this;" "The rumor *that* he is insane is unfounded."

EXERCISES.
To be parsed.

1. Come as the winds come, when navies are stranded. 2. I never thought that it could be so. 3. He locks the door after the horse is stolen. 4. I now know why you deceived me. 5. He will have friends wherever he may be.

6. I could distinguish the merchant to whom the ship was consigned. 7. However stern he may seem, he is a good man. 8. While there is life, there is hope. 9. Blessed are the merciful: for they shall obtain mercy. 10. He rushes to the fray as if he were summoned to a banquet.

11. Whether the planets are inhabited, was discussed last evening. 12. I consent to the constitution, because I expect no better, and because I am not sure it is not the best. 13. I do not know where he is. 14. There was so much noise that I could not sleep.

218. Interjections.

Rule XXII.—An interjection has no dependence upon other words.

EXERCISES.
To be parsed.

1. What! might Rome have been taken? 2. Ha! laughest thou, Lochiel, my vision to scorn? 3. Ho! warden! 4. Oh, fearful woe! 5. Ah, my saying was true.

6. Hark! hark! to God the chorus breaks. 7. Halloo! my boys, halloo! 8. Pshaw! there's no distress in that. 9. Hem! what is it? 10. Aha, is that you?

11. Alas, poor Yorick! 12. Adieu, adieu, my native land!

13. Hark! they whisper: angels say,
    Sister spirit, come away.

FALSE SYNTAX.

219. Definition.

1. **False Syntax** is any violation of the laws of good usage, in the application of words or in the construction of sentences.

2. Errors in the use of language arise from,

1. The use of Improper Words, Forms, and Expressions:
2. The Insertion of Unnecessary Words:
3. The Omission of Necessary Words:
4. The Improper Arrangement of the parts of a Sentence.

220. Model for Correcting False Syntax.

1. State that the sentence is not correct.
2. State in what respect it is incorrect.
3. Correct it.
4. Give reasons for the correction.

221. Improper Words, Forms, and Expressions.

I. IMPROPER WORDS.

Caution.—Avoid the use of words with a *wrong meaning.*

Ex.—Nouns.—1. He treated me with great negligence. 2. It is a matter of no consequence. 3. I have sold the balance of the goods. 4. The new play is attributed to the pen of Bulwer. 5. You may take either alternative. 6. I bought a couple of ducks. 7. He went up two pair of stairs. 8. Our ice companies are getting in their crops for the season.

Verbs.—1. I expect he has gone home. 2. I suspect the farm is a good one. 3. He donated $5000 to the college. 4. They teamed a large quantity of ice to the Boston Highlands. 5. The sun is sitting. 6. Set down on that chair. 7. The teacher sat him on the platform.

8. He learned me to read. 9. I love buckwheat cakes. 10. He laid down on the hay. 11. Where were you raised? 12. He enjoys

very bad health. 13. The medicine affected a cure. 14. The Ohio empties into the Mississippi, which has now overflown its banks. 15. If you will not go, I will come to you. 16. He has carried the horses to water.

ADJECTIVES AND PRONOUNS.—1. They resemble each other. 2. He has ne'er a [*nary*] horse, nor e'er a [*ary*] wagon. 3. That very same man came here yesterday. 4. A proper fraction is less than one. 5. We are incident to late frosts. 6. Do not call one another nicknames.

See also "Exercises to be corrected," § 55, 64.

ADVERBS AND CONJUNCTIONS.—1. Gravitation is where one body attracts another. 2. Anarchy is while no laws are enforced. 3. Mr. Elkins is such a nice man. 4. Snow seldom or ever falls in Florida. 5. I shall not forgive him be he never so penitent. 6. Home is home, be it never so homely. 7. He is a mighty mean man.

8. He came here about a week since. 9. He said nothing farther. 10. They went no further. 11. There are some styles of writing where too much ornament is used. 12. He walks like I do. 13. Henry is not tall like I am. 14. You should never do no mischief.

15. John is not as tall as I am. 16. He has neither money or credit. 17. I should like to know if you are going West. 18. Let me see if your face is clean. 19. I have no doubt but you can help him.

20. He was afraid lest he should be caught in the rain. 21. You shiver as though you had the ague. 22. Whether or no the charge can be sustained is questionable. 23. He was the more pleased that it was done cheerfully.

See also "Exercises to be corrected," § 141, 217.

PREPOSITIONS.—1. I have an abhorrence to such men. 2. We then witnessed a combat between a Bengal tiger with a Himalaya bear. 3. The vessel was turned out of the true course. 4. What need is there for so much preparation? 5. They make a great noise of nights. 6. The boy climbed up in a tree. 7. He was accused with forgery.

8. You will always find the old gentleman to home. 9. He rolled from his bed out on to the floor. 10. The bird flew in the window. 11. He put his hand in his pocket for his knife.

See also "Exercises to be corrected," § 134.

II. IMPROPER FORMS.

Note.—Sentences in which wrong forms of nouns, pronouns, adjectives, verbs, and participles are used may be found among "Exercises to be corrected," under appropriate heads. These should be carefully corrected.

Caution I.—Avoid the use of *A* before vowel sounds, and of *An* before consonant sounds.

Ex.—1. An hundred thousand. 2. An humorous person. 3. We are an united people. 4. Such an one is a honest man. 5. The regiment was formed in line in a open field. 6. She is an heroine. 7. That was a heroic deed. (Use **an** before *h* faintly sounded when the following syllable is accented.)

Caution II.—Observe that *the* denotes the class or a particular one, and *a* an indefinite one of several.

Ex.—1. The farthing is the fourth part of a penny. 2. A fox is cunning. 3. A horse is a useful animal. 4. The owl sleeps during a day. 5. A steam engine is a modern invention.

Caution III.—Do not use *them* for *those*, *this here* for *this*, *that 'ere* or *that there* for *that*, or *might of*, *should of*, &c., for *might have*, *should have*, &c.

Ex.—1. Give me them peaches. 2. I can not remember them rules. 3. That 'ere farm is very sandy. 4. What will you give for this here slate? 5. I do not like that 'ere way of doing things. 6. Did you buy them needles of this here peddler? 7. He might of helped me. 8. They should of told you.

Caution IV.—Avoid the use of *how* before *that*, or in its stead.

Ex.—1. He told me how that he was going to Oregon. 2. They said how they knew it was so. 3. She told me how that she had a new bonnet. 4. Father said how he believed the man was a swindler.

Caution V.—Never use *will* for *shall*, nor *would* for *should*.

Ex.—1. I was afraid I would be tardy. 2. I shall go; no one will prevent me. 3. If I would earn money, I would not spend it foolishly. 4. Whoever will swear falsely will be punished. 5. I should be sorry if you would be sick.

Caution VI.—Do not use adjectives as adverbs.

Ex.—1. You ought to value time higher. 2. The cars moved very slow. 3. I am exceeding glad to see you. 4. She dresses neat. 5. We walked silent through the cemetery. 6. I am tolerable well, I thank you. 7. He reads slow and distinct. 8. I came there previous to his coming. 9. He speaks German fluent. 10. The whisper was scarce audible. 11. They are near discouraged. 12. I am that sick I can not sit up any longer.

Caution VII.—Do not use adverbs as adjectives.

Ex.—1. We arrived safely. 2. The country looks beautifully after a shower. 3. I feel very poetically. 4. Things look more favorably this morning. 5. Ice feels coldly.

Caution VIII.—Avoid the use of different kinds of pronouns in the same construction.

Ex.—1. If you will go, I will pay thy expenses. 2. I hope you will put money into thy purse. 3. What we saw, and which frightened us very much, we thought was a ghost. 4. You have mine and I have thine. 5. A man who is industrious, and that is not extravagant, will prosper. 6. Finish thy task, then amuse yourself.

Caution IX.—Do not use the indicative mode where the subjunctive will be more elegant or expressive.

Ex.—1. He will take due heed lest he miscarries. 2. Be careful lest thou breakest some of the rules. 3. If he does but intimate his desire, it will be sufficient to produce obedience. 4. Though he falls, he shall not be utterly cast down. 5. Was I to tell the whole truth, I should not be believed.

Caution X.—Tense forms should denote time in harmony with that indicated by other parts of the sentence.

Ex.—1. They proposed to have visited Paris the following year. 2. After I learned my lesson, I took a walk. 3. He was absent this whole week. 4. He was under great obligations to have assisted me. 5. He will remain here if he could find employment.

6. They would readily believe this statement, if they can break away from their prejudices. 7. His step was then firm, and his figure erect, though he has seemed old and decrepit. 8. He declared himself to have been innocent of the charge brought against him. 9. He had neglected their dearest interest, but he strikes their imagination.

Caution XI.—In compound sentences, tense forms should generally be alike.

Ex.—1. He pays his taxes and liveth honestly. 2. He was here last week, and has been long expected. 3. Then did the officer lay hold on him, and executed him immediately. 4. Thou art the fellow who was at my house, and hast stolen my watch. 5. I went to town, and have heard some good news.

Caution XII.—Avoid the expression of universal truths or present facts in any other tense than the present.

Ex.—1. He demonstrated that the earth was round. 2. What did you say was the capital of Chili? 3. I should think it was time to hear from home. 4. He did not know that brass was made of zinc and copper. 5. I always thought that dew fell. 6. What did you say her name was? 7. Every one knows that air had weight. 8. Heat will radiate best from rough substances.

Caution XIII.—Do not use the perfect participle to express past time, nor the past-tense form instead of the perfect participle.

Ex.—1. I seen him yesterday. 2. He come here to-day. 3. He has ran home. 4. The boys all said he done it. 5. I have saw an old friend to-day. 6. After the storm, we found that the large oak had fell, and that it was broke in two.

Caution XIV.—Avoid the use of improper passive forms.

Ex.—1. He was retired from active service. 2. Evening was come when we reached the summit of the mountain. 3. He is possessed of a large number of farms. 4. The disputants were agreed on that. 5. The hour for adjournment is arrived.

Caution XV.—Avoid the improper use of compound participles.

Ex.—1. The new bridge is being built. 2. Such a foolish anecdote is not worth being repeated. 3. Butter is now being sold for thirty cents a pound. 4. That is not intended for being committed to memory. 5. A petition is being circulated. 6. Stores are now being closed at 8 o'clock P. M.

Caution XVI.—Avoid the inelegant use of participles in place of nouns, infinitives, and clauses.

Ex.—1. He failed fulfilling his promise. 2. He neglected the learning of his lesson. 3. One should be ashamed of being found in bad company. 4. What is the reason of your not having done your task to-day?

5. They who are set ruling over others should be just. 6. No one likes being made fun of. 7. Going to Congress is no evidence of greatness. 8. Such will ever be the consequences of youth associating with vicious companions.

Caution XVII.—Avoid the recurrence, at short intervals, of the same word in different senses.

Ex.—1. He turned to the left, and then left abruptly. 2. If the show of any thing be good for any thing, sincerity is better. 3. The truth is, that error and truth are blended in their minds. 4. His reason might have suggested better reasons. 5. The king communicated his intention to the minister, who disclosed it to the secretary, who made it known to the public.

III. IMPROPER EXPRESSIONS.

Caution I.—Avoid *provincialisms: i. e.*, expressions not national, but confined to certain districts in the same country.

Ex.—1. We raised a right smart chance of corn last year. 2. Our grapes are all done gone. 3. He has done spent all his money. 4. I reckon you have the ague, stranger. 5. I guess I will go home. 6. Watch out for the steamboat. 7. What time does school take up? 8. I am right glad to see you. 9. He toted his plunder on his back all the way from Virginia. 10. Sow the grain suant. 11. I disremember where you live. 12. I did n't go to do it. 13. Where did you loss it? 14. He is in cahoot with me. 15. Three goes in twelve four times.

Caution II.—Avoid *slang phrases*, and all low expressions used by the uneducated.

Ex.—1. That 's what 's the matter. 2. If any one insults you, go for him. 3. That 's tip-top. 4. He 's a brick with a gilt edge. 5. He can get every thing he wants: he has lots of tin. 6. They went at each other with their mauleys. 7. I closed his peepers for him. 8. Where shall I dump my cart? 9. She is setter 'n an old hen.

Caution III.—Avoid all *perversions: i. e.,* words habitually mispronounced or misapplied.

Ex.—1. This is a mountainious country. 2. I onc't went a miled to get some voilets. 3. He got into a voilent passion. 4. He is a candidate for the sheriffality. 5. How do you sell them cowcumbers? 6. I am necessitated to take medicine. 7. This is beautiful apple sauce. 8. He ēfected a cure. 9. The trees are clothed in green foilage. 10. We had some nice lattice (*lettuce*) and sparrow-grass (*asparagus*) for dinner.

Caution IV.—Avoid all improper contractions; as, *it 's* for *it is* or *'t is, is n't* or *aint* for *is not, have n't* or *haint* for *have not, 't aint* for *it is not, better 'n* for *better than,* &c.

Ex.—1. It 's now ready for use. 2. 'T aint my house that is burning. 3. I haint got my lesson. 4. Is n't she beautiful? 5. He aint a good skater. 6. My book is better 'n yours. 7. He is older 'n I am.

222. Insertion of Unnecessary Words.

Caution I.—Do not use unnecessary words.

Ex.—1. Amos Wilkins his book. 2. Henry he ran, and Samuel he ran. 3. They are very nice, these oranges. 4. The girls they all staid in at recess. 5. It took us two hours time to learn that lesson. 6. My father and mother are both of them sick. 7. She

is a poor widow lady.   8. It is above a year since the time I left
school.

9. Oil and water will not mix together.   10. You never denied
but that you came from Nova Scotia.   11. This is a pretty smart
sort of a place.   12. He may probably make the attempt, but he
can not possibly succeed.

13. There are but few other men like him.   14. He came here
about the latter end of last month.   15. Those who have not
bought tickets must now buy their tickets.   16. Who first invented
gunpowder?   17. It is six years ago since I saw you.   18. Whenever he sees me, he always inquires about your health.

19. He had ought to be more punctual.   20. He had not ought
to use profane language.   21. I have no doubt but that he will
come.   22. One is equally as beautiful as the other.   23. I learned
much by the listening to his conversation.   24. You will not never
have such a chance.

25. I am stronger than you think for.   26. We passed over
through the forest.   27. I will never enter into his house again.
28. He deserted from his friends.   29. Pharaoh and his host pursued after them.   30. They presented him with a gold watch.   31.
Mr. Ellison talks of buying of our farm.   32. He followed on
after us.

33. I do not recollect of hearing him say so.   34. You need not
to go to the post-office.   35. From whence came you?   36. He came
from thence last week.   37. You need not to have staid so long.
38. Their chagrin can hardly be conceived of.   39. They got angry
in their settling of their account.   40. He has got a long lesson to
learn.

Caution II.—Avoid double comparatives and super-
latives.

Ex.—1. He is the most unhappiest man I ever saw.   2. More
sharper than a serpent's tooth is vile ingratitude.   3. He seems
more cheerfuller since his return.   4. Choose the lesser of two
evils.   5. He is the most strictest teacher in the city.

Caution III.—Avoid the use of two negatives to express negation.

Ex.—1. He do n't know nothing about my affairs.   2. Time
and tide do n't wait for no one.   3. We did n't find nobody at

home. 4. The best way to keep a secret is to say nothing to nobody about it. 5. You do n't look no older than you did ten years ago. 6. She will never be no better: so the doctor says. 7. Neither her nor nobody else never saw a white blackbird. 8. There can not be nothing more insignificant than vanity.

Caution IV.—Omit the article before a word used as a title, as a mere name, or to denote a class generally.

Ex.—1. The king conferred on him the title of a duke. 2. What kind of a man is he? 3. I have a sort of a misgiving about it. 4. A rascal formerly meant a servant, and a knave a boy. 5. Riches and honor are the gifts of fortune.

6. Some think the Indians are the descendants of the ten lost tribes. 7. They voted for Mr. Weston as a senator. 8. They elected him a chairman. 9. She is not so good a cook as a milliner. 10. He is a better blacksmith than a doctor.

Caution V.—Avoid the needless repetition of words.

Ex.—1. The earth is a sphere, a globe, or a ball. 2. The days, the hours, and the minutes drag slowly along. 3. He went to St. Louis and to Chicago. 4. He is a man of wealth, and of character, and of influence. 5. That wise and that good man has many friends.

6. There is another and a better world. 7. Their idleness and their luxury and pleasures, their criminal deeds and their immoderate passions, and their timidity and baseness of mind, have dejected them to such a degree as to make them weary of life.

223. Omission of Necessary Words.

Caution I.—Avoid the omission of words necessary to complete the sense.

Ex.—1. I was amused at the way he told it. 2. What use would it be to me? 3. The remark is worthy the dunce that made it. 4. The insult does not admit of an apology. 5. That depends upon what precedes and follows. 6. What prevented him going?

7. This is the way I hold my pen. 8. That is the best can be said of him. 9. The steamboat is on the bar; I saw it stuck fast.

10. Having been condemned, there was no pardon. 11. This not only excited our hopes, but fears also. 12. He is an honest man, but unfortunate.

13. That is as hard a story to swallow as Gulliver himself. 14. He lives on the other side the river. 15. Our house is the other end of the street. 16. He was banished his native land. 17. The lazy fellow was expelled the college. 18. I would rather live in poverty than wealth acquired dishonestly.

19. Small farms are more profitable than large. 20. A squirrel can climb a tree quicker than a boy. 21. I could not refrain laughing. 22. The convict escaped the penitentiary. 23. The rich and poor are alike mortal. 24. All admire the beauties of nature and art.

25. I will be so candid to own I was mistaken. 26. It has or will be announced. 27. I have, nor shall not consent to such an arrangement. 28. Number the trees in the order they stand. 29. I help who help me. 30. The house in which I lived, and had long owned, was destroyed by fire. 31. I gave some to Edwin as well as Jonas. 32. I never read the book, and never mean to. 33. It is better to live on a little than outlive a great deal. 34. Please excuse Jane at recess. 35. How do you like out there? 36. He was seen go into a billiard saloon.

37. Using of tobacco is a bad habit. 38. Be careful in the spelling your words. 39. In building of houses there has been much improvement. 40. A modest man never indulges in praising of himself. 41. Gypsies are noted for telling of fortunes.

42. When the air is reduced to 32°, water will freeze. 43. I like to skate about as well as any thing. 44. By time they got that done it was noon. 45. Outdoor croquet is played on the ground instead of on a table, and also much larger.

Caution II.—Avoid the omission of words necessary to denote emphatic distinction.

Ex.—1. I like neither his principles nor practice. 2. He has checks for his valise and overcoat. 3. This is not only a question of policy, but right also. 4. Both his hat and umbrella were lost. 5. Neither his hat nor umbrella was found. 6. His hat, as well as umbrella, was stolen. 7. He has sold either his house or store. 8. He is beloved for his honesty and goodness.

Caution III.—Avoid the improper omission of modifiers and connectives in expressing a succession of particulars.

Ex.—1. We are in need of food, fuel, and of clothing.   2. He is the most zealous, most sanguine, and energetic man I ever knew. 3. In pain, trouble, and in sorrow, he wrote the treatise.   4. The country is full of idlers, swindlers, and of spendthrifts.   5. Farmers and mechanics, lawyers, doctors, and miners, are flocking to this new territory.

Caution IV.—Do not omit the subjects of declarative sentences, whether principal or subordinate.

Ex.—1. Hope to see you soon.   2. Sorry to hear you have been so unfortunate.   3. They knew what was best to do.   4. It is a long road has no turning.   5. After a long night's rest, rose much refreshed.   6. It was he discouraged the undertaking.   7. That there were any were dissatisfied I do not believe.

Caution V.—Avoid the improper omission of pronominals in making comparisons.

Ex.—1. Jacob loved Joseph more than all his children.   2. No one is so kind to me as he.   3. John thinks he is smarter than any body.   4. He owns more land than any man in the county. 5. No country is so cold as Greenland.   6. There is no land so fertile anywhere.

224. Improper Arrangement.

Caution I.—Modifying words, phrases, and clauses should be placed as near as may be to the parts which they modify.

Rem.—Adverbs and adjectives generally precede the words which they modify; but there are so many exceptions to this arrangement, that it can not be regarded as a general rule. In fact, no general rule for the position of modifiers can be given to which there are no exceptions. That position is always the best which conveys the meaning with the most precision.

H. G. 18.

Ex.—Single Words.—1. He was overcome totally by the sad intelligence. 2. Carefully scrutinize the sentiments contained in the books you read. 3. We always are controlled by circumstances. 4. I only saw him once. 5. Ice only forms during cold weather.

6. Theism can only be opposed by polytheism. 7. Only you have I known of all the nations of the earth. 8. Not only he found her employed, but pleased and tranquil also. 9. He read the book only, but did not return it. 10. I would prefer being hung a thousand times.

11. They called together their friends. 12. The officers arrested also the saloon keeper. 13. It is impossible constantly to study. 14. They were nearly dressed alike. 15. He chiefly spoke of himself, not of his employers.

16. By doing the same thing, it often becomes habitual. 17. The necessity of some new method has been felt long. 18. He was pleasing not often because he was vain. 19. The good man not only deserves the respect but the love of his fellow beings. 20. He is considered generally insane.

21. It is a general time of health. 22. Edward has a new pair of boots. 23. We have a young yoke of oxen. 24. All homes are not such as these. 25. You will hardly find such another man. 26. We have just received a fresh supply of fish.

27. The settler here the savage slew. 28. The advocate the court addressed. 29. The Divine Being heapeth favors on his servants, ever liberal and faithful. 30. An old, venerable, tall man just then broke in upon the circle. 31. Sing the four first verses of the hymn just read.

Phrases.—1. The witness had been ordered to withdraw from the bar, in consequence of being intoxicated, by the motion of an honorable member. 2. *Wanted*, a young man to take care of some horses of a religious turn of mind. 3. *Notice.*—A lecture on theater-going at eleven o'clock.

4. He went to town, and drove a flock of sheep, on horseback. 5. Study to unite with firmness gentle manners. 6. All anxiety about the issue divest yourselves of. 7. Hunting is a pastime many are very fond of. 8. These lines were written by a young man who has lain in his grave twelve years, for his own amusement.

9. We should carefully examine into, and candidly pass judgment on, our faults. 10. A good man may go beyond the evenness

of a wise Christian, in a sudden anger. 11. Reason is a ray, darted into the soul, of divinity.

12. The skin is closely allied to horny matter in its composition. 13. From the foregoing considerations, it will be seen that the influence of air is all-controlling over the human constitution. 14. Laughter, by the aid of phonetics, is easily taught as an art.

CLAUSES.—1. We must endure the follies of others, who will have their kindness. 2. He needs no spectacles that can not see, nor boots that can not walk. 3. From a habit of saving time and paper, which they acquired at the university, many write in so diminutive a manner, with such frequent blots and interlineations, that they are hardly able to go on without perpetual hesitation or extemporary expletives. 4. It is true what he says, but it is not applicable to the point. 5. These are the general's orders, who must be obeyed.

6. Mr. French needs a surgeon, who has broken his arm. 7. The figs were in small wooden boxes, which we ate. 8. *Found*, a silver fruit-knife, by a child, which has a broken back. 9. *For sale*, a cottage containing eight rooms, located in a respectable neighborhood, which has double parlors and a detached office.

Caution II.—Avoid any choice or arrangement of words subversive of clearness, precision, and elegance.

Rem. 1.—Looseness and vagueness of style should be guarded against with the greatest care. Hence, inversions, though allowable for rhetorical effect, should be avoided whenever they pervert or obscure the meaning.

Ex.—1. Nature mixes the elements variously and curiously sometimes, it is true. 2. They have the property of receiving rays of one refrangibility, and emitting them at a lower one. 3. They were persons of very moderate intellects, even before they were impaired by their passions. 4. He neither cares for you nor me. 5. Adversity both taught you to think and to reason.

6. The young now have many advantages which our forefathers were deprived of. 7. From what I have said, you will perceive readily the subject I am to proceed upon. 8. Having not known, or having not considered the subject, he declined expressing any opinion. 9. Cook the potatoes with their jackets, as I call them, on.

Rem. 2.—The leading proposition, in a contracted compound sentence, should generally be expressed fully. The parts contracted by ellipsis should be joined to the leading proposition, and to each other, by appropriate connectives.

Ex.—1. He is older, but not so influential, as his brother. [He is older than his brother, but not so influential.] 2. It is larger, but inferior to the other. 3. The camel has as much strength, and more endurance, than the horse. 4. I would rather spend the summer in traveling as in working.

5. He deemed himself, and meant to be, an honest man. 6. You can and ought to be more charitable. 7. The route has or will soon be surveyed. 8. It is our duty to protect this government and that flag from every assailant.

225. Miscellaneous Exercises.

1. If the mean temperature is low, it will require more days to ripen than if it were high. 2. We have done no more than it was our duty to have done. 3. I saw a white and brown bear at the menagerie. 4. The pleasures of the understanding are more preferable than those of the senses.

5. He is engaged in a monograph of the *Carices*. 6. It is difficult for him to speak three sentences together. 7. We have seen how fluids rise in tubes by wetting their sides. 8. I had hoped to have seen you ere this. 9. He is a man too vain to be proud. 10. He used to use many expressions not usually used, and which good usage will not permit one to use.

11. I could see that the desks had been scratched, with half an eye. 12. I seen the horse run away just as I come down street. 13. She married my uncle's first wife's brother. 14. They have heard from their cousins, they who live in Iowa. 15. They are much further north than us.

16. Charlotte seldom or ever comes to see us now. 17. Whether or no this is the man which committed the burglary is uncertain. 18. The time of John reciting his lesson is arrived. 19. The ungrateful man has forsook his friends. 20. I will show you another and a better way. 21. It's now most time for dinner. 22. The tree beareth fruit after his kind.

23. This style of architecture prevailed during the tenth and eleventh century. 24. His servants ye are to whom ye obey. 25. Having did the work satisfactorily, he is entitled to his pay. 26. Both minister and magistrate is compelled sometimes to choose

between his duty and reputation. 27. They are them strangers who come here yesterday. 28. You need not scarce mention it. 29. He is a better farmer than a lawyer.

30. John locked the door, and put the key in his pocket. 31. Some men prefer cold to warm weather, but I differ with them. 32. In learning of this lesson, study carefully the third and fourth section. 33. Come quick. 34. He did the work prompt. 35. I was almost froze when we arrove there.

36. Let each esteem the other better than themselves. 37. I found an empty old pocket-book this morning. 38. The posthumous volumes appeared in considerable intervals. 39. He is not only lazy, but improvident also. 40. I am resolved to try and accomplish the difficult undertaking. 41. There are certain miseries in idleness which the idle can only conceive.

42. The orator had just began, when the hissing commenced. 43. As time advances, it leaves behind him the traces of its flight. 44. Neither wealth nor honor confers happiness on their votaries. 45. He was purposed that he would not lie. 46. Hard work is not congenial with his disposition.

47. They wanted for the necessaries of life. 48. There are millions of people in China whose support is derived almost entirely from rice. 49. Thinks I to myself, symptoms. 50. So, says he, you are not going to pay me, are you? 51. The trial of these men take place to-morrow.

52. The public is requested to attend for their own benefit. 53. Nearly a thousand head of cattle was transported over this road yesterday. 54. Three cheers for our flag—the red, the white, and the blue. 55. Multiply each figure in the multiplier on to each figure in the multiplicand. 56. Take and add the subtrahend and remainder together.

57. He belongs to the very selectest circle in the city. 58. That report was very universally believed. 59. He took two spoonsful of laudanum. 60. He gave me three double handsful of cherries. 61. Deceiving is much the same thing as to lie. 62. I never have and never shall desert from my party: I allers votes the straight ticket. 63. I forgit the man's name; but he's the reverendest looking person I ever see.

64. Will you be to home this evening? 65. If you will go into too deep water, you shall be drownded. 66. I did not think that St. Petersburg was situated so fur north. 67. He can not lay still

or set still scarce a single minute, says she. 68. The enemy attackted us about three o'clock in the morning, before the day had began to break.

69. There is a great deal of good horses in this county. 70. I tried to learn him to cipher—but it aint no use. 71. I had rather not alit on my head, but it haint hurt me much: I feel tolerable hunky. 72. If any one has been missed, let them rise in their places. 73. I allude to Washington, who is a name for all which is just. 74. Next November, I shall be here twelve years.

75. The missionary gave an account of how Christianity has formerly been propagated among heathen nations. 76. Though he falls, he shall not be utterly cast down. 77. Though he be high, he hath respect to the lowly. 78. We have done no more than it was our duty to have done.

79. Can you not assign a more satisfactory and stronger reason than that? 80. The scandal is unworthy the least attention. 81. I have received no assistance from any source, neither from my friends nor from my relatives. 82. Punishments may, and often are, inflicted upon accessories to crimes.

83. He is liker to a half-breed than an Indian. 84. For lacking of diligent observing the clouds, we were caught in the rain. 85. Eve was the fairest of her daughters. 86. I found them in the same place I left them. 87. A poor widow woman drawed the highest prize in the lottery.

88. He has not broke his promise to confine himself to his speciality. 89. He left the *t* out in spelling chestnut, which ought not never to be done. 90. This is John Perkins his book. 91. She danced beautiful, and sang sweet. 92. I am in favor of an uniform system of taxation.

93. There is some hope of him recovering his senses. 94. Columbus had fondly hoped, at one time, to have rendered the natives civilized, industrious, and tributary subjects of the crown. 95. Them ghosts you was talking about, was they in white or black clothes?

96. They dared to bravely fight, or to nobly die, for their country. 97. He looked severe, and told them to quietly resume their seats. 98. He set his face against, and violently denounced, all innocent amusements. 99. Young industrious men can always find employment.

100. The mind of man can not continue long without some food

to nourish the activity of his thoughts. 101. A great variety of
fancy goods are offered for sale below cost. 102. *Lost*, a gutta-
percha cane, by a gentleman, with a gold head.

103. Rapt into future times, the bard begun.—*Pope.*

104. They are the lovely, them in whom unite
Youth's fleeting charms with virtue's lovely light.

105. Ah, Jockey, ill advises those, I wis,
To think of songs at such a time as this.

106. Ere you remark another's sin
Bid thy own conscience look within.—*Gay.*

107. Even now, where Alpine solitudes ascend,
I sit me down a pensive hour to spend.—*Goldsmith.*

WORDS VARIOUSLY CLASSIFIED.

226. Of the Use of Words.

1. The same word may belong to different parts of speech.

2. The manner in which a word is used determines its
classification.

3. The **normal** use of a word is its use according to
its ordinary meaning and classification.

4. The **abnormal** or *exceptional* use of a word is a
variation from its usual meaning or classification.

5. The **idiomatic** use of a word or expression is a
departure from the principles of universal grammar.

227. Examples.

A . . . . (1) **Adj.,** "*A* man;" "*An* ox." (2) **Prep.,** "I go *a* fish-
ing."

About . . . (1) **Adv.,** "He wanders *about*." (2) **Prep.,** "We talked
about the weather."

Above . . . (1) **Adv.,** "He soars *above*." (2) **Prep.,** "He soars *above*
the clouds."

Adieu ... (1) **Noun**, "He bade me *adieu.*" (2) **Interjection**, "*Adieu! adieu!* my native land."

After .... (1) **Adv.**, "I left soon *after.*" (2) **Prep.**, "He ran *after* me." (3) **Conj. adv.**, "He came *after* you left."

Again ... (1) **Adv.**, "Come *again.*" (2) **Conj.**, "*Again*, you have frequently seen," &c.

Alike .... (1) **Adj.**, "Those girls look *alike.*" (2) **Adv.**, "I am *alike* pleased with them both."

All ...... (1) **Noun**, "That is his *all.*" (2) **Adj.**, "*All* men;" "Good-by to you *all;*" "*All* were there" (3) **Adv.**, "He is *all* right;" "We were left *all* alone."

Any ..... (1) **Adj.**, "Have you *any* objections?" (2) **Adv.**, "He is not *any* better."

As ...... (1) **Adv.**, "*As* black as night." (2) **Conj. adv.**, "Do *as* I do," (*manner*); "He is as tall *as* I am," (*comparison*); "The men cheered *as* he passed," (*time*); "I will go now, *as* [*since*] I am a little lame," (*cause* or reason). (3) **Cor. Conj.**, "*As* the door turneth on its hinges, so doth the slothful man on his bed." (4) **Rel. pron.**, "They are such *as* I could find." (5) An **index of apposition**, "He shipped *as* second mate;" "*As* mayor of the city, I feel much aggrieved." (6) Part of a **comp. prep.**, "*As* to that;" "*As for* me," &c.

As follows may be parsed as an adverbial phrase, equivalent to *thus*, or the pronoun *it* may be supplied as the grammatical subject of "follows." Always supply *it* in parsing *as appears*, *as concerns*, and *as regards*.

Before ... (1) **Adv.**, "He went *before.*" (2) **Prep.**, "The hills rise *before* him." (3) **Conj. adv.**, "He spoke *before* I did."

Below ... (1) **Noun**, "I came from *below.*" (2) **Adj.**, "He is in one of the offices *below.*" (3) **Adv.**, "Go *below.*" (4) **Prep.**, "Stand *below* me."

Best ..... (1) **Noun**, "Now do your *best.*" (2) **Adj.**, "Covet the *best* gifts." (3) **Adv.**, "Who can *best* work and *best* agree?" (4) **Adv. phr.**, "Tones he loved *the best.*"

Better ... (1) **Noun**, "They scorn their *betters.*" (2) **Verb**, "Love *betters* what is best." (3) **Adj.**, "The gray mare is the *better* beast." (4) **Adv.**, "Never was monarch *better* feared."

Both .... (1) **Adj.**, "Hear *both* sides." (2) **Pron. adj.**, "*Both* of them made a covenant;" "They are *both* vagabonds." (3) **Cor. conj.**, "She is *both* young and beautiful."

But ..... (1) **Adv.**, "If they kill us, we shall *but* die." (2) **But a, Adj.**, "He is *but a* man." (3) **Prep.**, "All *but* two were drowned;" "None knew thee *but* to love thee;" "Whence all *but* him had fled." (4) Part of **comp. prep.**, "He would steal *but for* the law." (5) **Conj.**, "Knowledge comes, *but* wisdom lingers;" "When pride comes, then cometh shame; *but* with the lowly is wisdom."

By ...... (1) **Adv.**, "He passed *by* on the other side." (2) **Prep.**, "We have come *by* the valley road."

Close .... (1) **Adj.**, "From a *close* bower this dainty music flowed;" "He is a *close,* selfish man." (2) **Adv.**, "He followed *close* behind."

Each .... (1) **Pron. adj.**, "They searched *each* house;" "*Each* officer;" "They took one *each;*" "Wandering *each* his several way." "They resemble *each other.*" (Parse *each* as being in apposition with "they," or *each other* as a compound word.)

Else ..... (1) **Adj.**, "Do not call any one *else.*" (2) **Adv.**, "How *else* can this be done?" (3) **Conj.**, "Thou desirest not sacrifice, *else* would I give it."

Enough.. (1) **Noun**, "He has *enough.*" (2) **Adj.**, "I have trouble *enough.*" (3) **Adv.**, "I know you well *enough.*"

Except... (1) **Verb**, "Which our author could not *except* against." (2) **Prep.**, "I could see nothing *except* the sky;" "*Except* these bonds." (3) **Conj.**, "*Except* the Lord build the house, they labor in vain that build it."

Far ..... (1) **Noun**, "He came from *far.*" (2) **Adj.**, "We be come from a *far* country." (3) **Adv.**, "Over the hills and *far* away;" "*Far* from his home."

Farewell . (1) **Noun**, "A last *farewell.*" (2) **Adj.**, "A *farewell* concert." (3) **Int.**, "*Farewell!*"

Fast..... (1) **Noun**, "A surfeit is the father of much *fast.*" "An annual *fast.*" (2) **Verb**, "Thou didst *fast* and weep for thy child." (3) **Adj.**, "He is my *fast* friend." (4) **Adv.**, "We will bind thee *fast;*" "He runs *fast.*"

H. G. 19.

Few . . . . . (1) **Noun,** "A *few* escaped;" "The *few* and the. many."
    (2) **Adj.,** "We have a *few* copies left."

For . . . . . (1) **Prep.,** "We waited *for* you;" "He writes not *for*
    money nor *for* praise." (2) **Conj.,** "Give thanks unto
    the Lord; *for* he is good; *for* his mercy endureth for-
    ever." See **As.**

Full . . . . . (1) **Noun,** "The *full* of the moon." (2) **Verb,** "The
    moon *fulls* to-night;" "They *full* cloth at the factory."
    (3) **Adj.,** "The house was *full;*" "A *full* supply." (4)
    Adv., "He spake *full* well."

Hard . . . . (1) **Adj.,** "This is *hard* work." (2) **Adv.,** "He works
    hard;" "He lives *hard* by the river." (*Hard* modifies
    the phrase "by the river.")

However . (1) **Adv.,** "*However* great." (2) **Conj.,** "*However*, your
    house was not burned."

Ill . . . . . . (1) **Noun,** "Throw off the *ills;*" "The *ills* of life." (2)
    Adj., "I was quite *ill* yesterday." (3) **Adv.,** "*Ill* fares the
    land to hastening ills a prey."

Indeed . . . (1) **Adv.,** "It is *indeed* true." (2) **Conj.,** "*Indeed*, I was
    not aware of it."

Late . . . . . (1) **Adj.,** "A *late* frost destroyed the fruit." (2) **Adv.,**
    "We studied early and *late.*"

Like . . . . (1) **Noun,** "*Like* produces *like.*" (2) **Verb,** "I *like* frank
    people." (3) **Adj.,** "We have *like* chances;" "The staff
    of his spear was *like* a weaver's beam." (4) **Adv.,** "He
    ran *like* a deer;" "The Assyrian came down *like* a wolf
    on the fold." (Supply *coming* before "on.")

Low . . . . . (1) **Adj.,** "He is very *low* this evening." (2) **Adv.,** "Aim
    low;" "He speaks too *low.*"

More . . . . (1) **Noun,** "Have you any *more?*" "They saved some
    more, some less." (2) **Adj.,** "We want *more* men;" "Let
    us hear no *more* complaints." (3) **Adv.,** "Which returned
    not again unto him any *more.*"

Much . . . . (1) **Noun,** "They made *much* of the little they had."
    (2) **Adj.,** "He displayed *much* learning." (3) **Adv.,** "I
    am *much* disheartened;" "He reads *much.*"

Nay . . . . . (1) **Noun,** "The *nays* have it;" "I say *nay.*" (2) **Adv.,**
    "*Nay*, I said not so."

Ay, aye, yea, are similar to *nay* in use and construction; as, "The *ayes* have it;" "*Yea,* verily." *Yea* and *nay* are also used as conjunctions to denote emphatic addition; as, "What carefulness it wrought in you, *yea,* what clearing of yourselves, *yea,* what indignation, *yea,* what fear, *yea,* what vehement desire, *yea,* what zeal, *yea,* what revenge."—*2 Cor.* vii, 11.

No ......(1) **Noun,** "The *noes* have it." (2) **Adj.,** "This is *no* place for mirth." (3) **Adv.,** "I can walk *no* faster."

Notwithstanding. (1) **Prep.,** "We walked *notwithstanding* the rain." (2) **Conj.,** "He is kind, *notwithstanding* he is stern."

Now..... (1) **Noun,** "*Now* is the accepted time;" "Eternity is a never-ending *now.*" (2) **Adv.,** "Come *now.*" (3) **Conj.,** "*Now,* Barabbas was a robber."

Once .... (1) **Noun,** "Forgive me just this *once.*" (2) **Adv.,** "He visits us *once* a year."

Only . ... (1) **Adj.,** "Is this the *only* hotel in town?" (2) **Adv.,** "I sing *only,* I can not play."

Over . ... (1) **Adv.,** "They passed *over;*" "Turn *over* a new leaf." (2) **Prep.,** "We drove *over* the bridge;" "*Over* the hills." (3) Part of a **comp. prep.,** "*Over against* this mountain."

Right ... (1) **Noun,** "The *right* will finally triumph;" "I stand here on my *right;*" "Our *rights.*" (2) **Adj.,** "The *right* man in the *right* place;" "You are *right.*" (3) **Adv.,** "*Right* Reverend;" "Let thine eyes look *right* on."

Save..... (1) **Verb,** "Now *save* a nation and now *save* a groat." (2) **Prep.,** "Of the Jews, five times received I forty stripes *save* one." (3) **Conj.,** "And that no man might buy or sell *save* he that had the mark."—*Rev.* xiii, 17.

So.... ...(1) **Adv.,** "Why are you *so* angry?" "He said *so.*" (2) **Conj.,** "As in Adam all die, *so* in Christ shall all be made alive."

That .... (1) **Adj.,** "Watch *that* man;" "*That* house is sold;" "This is as good soil as *that.*" (2) **Rel. pron.,** "Ye *that* fear the Lord, bless the Lord;" "It was I, not he, *that* did it." (3) **Conj.,** "He heard *that* his friend was sick;" "Treat it kindly *that* it may wish with us to stay."

The . . . . . (1) **Article,** "*The* stars." (2) **Adv.,** "*The* more, *the* better." (3) When *the* modifies an adverb, it forms with it an **adv. phrase**; as, "I like you *the better* for that."

Then . . . . (1) **Noun,** "Alas, the change twixt *now* and *then*." (2) **Adv.,** "We *then* ascended the tower." (3) **Conj.,** "If you do not want it, *then* do not buy it."

There . . . (1) **Adv.,** "I live *there*;" "Grass grows *there* now." (2) **Expletive,** used to introduce a sentence in a particular way; as, "*There* were three of us."

Till . . . . . (1) **Noun,** "The money was in the *till*." (2) **Verb,** "Farmers *till* the ground." (3) **Prep.,** "Stay *till* next Monday." (4) **Conj. adv.,** "Stay *till* I return."

Up . . . . . . (1) **Noun,** "The *ups* and *downs* of life are many." (2) **Adv.,** "Go *up*, baldhead." (3) **Prep.,** "They sailed *up* the river."

Well . . . . . (1) **Noun,** "The *well* is sixty feet deep." (2) **Verb,** "Blood that *welled* from the wound." (3) **Adj.,** "Is it *well* with thee?" (4) **Adv.,** "The work was *well* done." (5) **Ind. adv.,** "*Well*, what do you say?"

What . . . . (1) **Rel. pron.,** "Pay *what* you owe." (2) **Int. pron.,** "*What* pleases you?" (3) **Adj.,** "*What* vessel is that?" (4) **Adv.,** "*What* [partly] with entreaty, *what* with threatening, I succeeded." (5) **Interj.,** "*What!* is thy servant a dog?"

When . . . . (1) **Noun,** "Since *when* was it?" (2) **Adv.,** "*When* you were there." (3) **Conj. adv.,** "Write *when* you reach Boston." So, *where*.

Which . . . (1) **Rel. pron.,** "The house in *which* I live." (2) **Int. pron.,** "*Which* is he?" (3) **Adj.,** "*Which* road shall I take?" So, *who*.

While . . . (1) **Noun,** "That is worth *while*." (2) **Verb,** "We will *while* away an hour." (3) **Adv.,** "*While* waiting for the train." (4) **Conj. adv.,** "We listened *while* he played."

Worse . . . (1) **Noun,** "For better or *worse*." (2) **Adj.,** "He is *worse* to-day." (3) **Adv.,** "He might do *worse*."

Worth . . . (1) **Noun,** "They have lost their dignity and *worth*." (2) **Verb,** an old imperative of a word meaning *to be*, "Woe *worth* the day." (3) **Adj.,** "He is *worth* a million."

Yet ..... (1) **Adv.**, "Our country *yet* remains." (2) **Conj.**, "I am disappointed, *yet* not discouraged."

Yonder .. (1) **Adj.**, "*Yonder* mountain." (2) **Adv.**, "Who beckons to us *yonder.*"

Rem. 1.—Nouns may perform an adjective use, and still be regarded as nouns; as, "The *sun's* rays;" "*Gen. Harrison's* residence;" "Peter the *Hermit;*" "Dionysius the *Tyrant.*"

Rem. 2.—By being placed before the words which they modify, nouns may be used as adjectives; as, "Our *Indian* summer;" "*Christmas* eve;" "*Strawberry* short-cake." Nouns thus used may be modified by adjectives; as, "The *High* Church Party;" "The *Protective* Tariff Bill."

A compound expression may be formed by uniting two nouns, or a noun and an adjective, by a hyphen; as, "*Fire-clay* brick;" "*air-pump* experiments;" "a *white-oak* pail;" "a white *oak-pail.*" In all cases, the limiting noun must be in the singular number; as, "A *four-rod* chain;" "a *ten-foot* pole." "This medicine cures *lung*-diseases;" "a *spectacle*-maker;" "a *scissor*-bill."

A compound expression may be formed of an indefinite number of words, joined by hyphens, the entire phrase being used as a single word; as, "The *Kansas-Nebraska* Bill;" "an *out-and-out* falsehood;" "He was dressed in *brown-once-black.*"

Rem. 3.—Nouns connected by conjunctions frequently form a compound term, which must be regarded as a *single* thing, though composed of distinct parts; as, "*Three dollars a day and board* is all I ask;" "A *horse and wagon* was stolen."

Rem. 4.—Phrases, inseparable in thought, may be formed by uniting prepositions with themselves or other parts of speech.

1. A *verb* and *preposition;* as, *to cast up, to buy off, to bring to, to come to, to go over,* &c. The preposition should be considered an inseparable part of the verb, but it may be parsed as an adverb.

2. A *preposition* and *adjective;* as, *on high, at large, in earnest, at most,* &c.: inseparable phrases, either adjective or adverbial.

3. *Preposition* and *preposition;* as, *over and over, by and by, in and in, through and through,* &c.: inseparable adverbial phrases.

4. *Noun, preposition,* and *noun;* as, *day by day, face to face, stride by stride, cheek by jowl,* &c. As the expressiveness of these phrases is destroyed by supplying any ellipsis, they should be

classed among inseparable adverbial phrases. If preferred, however, each word may be parsed separately, the first noun being made the object of a preposition understood.

Rem. 5—Two prepositions frequently come together: in which case they form a complex preposition; the first in order is an adverb, or both are adverbs; as, "He comes *from over* (*complex preposition*) the sea;" "They rode *by* (*adverb*) *in* a carriage;" "The whole subject was gone *over with*" (both *adverbs*.)

Rem. 6.—Two or more conjunctions may come together: in which case each has its use, which should always be regarded in parsing: as, "*Now when* even had come;" "*And so* I penned it down."

228. Exercises.

1. He has been ill since November. 2. I will go, provided he sends for me. 3. Can you not still this noise? 4. The rain still continues. 5. The before-mentioned facts are before you. 6. Does he live anywhere in Ohio? 7. This boy is full ten years old. 8. I never saw a saw saw a saw as that saw saws a saw. 9. What with the bread, and what with the water, he sustained himself for several weeks. 10. Give me such as I bargained for, and as much as I bargained for.

11. What, then, could be done? 12. He has come round. 13. That man purchased a round of beef. 14. The weight of this box is forty pounds. 15. The stars are out by twos and threes. 16. Whether is greater, the gold or the temple? 17. Sing unto the Lord, O ye saints of his. 18. No man can come unto me except the Father draws him. 19. He maketh me to lie down in green pastures. 20. They have promised, yet they do not perform. 21. One came, methought, and whispered in my ear.

22. He that catches at more than belongs to him, justly deserves to lose what he has. 23. All this, I heard as one half dead; but answer had I none to words so true, save tears for my sins. 24. Dreaming, she knew it was a dream. 25. I have told what, and how true thou art. 26. He thought only of his subject. 27. The path of glory leads but to the grave. 28. Kings will be tyrants from policy when subjects are rebels from principle. 29. Angling is somewhat like poetry: men are apt to be born so.— *Walton.*

30. And the final event to himself has been that, as he rose like a rocket, he fell like the stick.—*Paine.* 31. There shall

nothing die of all that is the children's of Israel. 32. We have just come from Brown and Starr's. 33. Three times seven are twenty-one. 34. I paid thirty-seven and a half cents for butter this morning. 35. Wheat is two dollars a bushel. 36. That hill is four miles off. 37. He ran the train at the rate of forty miles an hour. 38. The more I see of him the better I like him.

39. Let your communication be yea, yea, and nay, nay. 40. As far as the east is from the west, so far hath He removed our transgressions from us. 41. Therefore, if thine enemy hunger, feed him; if he thirst, give him drink: for in so doing, thou shalt heap coals of fire on his head. 42. It is good for us to be here. 43. Consider the lilies of the field, how they grow; they toil not, neither do they spin. 44. A little one shall become a thousand, and a small one a strong nation. 45. If I forget thee, O Jerusalem, let my right hand forget her cunning.

46. Hitherto shalt thou come, but no further. 47. Yet man is born unto trouble, as the sparks fly upward. 48. One fault he has; I know but only one. 49. "Madam," said I emphatically, "you are in an error." 50. In this case, it will vanish by degrees. 51. To be a foreigner, was always in England a reason of dislike. 52. How feeble were the attempts at planting towns, is evident from the nature of the tenure by which the lands near the Saco were held.—*Bancroft.* 53. This is—what shall we call it? 54. It is he, even he. 55. He was not even invited to be present.

56. Are you fond of skating?—Somewhat. 57. Is your health good, now?—Rather so. 58. The garret was filled with broken chairs, cast-off garments, and what not. 59. He gave me such a warm reception. 60. How long was it before the man came to?— About three-quarters of an hour. 61. How did he come by his property? 62. No quips, now, Pistol: indeed I am in the waist two yards about. 63. That's certain; I for my part knew the tailor that made the wings she flew withal.

64. He that will not when he may,
    When he would, he shall have nay.

65. Then say not man's imperfect, Heaven in fault;
    Say, rather, man's as perfect as he ought.—*Pope.*

66. For what is worth in any thing
    But so much money as 't will bring?—*Butler.*

67. O, what a tangled web we weave,
    When first we practice to deceive.—*Scott.*

68. The swan on still St. Mary's lake,
    Float double, swan and shadow.—*Wordsworth.*

69. In the hexameter rises the fountain's silvery column,
    In the pentameter aye falling in melody back.—*Coleridge.*

70. Here lies what once was Matthew Prior;
    The son of Adam and Eve:
    Can Bourbon or Nassau claim higher?—*Matt. Prior.*

71. "Moreover, it is written that my race
    Hewed Ammon, hip and thigh, from Aroer
    On Arnon unto Minnith." Here her face
    Glowed as I looked at her.—*Tennyson.*

72. I can not tell what you and other men
    Think of this life; but for my single self,
    I had as lief not be as live to be
    In awe of such a thing as I myself.—*Shakspeare.*

73. Think for thyself—one good idea,
    But known to be thine own,
    Is better than a thousand gleaned
    From fields by others sown.—*Wilson.*

74. So we were left galloping, Joris and I,
    Past Looz and past Tongres, no cloud in the sky:
    The broad sun above laughed a pitiless laugh;
    'Neath our feet broke the brittle bright stubble like chaff;
    Till over by Dalhem a dome-spire sprang white,
    And "Gallop," gasped Joris, "for Aix is in sight."
    Browning.

75. Fate seemed to wind him up for four-score years:
    Yet proudly ran he on ten winters more:
    Till like a clock worn out with eating time,
    The wheels of weary life at last stood still.—*Dryden.*

76.   This well may be
    The Day of Judgment which the world awaits;
    But, be it so or not, I only know
    My present duty, and my Lord's command
    To occupy till he come. So at the post
    Where he hath set me in his providence,
    I choose for one to meet him face to face,—
    No faithless servant frightened from my task,
    But ready when the Lord of the harvest calls.—*Whittier.*

FIGURES OF LANGUAGE.

229. Definitions.

1. A **Figure of Speech** is a departure from the ordinary form, regular construction, or literal signification of words.

2. A **Figure of Etymology** is a departure from the usual *form* of a word.

3. A **Figure of Syntax** is a departure from the usual *construction* of words.

4. A **Figure of Rhetoric** is a departure from the primitive or literal *sense* of a word.

230. Figures of Etymology.

1. **Apheresis** is the elision of a letter or syllable from the beginning of a word; as, *'gainst,* for *against; 'gan,* for *began.*

2. **Prosthesis** is the prefixing of a letter or syllable to a word; as, *adown,* for *down; beloved,* for *loved.*

3. **Syncope** is the omission of one or more letters in the middle of a word; as, *ne'er,* for *never; slumb'ring,* for *slumbering.*

4. **Tmesis** is the separation of a compound word by the insertion of a word between its parts; as, *to* us *ward,* for *toward* us; *how* high *soever,* for *howsoever* high.

5. **Apocope** is the omission of the last letter or syllable of a word; as, *th',* for *the; yond,* for *yonder.*

6. **Paragoge** is the addition of a letter or syllable to the end of a word; as, *bounden,* for *bound; withouten,* for *without.*

7. **Syneresis** is the contraction of two syllables into one; as, *do n't,* for *do not; can 't,* for *can not.*

8. **Dieresis** is the separation of two vowel letters which might otherwise form a diphthong or digraph; as, *aërial, preëminent.*

231. Figures of Syntax.

1. **Ellipsis** is the omission of a word, phrase, or clause which is necessary to complete the construction of a sentence.

Note.—For examples of Ellipsis, see § 190.

2. **Pleonasm** is the use of more words than are necessary.

Ex.—"I saw it *with these eyes.*" "All ye *inhabitants* of the world, and *dwellers on the earth.*"

Rem. 1.—**Polysyndeton** is the repetition of a conjunction; as, "He is good, *and* wise, *and* generous."

Rem. 2.—**Asyndeton** is the omission of connective words in a sentence.

Ex.—"I came, I saw, I conquered;" "He is wise, honest, faithful;" "We walked slowly, noiselessly, with bated breath."

Rem. 3.—**Anadiplosis** is the use of the same word or expression in the termination of one clause of a sentence, and at the beginning of the next.

Ex.—"Has he a gust for *blood? Blood* shall fill his cup."

Rem. 4.—**Epizeuxis** is the emphatic repetition of the same word or words.

Ex.—*Alone, alone, all, all alone,*
Alone on a wide, wide sea.—*Coleridge.*

3. **Enallage** is the use of one part of speech, or of one form, for another.

Ex.—*We,* for *I; you,* for *thou; "Slow* [*slowly*] rises worth;" "What is *writ* is *writ.*"

4. **Hyperbaton** is the transposition of words from the plain grammatical order.

Ex.—"He wanders *earth around;*" "From peak to peak, *the rattling crags among;*" "*Lightly* from fair to fair *he flew.*"

5. **Syllepsis** is the agreement of one word with the figurative sense of another.

Ex.—"The *Word* was made flesh, and dwelt among us: and we beheld *his* glory."—*John* i, 14. "A dauntless *soul* erect, *who* smiles on death."—*Thomson.*

6. **Parenthesis** is the insertion of a word or sentence between the parts of another sentence.

Ex.—"Every planet, (for God has made nothing in vain,) is most probably inhabited."

7. **Zeugma** is a figure by which an adjective or verb, which agrees with a nearer word, is referred to one more remote.

Ex.—"Lust overcame shame; boldness, fear; and madness, reason."

232. Figures of Rhetoric.

1. **Simile** is an express or formal comparison.

Ex.— *Like a dog,* he hunts in dreams.—*Tennyson.*

> Then felt I *like some watcher of the skies*
> When a new planet swims into his ken;
> Or *like stout Cortez,* when with eagle eyes
> He stared at the Pacific.—*Keats.*

2. **Metaphor** is the expression of similitude without the signs of comparison.

Ex.—"A *flash* of wit;" "A *sea* of troubles;" "The moralist is a *scout* for consequences;" "The wish is *father* to the thought."

3. **Personification** consists in attributing life and mind to inanimate objects.

Ex.—"O *Winter!* ruler of the inverted year;" "The *earth* mourneth and fadeth away."

> "Yes, the *Year* is growing old,
> And his eye is pale and bleared:
> *Death,* with frosty hand and cold,
> Plucks the *old man* by the beard,
> Sorely, sorely!"—*Longfellow.*

4. Allegory is a discourse in which one subject is described by another resembling it.

Ex.—The Pilgrim's Progress; Spencer's Faerie Queene; Swift's Tale of a Tub; The Vision of Mirza.

Rem. 1.—A **Fable** is a short allegory.

Ex.—Æsop's and La Fontaine's Fables. Most fables are short stories about certain animals that are regarded as representatives of particular qualities; as, the fox, of cunning; the lion, of strength.

Rem. 2.—A **Parable** is a relation of something real in nature from which a moral is drawn.

Ex.—Parable of the Poor Man and his Lamb.—2 *Sam.* xii, 1–5. Of the Sower.—*Matt.* xiii. Of the Ten Virgins.—*Matt.* xxv.

5. Synecdoche is a figure by which the whole is put for a part, or a part for the whole; a species for a genus, or a genus for a species, &c.

Ex.—*Roof,* for house or dwelling; *bread,* for food generally; *cut-throat,* for assassin.

> "Belinda smiled and *all the world* was gay."—*Pope.*

Rem. 1.—**Antonomasia** is the use of a proper name for a common name, or the name of some office, rank, profession, trade, or peculiarity, instead of the true name of a people or class.

Ex.—"He is a *Buckeye*," *i. e.,* an Ohioan; "The *Crescent City,*" *i. c.,* New Orleans.

> "Some mute, inglorious *Milton* here may rest,
> Some *Cromwell,* guiltless of his country's blood."

Rem. 2.—**Euphemism** is the substitution of a delicate word or expression for one which is harsh or offensive.

Ex.—*Departed, gone to rest, fallen asleep,* for *dead; stopped payment,* for *become bankrupt; embezzlement,* for *theft.*

> "Sleep had seized her senses.
> There did the traveler find her in the morning:
> *Death had released her.*"—*Southey.*

6. Metonymy is a change of names, or a figure by which one word is put for another.

Ex.—*Gray hairs,* for *old age; purse,* for *money; fare,* for a *passenger; city,* for its *inhabitants;* "Ye devour widow's *houses;*" "They have *Moses* and the *prophets.*"

7. Antithesis is the opposition of words and sentiments contained in the same sentence.

Ex.—"*Excess* of ceremony shows *want* of breeding;" "Wit laughs *at* things; Humor laughs *with* them."—*Whipple.*

> "Men may come and men may go,
> But I go on *forever.*"—*Tennyson.*

8. Epigram is a sentence in which the form of the language contradicts the meaning conveyed.

Ex.—"I can not see the city for the houses." "Summer has set in with its usual severity."—*Walpole.* "Any thing awful always makes me laugh."—*Lamb.* "Nothing so fallacious as facts, except figures."—*Canning.* "I believe it, because it is impossible."

Rem. 1.—The Epigram awakens attention by the seeming irrelevance of the assertion, or by the form given to it.

Rem. 2.—The **Paronomasia,** or **Pun,** is a play on the various meanings of the same word.

Ex.—A friend of Curran, hearing a person near him say *curosity* instead of *curiosity,* exclaimed, "How that man murders the English language!" "Not so bad," said Curran, "He has only knocked an *i* out."

Rem. 3.—The **Conundrum** is a sort of riddle, in which some odd resemblance between things unlike is proposed for discovery.

9. Hyperbole is an exaggeration of the meaning in-

tended to be conveyed, by magnifying objects beyond their proper bounds.

Ex.—"Rivers of water run down mine eyes because they keep not thy law." "The land flows with milk and honey." "The English gain two hours a day by clipping words."—*Voltaire*.

10. **Interrogation** is the putting in the form of a question what is meant to be strongly affirmative.

Ex.—"Canst thou by searching find out God?"

"Oh, who can hold a fire in his hand,
By thinking on the frosty Caucasus?
Or cloy the hungry edge of appetite
By bare imagination of a feast?"—*Shakspeare*.

11. **Climax** is an arrangement of the parts of a sentence, by which they are made to rise step by step in interest or importance.

Ex.—"It is an outrage to *bind* a Roman citizen; to *scourge* him is an atrocious crime; to *put him to death* is almost a parricide; but to *crucify* him—what shall I call it?"—*Cicero*.

Rem.—**Anti-climax** is any great departure from the order required in climax.

Ex.—"That all-softening, overpowering knell,
The tocsin of the soul—the dinner-bell."—*Byron*.

"Die, and endow a college or a cat."—*Pope*.

12. **Exclamation** is the animated or impassioned expression of sudden and intense emotion.

Ex.—"Oh, what a pity!" "A horse, a horse, my kingdom for a horse!" "Blow, winds, and crack your cheeks!"

13. **Apostrophe** is the turning away from the real auditory, and addressing an absent or imaginary one.

Ex.—"Ye winds that wafted the Pilgrims to the land of promise, fan, in their children's hearts, the love of freedom!"—*Everett*.

"Ye toppling crags of ice!
Ye avalanches, whom a breath draws down,
In mountainous overwhelming, come and crush me."—*Byron*.

Rem.—Hypotyposis, or **Vision,** is a description of things in such strong and lively colors, as to bring the absent before the mind with the force of present reality.

Ex.—"I see the rural virtues leave the land."—*Goldsmith.* "Greece cries to us by the convulsed lips of her poisoned, dying Demosthenes."—*Everett.*

14. **Innuendo** is a covert suggestion of an author's meaning, instead of an open expression of it.

Ex.—"What evil have I done that *he* should *praise* me?" "He did his party all the harm in his power: he *spoke for it,* and *voted against it."*

15. **Irony** is a mode of expression by which what is said is contrary to what is meant.

Ex.—"No doubt but ye are the people, and wisdom will die with you."

"And on our City Hall a justice stands:
  A neater form was never made of board;
Holding majestically in her hands
  A pair of steelyards and a wooden sword,
And looking down with complaisant civility—
Emblem of dignity and durability."—*Halleck.*

Rem.—Sarcasm is a keen, reproachful, and scornful expression.

Ex.—"Who but must laugh, if such a man there be?
  Who would not weep if Atticus were he?"—*Pope.*

16. **Litotes** is a mode of expressing something by denying the contrary.

Ex.—"Nor are thy lips ungrateful, sire of men,
  Nor tongue inadequate: for God on thee
Abundantly his gifts hath also poured."—*Milton.*

17. **Catachresis** is wresting a word from its original signification, and making it express something at variance with its true meaning.

Ex.—"*Silver* curling-*irons;*" "A *glass* ink-*horn;*" "Her voice as but the *shadow of a sound."*—*Young.*

PUNCTUATION.

233. Definition.

1. **Punctuation** is the art of dividing written dis-course into sentences and parts of sentences, by means of points or marks.

Rem. 1.—Points are principally used for the purpose of ren-dering the sense more intelligible. They do not mark all the pauses made in reading, though a pause is generally made where a point is used.

Rem. 2.—A change in the punctuation of a sentence, generally produces a change in the meaning.

Ex.—John Keys the lawyer says he is guilty.
John, Keys the lawyer says he is guilty.
John Keys, the lawyer says he is guilty.
"John Keys the lawyer," says he, "is guilty."

2. The principal marks used in punctuation are the following:

Comma, ... ,	Exclamation Point, **!**
Semicolon, . . . ;	Dash, ... ―
Colon, ... :	Curves, ... ( )
Period, ...	Brackets, ... [ ]
Interrogation Point, ?	

234. The Comma.

The **Comma** denotes the slightest degree of separation between the elements of a sentence.

Rule I.—A complex subject, if long, should be sep-arated from the predicate by a comma.

Ex.—The patriarchal church, inconsiderable in size and mean in decoration, stands on the outermost islet of the Venetian group.—*Ruskin.*

Rule II.—A clause used as subject, if it ends with a verb, should be separated from the predicate by a comma.

Ex.—1. Whatever is, is right. 2. Whosoever perseveres, will succeed.

Rule III.—Nouns and pronouns in the absolute case by pleonasm or direct address, should be separated from the rest of the sentence by commas.

Ex.—1. Our souls, how heavily they go, to reach immortal joys. 2. Take, O boatman, thrice thy fee. 3. Think of that, Master Brook.

Rule IV.—Adjective, participial, appositive, and absolute phrases, should be separated from the context by commas.

Ex.—1. Faithful to his promise, he assisted me in obtaining employment. 2. Having once lost the good opinion of our friends, it is difficult for us to reclaim it. 3. The maxim, "Enough is as good as a feast," has silenced many a vain wish. 4. The storm having ceased, we weighed anchor and set sail.

Rem. 1.—Nouns in apposition, unmodified, or modified by *the* only, are not separated by commas; as, "The Emperor Nero was a cruel tyrant;" "Thomson the poet was indolent."

Rem. 2.—An appositive word or expression introduced by *as* or *or*, should be set off by a comma; as, "So that he, as God, sitteth in the temple of God;" "Maize, or Indian corn, is a staple production of the United States."

Rule V.—Transposed words, phrases, and clauses are usually set off by commas.

Ex.—1. Doubtless, the man is guilty: the evidence, however, is not conclusive. 2. Now, faith is the substance of things hoped for, the evidence of things not seen. 3. Integrity is, no doubt, the first requisite. 4. Whom ye ignorantly worship, Him declare I unto you.

Rem. 1.—A transposed objective element is not usually set off by a comma; as, "That book he has never returned."

Rem. 2.—When an inverted expression begins with *it is* or *only*, it is not set off by a comma; as, "It is a pleasant thing to see

H. G. 20.

the sun;" "Only on slight occasions they felt disposed to be merciful."

Rule VI.—Parenthetical words, phrases, and clauses should be separated from the rest of the sentence by commas.

Rem.—A parenthetical word or expression is one which is not essential to the grammatical construction of a sentence, but is required to express its full meaning.

Ex.—1. He invented, it is said, the theory of moral science. 2. That excitement, too, was of the most dangerous kind. 3. Their great predecessors, it is true, were as bad critics as themselves.

Rule VII.—Adverbs used independently, or modifying an entire proposition, should be set off by commas.

Ex.—1. Yea, the earth itself shall pass away. 2. Well, if this is law, I want no more of it. 3. Indeed, you must wait awhile.

Rule VIII.—When a verb is omitted to avoid repetition, its place is usually supplied by a comma.

Ex.—1. One murder makes a villain; millions, a hero. 2. War is the law of violence; peace, the law of love. 3. The young are slaves to novelty; the old, to custom; the middle-aged, to both; the dead, to neither.

Rem.—There are many exceptions to this rule. The general practice is, to omit the comma unless clearness and precision demand its insertion; as, "Reading maketh a full man, conference a ready man, and writing an exact man."—*Bacon.*

Rule IX.—Antithetical words, phrases, and clauses should be separated by commas.

Ex.—1. Talent has many a compliment from the bench, but tact touches fees. 2. Strong proofs, not a loud voice, produce conviction. 3. Though deep, yet clear; though gentle, yet not dull.

Rule X.—The members of compound sentences, when short and connected by conjunctions, should be separated by commas.

Ex.—The simplicity of his character inspired confidence, the ardor of his eloquence roused enthusiasm, and the gentleness of his manners invited friendship.

Rule XI.—Two correlative clauses should be separated by commas.

Ex.—As the lightning that lighteneth out of the one part under heaven, shineth unto the other part under heaven, so shall the Son of Man be in his day.

Rem.—Two correlative clauses, joined by *as* or *than*, should not be separated by a comma; as, "She is as old as he?" "A good name is rather to be chosen than great riches."

Rule XII.—The clauses of complex sentences should be separated by commas, unless the dependent clauses are very short and the connection very close.

Ex.—1. Men of great and stirring powers, who are destined to mold the age in which they are born, must first mold themselves upon it.—*Coleridge.* 2. I took notice, in particular, of a very profligate fellow, who, I did not question, came loaded with his crimes; but upon searching his bundle, I found that, instead of throwing his guilt from him, he had only laid down his memory.—*Addison.*

Rule XIII.—When words are arranged in pairs, each couplet should be set off by commas.

Ex.—1. Hope and fear, pleasure and pain, diversify our lives. 2. Sink or swim, live or die, I give my hand and my heart to this vote.

Rule XIV.—Each term of a series of words in the same construction, should be set off by commas.

Ex.—1. War, peace, darts, spears, towns, rivers, every thing, in his writings, is alive.

2. Sky, mountains, river, winds, lake, lightnings! ye
    With night, and clouds, and thunder, and a soul
  To make these felt and feeling, well may be
    Things that have made me watchful.—*Byron.*

Rem.—Two words, closely connected by a conjunction, should not be separated; as, "Honor and fame from no condition rise."

Rule XV.—The terms of a coördinate series, used as the antecedent of a relative pronoun, should be set off by commas, to show that the relative belongs equally to each term.

Ex.—The oxygen, nitrogen, and carbonic acid, which unite to form the atmosphere, are mingled in unequal proportions.

Rule XVI.—A direct quotation, separated by a principal clause, should be set off by commas.

Ex.—1. "Oh, Mr. Pickwick," said Mrs. Bardell, trembling with agitation, "you're very kind, sir." 2. "Sir," said Mr. Adams, "my definition of charity is, a generous disposition to relieve the distressed."

Rule XVII.—A quoted sentence, a long infinitive phrase, or an indirect quotation, introduced by *that*, should usually be set off by a comma.

Ex.—1. He asked, "Why are you so melancholy?" 2. I have heard say of thee, that thou canst understand a dream to interpret it. 3. To correct such gross vices as lead us to commit a real injury to others, is the part of morals, and the object of the most ordinary education.—*Hume.*

Rule XVIII.—Words repeated for emphasis should be set off by commas.

Ex.—1. Verily, verily, I say unto you. 2. "Treason, treason, treason," reëchoed from every part of the house.

Rule XIX.—Whenever ambiguity would arise from its omission, a comma should be inserted.

Ex.—1. I have a house with nine rooms, and out-buildings. 2. He has seven yoke of oxen, and horses.

EXERCISES.

Insert commas wherever required in these sentences:

1. A man who does so care has a garment embroidered with hooks which catches at every thing that passes by. 2. There were burly tradesmen with an air of quiet satisfaction sauntering about or leaning against railings. 3. Come Rollo—let us take a walk.

4. Ill-sorted marriages will hardly bring agreement and from those of convenience will hardly come love. **5.** We often commend as well as censure imprudently.

6. The deaf and the blind and the lame were there. **7.** The rich and the poor—the high and the low—the learned and the unlearned—have access alike to this fountain of peace. **8.** It shows a love breaking through the reserve and distance which we all feel to belong to the method of teaching us by his works alone. **9.** I see then in revelation a purpose corresponding with that for which human teaching was instituted. **10.** The oranges, lemons and figs which grow in the northern range of the Southern States are of an inferior quality.

11. "Think you Abel" said Paul at last " that the storm drove thither?" **12.** Yes, I am sure it is so. **13.** As it was then so it is now. **14.** If one burden can be borne so can another and another. **15.** He that seeketh findeth. **16.** I lisped in numbers for the numbers came. **17.** Concession is no humiliation nor admission of error any disgrace. **18.** The idle want steadiness of purpose; the indolent power of exertion. **19.** It was said of Socrates that he brought philosophy down from heaven to dwell among men.

20. "No no no," said she greatly agitated. **21.** He plagues you with no doubts no half views no criticism. **22.** Daniel Webster the great American statesman died at Marshfield Mass. **23.** An indirect advantage but a very considerable one attendant upon various modes of recreation is that they provide opportunities of excelling in something to boys and men who are dull in things which form the staple of education.

235. The Semicolon.

The **Semicolon** denotes a degree of separation greater than that denoted by the comma.

Rule I.—The semicolon should be used before *as, namely, to wit, viz.,* introducing an example or an illustration.

Ex.—1. One part only of an antithesis is sometimes expressed; as, "A friendly eye would never see such faults." 2. Some men distinguish the period of the world into four ages; viz., the golden age, the silver age, the brazen age, and the iron age.

Rule II.—The semicolon is used to separate the members of a compound sentence, when the connective is omitted.

Ex.—The earth glows with the colors of civilization; the banks of the stream are enameled with the richest grasses; woodlands and cultivated fields are harmoniously blended; the birds of spring find their delight in orchards and trim gardens, variegated with choicest plants from every temperate zone; while the brilliant flowers of the tropics bloom from the windows of the green-house and the saloon.—*Bancroft.*

Rule III.—The members of a compound sentence, if long, or if their parts are set off by commas, should be separated by semicolons, even when joined by connectives.

Ex.—1. And he gave some, apostles; and some, prophets; and some, evangelists; and some, pastors and teachers. 2. I only know that I had been torn from my dromedary, borne along, and buried by the sand; and that the young child was still in my arms.—*Ware.*

Rule IV.—Successive clauses having a common dependence, should be separated by semicolons.

Ex.—My imagination would conjure up all that I had heard or read of the watery world beneath me; of the finny tribes that roam in the fathomless valleys; of shapeless monsters that lurk among the very foundations of the earth; and those wild phantasms that swell the tales of fishermen and sailors.—*Irving.*

Rem.—This rule applies, also, to a series of phrases, some one of which is composed of parts separated by commas; as, "To be delivered from trouble; to be relieved from power; to see oppression humbled; to be freed from sickness and distress; to lie down as in a bed of security, in a long oblivion of our woes; to sleep in peace without the fear of interruption;—how pleasing the prospect!"

Rule V.—An inferential, contrasted, or explanatory clause, introduced by *for, but, and,* or an equivalent connective, is usually set off by a semicolon.

Ex.—1. Rejoice the soul of thy servant; for unto thee, O Lord,

I lift up my soul. 2. The person he chanced to see, was, to appearance, an old, sordid, blind man; but upon his following him from place to place, he at last found, by his own confession, that he was Plutus, the god of riches, and that he was just come out of the house of a miser.

Rem.—When the clauses are short, the semicolon is frequently replaced by the comma; as, "I go, but I return;" "They had not come in search of gain, for the soil was sterile and unproductive."

EXERCISES.

Insert semicolons wherever required in these sentences:

1. A Scotch mist becomes a shower, and a shower, a flood, and a flood, a storm, and a storm, a tempest, and a tempest, thunder and lightning, and thunder and lightning, heaven-quake and earth-quake.

2. And besides this, giving all diligence, add to your faith, virtue, and to virtue, knowledge, and to knowledge, temperance, and to temperance, patience, and to patience, godliness, and to godliness, brotherly kindness, and to brotherly kindness, charity.

3. Wit is abrupt, darting, scornful, and tosses its analogies in your face, Humor is slow and shy, insinuating its fun into your heart. 4. An enigma is a dark saying, an obscure question, a riddle.

5. I take no notice of his brutal conduct, I do not speak of his treachery and malice. 6. Never value yourself upon your fortune for this is the sign of a weak mind. 7. He has two farms namely a large one and a small one.

236. The Colon.

The **Colon** denotes a degree of separation greater than that indicated by the semicolon.

Rule I.—The colon should be used after the formal introduction to a speech, a course of reasoning, a lengthy quotation, or an enumeration of particulars.

Ex.—1. Then closing the book, he proceded in a lower tone: "The philosophers of whom you have read in the dictionary, possessed this wisdom only in part, because they were heathens."

2. The reason of things, also, doth help to explain these words, and to show why they are prohibited: because these harsh terms are needless; because they are commonly unjust; because they are uncharitable; because, also, they produce mischievous effects.

3. Be our plain answer this: the throne we honor is the people's choice; the laws we reverence are our brave father's legacy; the faith we follow teaches us to live in bonds of charity with all mankind, and die with hope of bliss beyond the grave.

Rule II.—The colon should be used before an explanatory remark, or one which presents the meaning of the preceding sentence in another form.

Ex.—1. All reasoning is retrospective: it consists in the application of facts and principles previously known. 2. By degrees he infuses into it the poison of his own ambition: he breathes into it the fire of his own courage.

Rule III.—The members of a compound sentence, whose parts are phrases or clauses set off by semicolons, should be separated by colons.

Ex.—We do not say that his error lies in being a good member of society; this, though only a circumstance at present, is a very fortunate one: the error lies in his having discarded the authority of God, as his legislator; or, rather, in his not having admitted the influence of that authority over his mind, heart, or practice.

EXERCISES.

Insert colons wherever required in these sentences:

1. There are five senses, sight, hearing, feeling, taste, and smell. 2. The discourse consisted of two parts, in the first was shown the necessity of exercise; in the second, the advantages that would result from it. 3. Men's evil manners live in brass, their virtues we write in water. 4. Write on your slates the following example, the lake is very deep.

5. He sunk to repose where the red heaths are blended;
   One dream of his childhood his fancy passed o'er,
   But his battles are fought, and his march it is ended;
   The sound of the bagpipe shall wake him no more.

237. The Period.

The **Period** denotes the greatest degree of separation.

Rule I.—The period should be placed at the end of a declarative or imperative sentence.

Ex.—1. Contrivance proves design.   2. Study diligently.

Rem.—A period is sometimes placed at the end of the first of two or more complete sentences joined by conjunctions; as, "Seeing, then, that these things can not be spoken against, ye ought to be quiet, and to do nothing rashly. For ye have brought hither these men, who are neither robbers of churches, nor yet blasphemers of your goddess."

Rule II.—The period should be placed at the end of every abbreviated word.

Ex.—1. H. M. Swainson, Esq., b. Feb. 10, 1757, d. Ap. 3, 1812. 2. See Ms., pp. 5 and 6.

Rem. 1.—The period, thus used, is a part of the abbreviation. Except at the end of a sentence, the point required by the construction should be used after it; as, "Sir Humphrey Davy, F. R. S., &c.;" "Ohio is bounded N. by Mich. and L. E.; E. by Pa. and Va.; S. by Va. and Ky.; W. by Ind."

Rem. 2.—Some proper names, though shortened, should not be regarded as abbreviations; as, "Tom Moore;" "Will Shakspeare;" "O rare Ben Jonson."

Rem. 3.—Such expressions as 4to, 8vo, 12mo, 1st, 2d, 3d, 5's, 11's, 4°, 7′, &c., are not abbreviations. The figures supply the place of the first letters of the words, and the signs or indices supply the place of words.

Rem. 4.—The period should be placed before decimals, and between the denominations of sterling money; as, $35.75; £5. 12s. 6d.

Rem. 5.—The period should always be placed after letters used as numerals; as, Ps. lxxv., 6, 7.; George III., King of England.

Rem. 6.—The period should be placed at the end of titles, headings, &c.; as, "Concerning Veal." "Hopkins & Co." "The Preposition." "Chap. XXVII."

H. G. 21.

EXERCISES.

Insert periods wherever required in these sentences:

1. It was a past that never was present   2. By indignities men come to dignities   3. D. K. Merwin Esq was chosen chairman   4. H C Cartwright b A D 1825, d Feb 2, 1854   5. See Rev xii 11.   6. Chapter XX § IV Part II   7. It cost in London, £6, 7s, 8d.

238. The Interrogation Point.

The **Interrogation Point** denotes that a question is asked.

Rule I.—The interrogation point should be used at the end of an interrogative sentence.

Ex.—1. Were you there?   2. By whom was this extraordinary work of art executed?

Rem. 1.—When a question is composed of several parts, and when several questions are contained in one sentence, one answer only being required, the interrogation point is placed only at the end; as, "By whom is this profession praised, but by wretches who consider him as subservient to their purposes; sirens that entice him to shipwreck; and cyclops that are gaping to devour him?"

Rem. 2.—The interrogation point should be used after each successive particular of a series of questions, related in sense, but distinct in construction; as, "Why was the French revolution so bloody and destructive? Why was our revolution of 1641 comparatively mild? Why was our revolution of 1688 milder still? Why was the American revolution, considered as an internal movement, the mildest of all?"

239. The Exclamation Point.

The **Exclamation Point** denotes passion or emotion.

Rule I.—The exclamation point should be placed after expressions denoting strong emotion.

Ex.—1. Avaunt, thou witch!   2. Mercy, sir, how the folks will talk of it!   3. Alas, poor Yorick!

Rem.—The exclamation point should not be used after interjections closely connected with other words, but at the end of each expression of which the interjections form a part; as, "Fie upon you!" "All hail, ye patriots brave!"

EXERCISES.

Insert the points required in these sentences:

1. What did my father's godson seek your life He whom my father named 2. See there behold look lo if I stand here I saw him 3. Is this a vision Is this a dream Do I sleep Master Ford awake awake 4. What is civilization—where is it—what does it consist in—by what is it excluded—where does it commence—where does it end—by what sign is it known—how is it defined—in short, what does it mean

240. The Dash.

The **Dash** is a straight, horizontal line, placed between the parts of a sentence.

Rule I.—The dash should be used where there is a sudden break or stop in a sentence, or a change in its meaning or construction.

Ex.—1. Dim—dim—I faint—darkness comes over my eyes. 2. It glitters awhile—and then melts into tears. 3. He stamped and he stormed—then his language!—Oh, dear! 4. Miss frowned, and blushed, and then was—married. 5. The flowers, the fruits, the birds, the woods, the waters, the course, the vicissitudes, and the vast phenomena of nature, created, regulated, and preserved by the mighty hand of an Omnipotent Being—all are legitimate and reasonable sources of enjoyment, within the reach of every rational being.—*Paulding.*

Rule II.—The dash is frequently used before words repeated in an emphatic manner.

Ex.—1. Why should I speak of his neglect—*neglect* did I say? call it rather *contempt*. 2. The consequences which resulted from the events of that day, to us, to this continent, and to the world—consequences which we know must continue, and rain their influ-

ence on the destinies of mankind to the end of time, surpass all
the most arduous study of the closet, and even the inspiration of
genius.— *Webster*.

Rule III.—The dash is frequently placed both before
and after a parenthesis—the curves being omitted.

Ex.—They see three of the cardinal virtues of dog or man—
courage, endurance, and skill—in intense action.

Rem.—A comma should precede each dash used to set off a
parenthetical expression; as, "The archetypes, the ideal forms of
things without,—if not, as some philosophers have said, in a meta-
physical sense, yet in a literal one,—exist within us."

Note.—An interrogation or an exclamation point should precede the second dash, when the parenthetical expression is a
question or denotes emotion.

Rule IV.—The dash is often used where there is an
omission of letters or figures, or of words commonly used
to introduce an enumeration of particulars.

Ex.—1. L—d B—n; *i. e.*, Lord Byron. 2. Ps. xxxv., 6—10; *i. e.*,
Ps. xxxv., 6, 7, 8, 9, 10. 3. Amongst us men, these three things
are a large part of our virtues,—to endure, to forgive, and ourselves to get pardon. 4. He looked like his works,—nimble,
vigorous, and gentle; open, and yet reserved; seeing every thing,
saying not much; capable of heartiest mirth, but generally
quiet.—*Dr. Brown*.

241. The Marks of Parenthesis.

The **Curves** include an expression which has no necessary connection, in sense or construction, with the sentence
in which it is inserted.

Rem.—Such an expression is called a *parenthesis*.

Rule.—The curves should include those words which
may be omitted without injury to the sense, or without
affecting the grammatical construction of the sentence.

Ex.—1. Shall we continue (alas, that I should be constrained to ask the question!) in a course so dangerous to health, so enfeebling to mind, so destructive to character?

    2. The tuneful Nine (so sacred legends tell)
       First waked their heavenly lyre these scenes to tell!

Rem. 1.—When any point is required after the word preceding a parenthesis, it should be placed after the second curve; as, "My gun was on my arm (as it always is in that district), but I let the stoat kill the rabbit."

But, should the parenthesis be a question or an exclamatory expression, the point should be placed before the first curve, and that which belongs to the parenthesis before the second; as, "She had managed this matter so well, (oh, she was the most artful of women!) that my father's heart was gone before I suspected it was in danger."

Rem. 2.—The words included by the curves should be punctuated as an independent expression; as,

    "The Frenchman, first in literary fame,
      (Mention him, if you please.   Voltaire?—The same.)
      With spirit, genius, eloquence supplied,
      Lived long, wrote much, laughed heartily, and died."

Rem. 3.—The curves sometimes include letters or figures used to enumerate subjects or divisions of a subject, treated of in didactic or scientific works; as, "(a.) What it does; (b.) What it is." "The beds of the Jackson epoch, or Upper Eocene, are (1) Lignitic clay; (2) White and blue marls, the former often indurated." They are also used to include references; as, "(See page 21.)" "(§ V., Rem. 7.)" "(247, a., b.)"

EXERCISES.

Insert the dash and the curves wherever required in these sentences:

1. He had a large blunt head; his muzzle black as night, his mouth blacker than any night; a tooth or two, being all he had, gleaming out of his jaws of darkness.   2. The faithful man acts not from impulse but from conviction, conviction of duty, the most stringent, solemn, and inspiring conviction that can sway the mind.

3. Know ye not, brethren, for I speak to them that know the law, that the law hath dominion over a man as long as he liveth?

4. The Egyptian style of architecture see Dr. Pocock, not his discourses, but his prints was apparently the mother of the Greek.

242. Brackets.

Brackets are used to inclose words, phrases, and clauses explanatory of what precedes them, or to correct an error.

Ex.—1. They [the Indians] are fast disappearing. 2. I wish you would do like [as] I do.

243. Other Marks Used in Writing.

I. The **Apostrophe** ['] is used to denote the omission of one or more letters, or to mark the possessive case.

Ex.—1. You 're overwatched, my lord. 2. Variety 's the very spice of life. 3. The King's English. 4. Webster's Dictionary.

Rem.—The apostrophe is also used in forming the plurals of letters, figures, marks, &c.; as, "Dot your i's and cross your t's." "Cast out the 9's." "¶'s and ₰'s."

II. The **Hyphen** [-] is used (1) to join the parts of compound words and expressions; (2) to divide words into syllables; (3) after a syllable at the end of a line, when the rest of the word is carried to the next line.

Ex.—1. Heaven-born band. 2. Thou many-headed monster thing.—*Scott.* 3. He is my father-in-law, and always wears a pepper-and-salt suit. 4. Com-mu-ni-ca-tive-ness.

III. The **Quotation Marks** [" "] are used to show that a passage is taken *verbatim* from some author.

Ex.—Cowper says, "Slaves can not breathe in England."

Rem.—A quotation included within another should be preceded by a single inverted comma and closed by a single apostrophe; as, "'War, war,' is still the cry, 'war even to the knife.'"

IV. The **Index** [☞] and **Asterism** [⁂] point out a passage to which special attention is directed; as, "☞ Do not forget the time and place of meeting."

V. The **Asterisk** [*], the **Obelisk, or Dagger,** [†], the **Double Dagger** [‡], the **Section** [§], the **Parallels** [‖], and the **Paragraph** [¶] refer to notes in the margin, or at the bottom of the page.

Rem.—Lower case letters and figures, of a smaller size, or letters and figures included in curves, are used for reference marks.

VI. A **long dash** [——] or several **asterisks** [* * * *] denote the omission of letters in a word, of words in a sentence, or sentences in a paragraph.

Ex.—Miss M * * * * n. Mr. A——h.

VII. The **Brace** [⏜] connects a number of words with a common term.

VIII. The **Paragraph** [¶] denotes the beginning of a new subject.

IX. The **Section** [§] denotes the divisions of a treatise.

X. The **Tilde** [ñ],—a Spanish mark placed over *n,*— annexes to it the sound of *y; as, cañon,* pronounced *can-yon.*

XI. The **Cedilla** [ç],—a French mark, joined to *c,*—gives to this letter the sound of *s; as, façade.*

XII. The **Caret** [∧] is used in writing, to show that some letter, word, or phrase has been omitted.

                a   not   countries
Ex.—The se sons are alike in all of the same region.
           ∧   ∧   ∧

XIII. The **Macron** [ˉ] marks a long sound, as in *lōne;* the **Breve** [˘], a short sound, as in *nŏt;* the **Dieresis** [¨] separates two vowels into two syllables, as *aëriform.*

XIV. The **Acute Accent** [´] commonly denotes a sharp sound; the **Grave Accent** [`], a depressed sound; the **Circumflex Accent** [⌐ or ⌐], a broad sound.

Rem.—In most works on elocution, the *acute* accent denotes the rising inflection; the *grave* accent, the falling inflection; the *circumflex*, a union of the acute and the grave.

EXERCISES.

Note to Teachers.—Exercises in punctuation may be selected from the Readers in general use. Require pupils to give rules or cite remarks for the use of all the points they may find. Select, also, passages from good authors, and pronounce the words in consecutive order, slowly and distinctly, as in a spelling lesson, without indicating the grammatical construction by tone or inflection. Require pupils to write these as pronounced, and to separate them into sentences and parts of sentences by the proper points.

Punctuate properly the following examples, and observe the rules for the use of capitals:

the noonday sun came slanting down the rocky slopes of la riccia and its masses of entangled foliage whose autumnal tints were mixed with the wet verdure of a thousand evergreens were penetrated with it as with rain I can not call it color it was conflagration purple and crimson and scarlet like the curtain of God's tabernacle the rejoicing trees sank into the valley in showers of light every separate leaf quivering with buoyant and burning life each as it turned to reflect or to transmit the sunbeam first a torch and then an emerald. *ruskin*

What tubero did that naked sword of yours mean in the battle of pharsalia at whose breast was its point aimed what was then the meaning of your arms your spirit your eyes your hands your ardor of soul what did you desire what wish for I press the youth too much he seems disturbed let me return to myself I too bore arms on the same side *cicero*

presently my soul grew stronger hesitating then no longer
sir said I or madam truly your forgiveness I implore
but the fact is I was napping and so gently you came rapping
and so faintly you came tapping tapping at my chamber door
that I scarce was sure I heard you here I opened wide the door
darkness there and nothing more *poe*

PART IV.

PROSODY.

244. Definitions.

1. **Prosody** treats of the quantity of syllables, of accent, and of the laws of versification.

2. **A Verse** is a line consisting of a certain number of accented and unaccented syllables, disposed according to metrical rules.

3. **Versification** is the art of metrical composition.

4. **Discourse** is written either in *Prose* or *Verse*.

5. **Prose** is discourse written in language as ordinarily used, having reference, mainly, to a clear and distinct statement of the author's meaning.

6. **Poetry** is discourse written in metrical language. Its aim is to please, by addressing the imagination and the sensibilities.

7. Poetry is written either in *Rhyme* or in *Blank Verse*.

8. **Rhyme** is a correspondence of sound in the last syllables of two or more lines, succeeding each other immediately, or at no great distance.

Ex.—"Onward its course the present *keeps;*
    Onward the constant current *sweeps.*"

Rem. 1.—*Perfect rhymes* require, (1) that the syllables be accented, and that the vowel sounds be the same; (2) that the sounds following the vowels be the same; (3) that the sounds preceding the vowels be different.

Ex.—*Talk* and *walk, town* and *crown* are perfect rhymes. *Breathe* and *teeth, home* and *come* are imperfect rhymes.

Rem. 2.—A *single rhyme* is an accented syllable standing alone at the end of a line; as, *mind*, re*fined*.

A *double rhyme* consists of an accented syllable, followed by an unaccented one; as, *dreaming*, *seeming*.

A *triple rhyme* consists of an accented syllable, followed by two unaccented ones; as, *fearfully*, *cheerfully*.

Rem. 3.—A **couplet,** or *distich*, consists of two lines rhyming together.

A **triplet** consists of three lines rhyming together.

Rem. 4.—*Middle rhyme* is that which exists between the last accented syllables of the two sections of a verse or line.

Ex.—"We were the *first* that ever *burst*
Into that silent sea."—*Coleridge*.

"Come weal, come *woe*, we'll gather and *go*,
And live and die wi' Charlie."—*Burns*.

9. Blank Verse is verse without rhyme.

Ex.—"The primal duties shine aloft, like stars;
The charities that soothe, and heal, and bless,
Are scattered at the feet of man, like flowers."
Wordsworth.

Rem.—In blank verse, every line should end with an important word.

10. A Stanza is a group of lines forming a division of a poem.

245. Poetic Feet.

1. A **Foot** is a certain portion of a line in poetry, combined according to *accent*.

2. **Accent** is a stress of voice on a certain syllable of a word or foot.

Rem. 1.—In Greek and Latin, verse is made according to the *quantity* of syllables; *i. e.*, the relative time employed in pronouncing them. A *long* syllable requires twice the time in uttering it that a *short* one requires.

In English, verse is composed wholly according to accent. An accented syllable is considered *long ;* an unaccented syllable, *short.*

Rem. 2.—In poetry, monosyllables receive accent.

Ex.—"And to′ | and fro′, | and in′ | and out′
The wan′ | stars danced′ | between."

3. The principal feet used in English verse, are the *Iambus,* the *Trochee,* the *Pyrrhic, the Spondee,* the *Anapest,* the *Dactyl,* and the *Amphibrach.*

Rem.—In the formulas, an accented, or long syllable, is represented by *a ;* an unaccented, or short syllable, by *u.*

4. The **Iambus** consists of an unaccented and an accented syllable.   Its formula is *u a.*

Ex.—"A mind′ | not to′ | be changed′ | by place′ | or time′."

5. The **Trochee** consists of an accented and an unaccented syllable.   Its formula is *a u.*

Ex.—"Ru′in | seize′ thee, | ruth′less | king′."

6. The **Spondee** consists of two accented syllables. Its formula is *a a.*

Ex.—"Rocks′, caves′, | lakes′, fens′, | bogs′, dens′, | and shades′ | of death′."

7. The **Pyrrhic** consists of two unaccented syllables. Its formula is *u u.*

Rem.—The pyrrhic is sometimes used in iambic verse, to avoid accenting an unimportant word.

Ex.—"What could′ | be less′ | *than to* | afford′ | him praise′?"

Instead of resting on a short syllable, the accent is sometimes allowed to pass to the first syllable of the next foot, making that foot a spondee.

Ex.—"*Of the* | low, sun′- | set clouds′, | *and the* | blue′ sky′."

8. The **Anapest** consists of two unaccented and an accented syllable.   Its formula is *u u a.*

Ex.—"All at once′ | and all o'er′ | with a might′- | y uproar′."

9. The **Dactyl** consists of one accented and two unaccented syllables. Its formula is *a u u.*

> **Ex.**—"Heed′ not the | corpse′, though a | king's′, in your | path′."

10. The **Amphibrach** consists of one unaccented, one accented, and one unaccented syllable. Its formula is *u a u.*

> **Ex.**—"A pret′ti- | er din′ner | I nev′er | set eyes′ on."

11. A long or accented syllable used as one foot is called a **Cæsura.**

> **Ex.**—Gold′, | gold′, | gold′, | gold′!
> Hea′vy to | get′ and | light′ to | hold′.—*Hood.*

12. A foot of three unaccented syllables is called a **Tribrach.** It is rarely found in English poetry.

Rem. 1.—The iambus and the anapest,—the accent falling on the same part of the foot in each,—are interchangeable feet.

> **Ex.**—"There were grace′- | ful heads′, | with their ring′- | lets bright′,
> Which tossed′ | in the breeze′, | with a play′ | of light′."

Rem. 2.—For a similar reason, the trochee and the dactyl are sometimes used promiscuously.

> **Ex.**— "Joy′ to the | spir′it | came′,
> Through′ the wide | rent′ in | Time's e- | ter′nal | veil′."

Rem. 3.—The following lines by Coleridge will assist in remembering the character of the different kinds of feet:

> "**Tro′chees** | trip′ from | long′ to | short′.
> From long′ | to long′, | in sol′- | emn sort′,
> Slow **Spon′** | dee′stalks′; | strong foot′, yet | ill′ able
> Ev′er to | come′ up with | **Dac′tyl** tri- | syl′lable.
> **Iam′** | **bics** march′ | from short′ | to long′.
> With a leap′ | and a bound′, | the swift **An′** | apests throng′.
> One syl′la- | ble long′, with | one short′ at | each side′
> **Amphi′brach-** | **ys** hastes′ with | a state′ly stride."

246. Kinds of Verse.

1. Verse is named from the kind of foot which predominates in a line; as, the *Iambic*, from the iambus; the *Trochaic*, from the trochee; the *Anapestic*, from the anapest; the *Dactylic*, from the dactyl.

2. A verse containing one foot is called a *Monometer;* one containing two, a *Dimeter;* one containing three, a *Trimeter;* one containing four, a *Tetrameter;* one containing five, a *Pentameter;* one containing six, a *Hexameter;* one containing seven, a *Heptameter;* and one containing eight, an *Octometer*.

3. Verse, therefore, may be *Iambic Monometer, Iambic Dimeter,* &c.; *Trochaic Monometer, Trochaic Dimeter,* &c.; *Anapestic Monometer, Anapestic Dimeter,* &c.; *Dactylic Monometer, Dactylic Dimeter,* &c.

4. A verse or foot in which a syllable is wanting at the end, is called *catalectic:* a full verse or foot is called *acatalectic:* a verse or foot in which a syllable is wanting at the beginning, is called *acephalous:* a line which has a redundant syllable at the end, is called *hypermeter, or hypercatalectic*.

247. Poetic Pauses.

1. There are two pauses in every verse: a *Final* and a *Cæsural*.

2. The **Final Pause** is a pause made at the end of a line, in reading.

Rem.—Some kinds of verse can be distinguished from prose only by means of the final pause. This pause should always be observed in reading verse, even when not required by the grammatical construction.

3. The **Cæsural Pause** is a pause in a verse.

Rem.—The cæsural pause is a natural suspension of the voice in reading. The shorter kinds of verse are without it. Its natural place is near the middle of the line; but the sense often requires that it be placed elsewhere. In well-constructed verse, it always occurs where the thought requires a pause.

Ex.—"Warms in the sun, ‖ refreshes in the breeze,
    Glows in the stars, ‖ and blossoms in the trees."—*Pope.*

"And now ‖ my tongue the secret tells."

"And on the sightless eyeballs ‖ pour the day."

EXERCISES.

Show the place of the cæsural pause in the following:

Many are poets who have never penned
    Their inspirations, and, perchance, the best.
They felt, and loved, and died, but would not lend
    Their thoughts to meaner beings; they compressed
The God within them, and rejoined the stars
    Unlaurel'd upon earth, but far more bless'd
Than those who are degraded by the jars
    Of passion, and their frailties linked to fame,
Conquerors of high renown, but full of scars.—*Byron.*

248. Iambic Measures.

1. *Iambic Monometer* . . . . u a.
    Invite′,
    Delight′.

2. *Iambic Dimeter* . . . . u a × 2.
    And called′ | the brave′
    To blood′- | y grave′.

3. *Iambic Trimeter* . . . . . u a × 3.
    What sought′ | they thus′ | afar′?
    Bright jew′- | els of′ | the mind′?

4. *Iambic Tetrameter* . . . . u a × 4.
    Majes′ | tic mon′- | arch of′ | the cloud′!
    Who rear'st′ | aloft′ | thy re′- | gal form′.

5. *Iambic Pentameter* . . . . u a × 5.
    O then′, | methought′, | what pain′ | it was′ | to drown′!
    What dread′- | ful noise′ | of wa′- | ters in′ | my ears′!

Rem.—This is often called **Heroic Measure,** because *epic* or *heroic* poetry is written in it. Rhymed iambic pentameter is sometimes called **Heroic Couplet.**

6. *Iambic Hexameter* . . . . $u\,a \times 6.$

> Then from′ | her bur′- | nished gate′, | the good′-ly glit′- | tering East′
>
> Gilds ev′- | ery loft′- | y top′, | which late′ | the hu′- | morous Night′
>
> Bespan′- | gled had′ | with pearl′, | to please | the Morn′- | ing's sight′.

Rem.—This verse is called **Alexandrine.**

7. *Iambic Heptameter* . . . . $u\,a \times 7.$

> How hard′ | when those′ | who do′ | not wish′ | to lend′, | thus lose′, | their books′,-
>
> Are snared′ | by an′- | glers,—folks′ | that fish′ | with lit′- | era′- | ry hooks′!

8. **Long Meter** is iambic tetrameter, arranged in stanzas of four lines, rhyming in couplets or alternately.

> **Ex.**—Praise God′ | from whom′ | all bless′- | ings flow′:
> Praise him′ | all creat′- | ures here′ | below′;
> Praise him′ | above′, | ye heaven′- | ly host′;
> Praise Fath′- | er, Son′, | and Ho′- | ly Ghost′.

9. **Common Meter** is a stanza of four iambic lines, the first and third being tetrameter, the second and fourth, trimeter.

> **Ex.**—Come let′ | us join′ | our cheer′- | ful songs,′
> With an′- | gels round′ | the throne′:
> Ten thou′- | sand thou′- | sand are′ | their tongues′,
> But all′ | their joys′ | are one′.

10. **Short Meter** is a stanza of four iambic lines, the first, second, and fourth being trimeter, the third, tetrameter.

> **Ex.**—There sin′ | and sor′- | row cease′,
> And ev′- | ery con′- | flict's o'er′;
> There we′ | shall dwell′ | in end′- | less peace
> Nor thirst′ | nor hun′- | ger more′

11. **Hallelujah Meter** is a stanza of six iambic lines, the first four being trimeter, the last two, tetrameter.

Ex.—Now may′ | the king′ | descend′,
  And fill′ | his throne′ | of grace′;
Thy scep′- | ter, Lord′! | extend′,
  While saints′ | address′ | thy face′:
Let sin′- | ners feel′ | thy quick′- | 'ning word′,
And learn′ | to know′ | and fear′ | the Lord′.

Rem.—The last two lines are frequently separated into four, containing two iambics each.

12. **Gay's Stanza** has the formula $u\,a \times 3 +$ for the odd lines; for the even lines, $u\,a \times 3$.

Ex.—'T was when′ | the sea′ | was roar′- | ing
  With hol′- | low blasts′ | of wind′,
A dam′- | sel lay′ | deplor′- | ing
  All on′ | a rock′ | reclined′.—*Gay.*

13. **Burns's Stanza** consists of six lines, having the formula $u\,a \times 4$ for the first, second, third, and fifth, and $u\,a \times 2$ for the fourth and sixth.

Ex.—Some hint′ | the lov′- | ers harm′- | less wile′;
  Some grace′ | the maid′- | en's art′- | less smile′;
Some soothe′ | the la′- | b'rer's wea′- | ry toil′,
    For hum′- | ble gains′,
And make′ | his cot′- | tage scenes′ | beguile′
    His cares′ | and pains′.—*Burns.*

13. **Byron's Stanza,** (the *Ottava Rima* of the Italians,) consists of eight lines, the first six rhyming alternately, the last two, in couplets. Its formula is usually $u\,a \times 5$.

Ex.—'T is sweet′ | to hear′ | the watch′- | dog's hon′- | est bark′
    Bay deep-′ | mouth'd wel′- | come as′ | we draw′ | near
      home′;
  'T is sweet′ | to know′ | there is′ | an eye′ | will mark′
    Our com′- | ing, and′ | look bright′- | er when′ | we come′;
  'T is sweet′ | to be′ | awak′- | en'd by′ | the lark′,
    Or lull'd′ | by fall′- | ing wa′- | ters; sweet′ | the hum′
  Of bees′, | the voice′ | of girls′, | the song′ | of birds′,
  The lisp′ | of chil′- | dren, and′ | their ear′- | liest words′.

14. The **Elegiac Stanza** consists of four iambic lines, rhyming alternately, with the formula $u\,a \times 5$.

Ex.—The cur'- | few tolls' | the knell' | of part'- | ing day';
　　　The low'- | ing herds' | wind slow'- | ly o'er' | the lea';
　　　The plow'- | man home'- | ward plods' | his wea'- | ry way';
　　　And leaves' | the world' | to dark'- | ness and' | to me'.

Gray.

15. The **Spenserian Stanza** (so called because invented by Spenser, author of the *Fairy Queen,* which poem is written in this stanza,) consists of nine iambic lines, the first eight having the formula $u\,a \times 5$, the last, $u\,a \times 6$; the first and third rhyming; the second, fourth, fifth, and seventh; and the sixth, eighth, and ninth.

Ex.—A lit'- | tle low'- | ly her'- | mitage' | it was'
　　　Down in' | a dale', | hard by' | a for'- | est's side',
　　　Far from' | resort' | of peo'- | ple that' | did pass'
　　　In trav'- | el to' | and fro': | a lit'- | tle wide'
　　　There was', | a ho'- | ly chap'- | el ed'- | ified',
　　　Wherein' | the her'- | mit du'- | ly wont' | to say
　　　His ho'- | ly things' | each morn' | and ev'- | en-tide';
　　　Thereby' | a crys'- | tal stream' | did gen'- | tly play',
　Which from'|a sa'-|cred fount'-|ain well'-|ed forth'|alway'.

Spenser.

16. A **Sonnet** is a poem complete in fourteen iambic lines. Its formula is $u\,a \times 5$.

17. *Iambic Hypermeters.*

$u\,a +$ . . . . Relent'- | ing.
$u\,a \times 2 +$ . . . . . Thine eye'- | lids quiv'- | er.
$u\,a \times 3 +$ . . . . . 'T is sweet' | to love' | in child'- | hood.
$u\,a \times 4 +$ . . . . What seek' | ye from' | the fields' | of heav'- | en?
$u\,a \times 5 +$ . . The air' | is full' | of fare'- | well to' | the dy'- | ing.
$u\,a \times 6 +$. Thine eye' | Jove's light'- | ning seems', | thy voice' | his dread'- | ful thun'- | der.
$u\,a \times 7 +$ I think' | I will' | not go' | with you' | to hear' | the toasts' | and speech'- | es.

249. Trochaic Measures.

1. *Trochaic Monometer* . . . $a\,u.$	2. *Trochaic Dimeter* . . . $a\,u \times 2.$
Chang'ing, Rang'ing.	Hope' is | van'ished, Joys' are | ban'ished.

H. G. 22.

3. *Trochaic Trimeter*......$a\,u\times 3$.

> Then' let | mem″ry | bring' thee
> Strains' I | used' to | sing' thee.

4. *Trochaic Tetrameter*....$a\,u\times 4$.

> Tell' me | not' in | mourn' ful | num″bers,
> Life' is | but' an | emp'ty | dream'.

5. *Trochaic Pentameter*....$a\,u\times 5$.

> Nar'rowing | in'to | where' they | sat' as- | sem'bled,
> Low' vo- | lup'tuous | mu'sic | wind'ing | trem'bled.

6. *Trochaic Hexameter*....$a\,u\times 6$.

> On' a | mount'ain | stretched' be- | neath' a | hoar'y | wil'low,
> Lay' a | shep'herd ⎩ swain', and | viewed' the | roll'ing |
>   bil'low.

7. *Trochaic Heptameter*....$a\,u\times 7$.

> In' the | spring' a | fee'ble | crim'son | comes' up- | on' the |
>   rob'in's | breast';
> In' the | spring' the | wan'ton | lap'wing | gets' him- | self'
>   an- | oth'er | nest'.

8. *Trochaic Hypermeters.*

$a\,u+$ . . . . Mer'ry | May'.

$a\,u\times 2+$ . . . . . . All' that's | bright' must | fade'.

$a\,u\times 3+$ . . . . . Chill'y | win'ter's | gone' a- | way'.

$a\,u\times 4+$ . . . . I'dle | af'ter | din'ner | in' his | chair.'

$a\,u\times 5+$ . . . Hail' to | thee', blithe | spir'it ! | bird', thou |
  nev'er | wert'.

$a\,u\times 6+$ . . Half' the | charms' to | me' it | yield'eth, | mon'ey |
  can' not | buy'.

$a\,u\times 7+$ Bet'ter | fif'ty | years' of | Eu'rope | than' a | cy'cle | of'
  Cath- | ay'.

250. Anapestic Measures.

1. *Anapestic Monometer*....$u\,u\,a$.

> Move your feet'
> To our sound'.

2. *Anapestic Dimeter*......$u\,u\,a\times 2$.

> In my rage', | shall be seen'
> The revenge' | of a queen'.

3. *Anapestic Trimeter* . . . . . . $uua \times 3$.

> I have found' | out a gift' | for my fair'.
> I have found' | where the wood'- | pigeons breed'.

4. *Anapestic Tetrameter* . . . . $uua \times 4$.

> Through the ranks' | of the Sax'- | ons he hew'd' | his red
> way',—
> Through lan'- | ces, and sa'- | bers, and hos'- | tile array'.

Rem.—The first foot of an anapestic verse may be an iambus.

Ex.—Our life' | is a dream',
> Our time', | as a stream',
> Glides swift'- | ly away'.—*Wesley.*

5. *Anapestic Hypermeters.*

$uua \times 2 + $ . . . . Like the dew' | on the mount'- | ain.
> Like the foam' | on the riv'- | er.

$uua \times 3 + $ . . . . If they rob' | us of name', | or pursue' | us with
> bea'- | gles,
> Give their roof' | to the flame' | and their flesh' |
> to the ea'- | gles.

251. Dactylic Measures.

1. *Dactylic Monometer* . auu. | 2. *Dactylic Dimeter* . $auu \times 2$.
> Fear'fully. | Cor'al reefs | un'der her,
> Tear'fully. | Read'y to | sun'der her.

3. *Dactylic Trimeter* . . . . $auu \times 3$.

> Wear'ing a- | way' in his | use'fulness,
> Love'liness, | beau'ty, and | truth'fulness.

4. *Dactylic Tetrameter* . . . . . $auu \times 4$.

> Boy' will an- | tic'ipate, | lav'ish, and | dis'sipate
> All' that your | bu'sy pate | hoard'ed with | care.

5. *Dactylic Hexameter* . . . . . $auu \times 5 + au$.

> This' is the | for'est pri- | me'val; but | where' are the |
> hearts' that be- | neath' it
> Leaped' like the | roe', when he | hears' in the | wood'land
> the | voice' of the | hunt-er?

Rem.—A dactylic verse rarely ends with a dactyl. It is some-times catalectic, or ends with a trochee; sometimes hypermeter, or ends with a long syllable.

Ex.—Bright′est and | best′ of the | sons′ of the | morn′ing,
Dawn′ on our | dark′ness, and | lend′ us thine | aid′.

252. Amphibrach Measures.

1. *Amphibrach Monometer* . . . . *u a u.*

Hearts beat′ing,   Tears start′ing,
At meet′ing;   At part′ing.

2. *Amphibrach Dimeter* . . . . *u a u* × 2.

O would′ I | were dead′ now,
Or up′ in | my bed′ now,
To cov′er | my head′ now,
    And have′ a | good cry′.

3. *Amphibrach Trimeter* . . . . *u a u* × 3.

A breath′ of | submis′sion | we breathe′ not;
The sword′ we | have drawn′ we | will sheathe′ not.

4. *Amphibrach Trimeter Catalectic* . . . . *u a u* × 3 —.

Ye shep′herds | so cheer′ful | and gay′,
Whose flocks′ nev- | er care′less- | ly roam′.

5. *Amphibrach Tetrameter* . . . . *u a u* × 4.

The flesh′ was | a pict′ure | for paint′ers | to stud′y,
The fat′ was | so white′ and | the lean′ was | so rud′dy

6. *Amphibrach Tetrameter Catalectic* . . . *u a u* × 4 —.

But hang′ it,— | to po′ets | who sel′dom | can eat′,
Your ver′y | good mut′ton′s | a ver′y | good treat′.

253. Mixed Verse.

1. Different kinds of feet are often found in the same line.

2. Different measures are frequently used in the same poem.

EXERCISES.

Tell what feet compose each line of the following examples:

1. My heart was a river
      Without a main,—
    Would I had loved thee never,
      Florence Vane.—*Cooke.*

2. Merrily swinging on briar and weed,
      Near to the nest of his little dame,
    Over the mountain-side or mead,
      Robert of Lincoln is telling his name,
        Bob-o-link, Bob-o-link;
        Spink, spank, spink;
    Snug and safe is that nest of ours,
    Hidden among the summer flowers.
        Chee, chee, chee.—*Bryant.*

3. My tears must stop, for every drop
      Hinders needle and thread.—*Hood.*

4. No matter, no matter! the path shines plain
    These pure snow-crystals will deaden pain;
    Above, like stars in the deep blue dark,
    Eyes that love us look down and mark.
        Let us go, let us go
    Whither heaven leads in the path through the snow.
                     Miss Muloch.

254. Poetic License.

Poetic License is an indulgence in the use of peculiar words, forms, and expressions, allowed to poets by common consent.

Rem. 1.—The requirements of versification render poetic license necessary.

Rem. 2.—Poetic license permits the use of antiquated words and phrases, foreign words, and common words shortened, lengthened, or changed in pronunciation.

Ex.—*Eke, erst, eyne, eve, beweep, evanish, albeit, fount, trow, hight* (called), *vastly, wis, ween, wight,* &c. "A train-band captain *eke* was he;" "His timeless death *beweeping.*"

Rem. 3.—It permits the use of compound epithets to a greater extent than prose.

Ex.—*Sphere-descended, violet-embroidered, dim-discovered, broad-eyed,* &c. "O Music! *sphere-descended* maid;" "*Pun-provoking* thyme."

Rem. 4.—It permits intransitive verbs to be used transitively.

Ex.—They *lived* the rural *day,* and *talked* the flowing *heart.*

Rem. 5.—It permits the use of foreign idioms.

Ex.—"He came; and, standing in the midst, explained
The *peace rejected,* and the *truce detained.*"

Rem. 6.—Poets make use of an inverted order of arrangement more frequently than prose writers.

Ex.—*Predicate . . Subject;*   as, "*Sunk* was the *sun.*"
Object . . . . Predicate;   as, "His *voice* they *heard.*"
Noun . . . . Adjective;   as, "Visions *fair;*" "Twilight *gray.*"
Object . . . . Preposition;   as, "The rattling *crags among.*"

Rem. 7.—Poetic license permits any ellipsis which will not pervert or destroy the sense.

Ex.—Of the antecedent; as, "Who steals my purse, steals trash."
Of the relative; as, "There's nothing ill can dwell in such a temple."
Of the pronoun *it;* as, "Suffice to-night, these orders to obey."
Of the article; as, "Like shipwrecked mariner on desert coast."

255. Scanning.

Scanning is an analysis of versification. To *scan* a line is to divide it into the feet of which it is composed.

Rem.—The following are intended to be used not only as scanning exercises, but as final *Review Exercises in Analysis and Parsing.*

EXERCISES.

1. Sweet day! so cool, so calm, so bright,
   The bridal of the earth and sky;
   The dews shall weep thy fall to-night;
   For thou must die.—*Herbert.*

2.   Under the greenwood tree
        Who loves to lie with me,
        And tune his merry note
        Unto the sweet bird's throat,—
     Come hither, come hither, come hither!
        Here shall he see no enemy
     But winter and rough weather.—*Shakspeare.*

3. Nature, attend! join, every living soul,
   Beneath the spacious temple of the sky;
   In adoration join; and, ardent, raise
   One general song! To Him, ye vocal gales,
   Breathe soft, whose Spirit in your freshness breathes;
   Oh, talk of Him in solitary glooms,
   Where, o'er the rock, the scarcely waving pine
   Fills the brown shade with a religious awe.—*Thomson.*

4. With fruitless labor, Clara bound
   And strove to stanch the gushing wound:
   The Monk, with unavailing cares,
   Exhausted all the church's prayers:
   Ever, he said, that, close and near,
   A lady's voice was in his ear,
   And that the priest he could not hear,
        For that she ever sung,
   "In the lost battle, borne down by the flying,
   Where mingles war's rattle with groans of the dying!"
        So the notes rung.—*Scott.*

5.   Bird of the wilderness,
          Blithesome and cumberless,
     Sweet be thy matin o'er moorland and lea!
          Emblem of happiness,
          Blest is thy dwelling-place,—
     Oh to abide in the desert with thee!—*Hogg.*

6. *What is this stanza called?*

   Full many a gem of purest ray serene,
        The dark, unfathomed caves of ocean bear;
   Full many a flower is born to blush unseen,
        And waste its sweetness on the desert air.—*Gray.*

7.   We look before and after, and pine for what is not:
        Our sincerest laughter with some pain is fraught;
     Our sweetest songs are those which tell of saddest thought.
                                         Shelley.

8. *What is this stanza called?*

> And this is in the night: most glorious night!
> Thou wert not sent for slumber! let me be
> A sharer in thy fierce and far delight,
> A portion of the tempest and of thee!
> How the lit lake shines, a phosphoric sea,
> And the big rain comes dancing to the earth!
> And now again 't is black,—and now the glee
> Of the loud hill shakes with its mountain mirth,
> As if they did rejoice o'er a young earthquake's birth.
>
> *Byron.*

9. Do you hear the children weeping, O my brothers!
> Ere the sorrow comes with years?
> They are leaning their young heads against their mother's,
> And *that* can not stop their tears.
> The young lambs are bleating in the meadows,
> The young birds are chirping in the nest,
> The young fawns are playing in the shadows,
> The young flowers are blooming from the west;
> But the young, young children, O my brothers!
> They are weeping bitterly!
> They are weeping in the play-time of the others,
> In the country of the free.—*Mrs. Browning.*

10. Our bugles sang truce, for the night-cloud had lowered,
> And the sentinel stars set their watch in the sky;
> And thousands had sunk on the ground overpowered;
> The weary to sleep, and the wounded to die.—*Campbell.*

11. Thou art!—directing, guiding all,—Thou art!
> Direct my understanding, then, to Thee;
> Control my spirit, guide my wandering heart;
> Though but an atom midst immensity,
> Still I am something fashioned by thy hand!
> I hold a middle rank 'twixt heaven and earth,
> On the last verge of mortal being stand,
> Close to the realms where angels have their birth,
> Just on the boundaries of the spirit land.—*Derzhaven.*